Drupal 10 Masterclass

Build responsive Drupal applications to deliver custom and
extensible digital experiences to users

Adam Bergstein

BIRMINGHAM—MUMBAI

Drupal 10 Masterclass

Group Product Manager: Alok Dhuri

Publishing Product Manager: Uzma Sheerin

Book Project Manager: Deeksha Thakkar

Senior Editor: Nisha Cleetus

Technical Editor: Rajdeep Chakraborty

Copy Editor: Safis Editing

Indexer: Tejal Soni

Production Designer: Joshua Misquitta

Business Development Executive: Puneet Kaur

DevRel Marketing Coordinators: Deepak Kumar and Mayank Singh

First published: December 2023

Production reference: 1221123

Published by Packt Publishing Ltd.

Grosvenor House

11 St Paul's Square

Birmingham

B3 1RB, UK

ISBN 978-1-83763-310-4

www.packtpub.com

To my girls, Leah and Nora, for their learning, to help their generation, and to show you can chase your dreams.

– Adam Bergstein

Contributors

About the author

Adam Bergstein is a product engineering leader and an architect. He has been a long-time Drupal community member, a routine speaker at Drupal community events around the globe, and provided keynotes for several events. He has maintained and contributed to many Drupal projects, including Password Policy, Taxonomy Menu, and more. Adam is the lead of Simplytest, a free service, and a project that offers testing sandboxes to Drupal community members. He has also worked for both—agencies building Drupal applications and Drupal service providers building Drupal-related products. He has led the Drupal Community Governance Task Force and is serving a term as a community board member of the Drupal Association.

Mike Herchel, author of Chapter 19, is the primary developer behind Drupal's default theme (called Olivero), as well as a maintainer of Drupal core's CSS subsystem. He's on a crusade to improve Drupal's front-end developer experience for those new to the Drupal ecosystem. If you have feedback on this, or thoughts on what's hard to accomplish, please reach out to him at mike@herchel.com. The work on this chapter was traded for beer, and in fact, if you find Mike at a local DrupalCamp, you can typically get him to do core development in exchange for beer.

About the reviewer

Rachel Lawson has been working in open source communities, primarily Drupal, for the last 17 years. Rachel has held diverse roles across education, defense, and pharmaceuticals, learning many of her community skills as a mentor, core mentoring coordinator of the Drupal open source project, and community liaison for the Drupal Association. She has most recently had the opportunity to take many of the good practices in open source into international development with the Digital Impact Alliance at the United Nations Foundation.When not working, Rachel can usually be found planning or enjoying her next overland adventure on her motorbike – 26 countries in 4 continents so far, where's next?

Table of Contents

Preface   xvii

Part 1: Foundational Concepts

1

What is Drupal?   3

What is a CMS?   3
Frameworks and extensibility   4
Basic Drupal concepts   5
Drupal's administrative backend   5

Drupal's frontend presentation layer   7
Popular Drupal case studies   8
Summary   8

2

Drupal Core, Modules, and Themes   9

Drupal core   9
What is core?   10
Core features   10
Core systems   11
Core development   12

Overview of Drupal projects   12
Drupal modules   13

What is a module?   13
Popular community modules   13

Drupal themes   14
What is a theme?   14
Core themes   14

Contribution   14
Summary   15

3

Infrastructure and Overview of Technical Architecture   17

Hosting Drupal and platform requirements	17	**Drupal management and operations**	24
Drupal architecture	18	Maintenance	24
Infrastructure technical stack	19	Operations	25
Application architecture	19	**Summary**	27
Backend architecture	21		
Frontend architecture	22		

4

Drupal Community   29

Understanding the open-source community	29	Projects on Drupal.org	32
Drupal.org basics	29	Contribution impact	37
Core on Drupal.org	31	**Other community resources and tools**	37
Core contribution	32	**Summary**	38

5

What's New in Drupal 10   39

Release methodology	39	Claro	42
Platform requirements	40	Starter kit themes	43
Upgrade considerations	40	**Built in Drupal 10**	44
Major releases	40	Automatic updates	44
New to Drupal 10	40	Recipes	44
Symfony 6.2	40	Decoupled menus	45
CKEditor 5	41	Project browser	45
Olivero	41	**Summary**	45

Part 2: Setting up - Installing and Maintaining

6

Bootstrapping, Installing, and Configuring a New Drupal Project   49

Establishing a new codebase	50	Site Building Concept	59
What is Composer?	50	Requirements Gathering	59
Composer projects	51	Beyond core features	60
Common commands	52	**Basic configuration**	**60**
Installing Drupal	**54**	Post-installation configuration	61
Installation preparation	54	Common configuration changes	61
UI-based installation	54	**Help, logs, and reporting**	**62**
Performing an installation with Drush	58	Help	62
Post-installation	58	Logs and Reporting	63
Out-of-the-box Drupal Building	**59**	**Summary**	**65**
Developer Classification	59		

7

Maintaining Drupal   67

Types of maintenance	**67**	Environment differences	73
Code-related maintenance	68	Managed platforms	74
Infrastructure platform maintenance	69	SaaS services	74
Code maintenance process	**69**	Update frequency	75
Reviewing code management and		Product life cycles	75
deployment concepts	69	System monitoring and tools	75
Typical code maintenance process	70	Edge systems	75
Best practices	**73**	**Summary**	**76**
Backups	73		

Part 3: Building - Features and Configuration

8

Content Structures and Multilingual   79

Importance of structured content	**79**	Example models	83
Relational database best practices	80	Configuration entities	83
		Under the hood	83
Structured content in Drupal	**81**	Site building	84
Entities, types, and bundles	81	Applying to other features	90
Fields and field types	81		
Base entities	82	**Multilingual features**	**91**
Content entities	82	Modules	91
Entity example for Node	82	**Summary**	**94**

9

Users, Roles, and Permissions   95

Users	**95**	Configuring roles	101
User entity	95	**Permissions**	**101**
Features	96	Access control	102
User management	97	Types of permissions	102
		Managing permissions	102
Roles	**100**	Permission definition	103
Role entity	100		
Default roles	100	**Summary**	**104**

10

Drupal Views and Display Modes   105

Defining Views	**105**	Popular use cases	110
Overview	106	**Using Views and display modes**	**110**
Views features	106	Creating a teaser display mode	
Customizing Views	108	for blogs	111
Defining display modes	**109**	Creating a View for a blog listing –	
Overview	109	option 1 with teaser display mode	113

Creating a View for a blog listing –
option 2 with fields   115
Explaining the Views editing interface   118

Creating an RSS feed display   120
Summary   121

11

Files, Images, and Media   123

Assets in Drupal   123
Use cases   124

Files   124
Subsystem   125
Modules and configuration   125

Images   129
Modules and configuration   129

Media   133
Modules and configuration   133

Use cases   138
Creating research papers   138
Icons for sports   138
Tutorials found in YouTube videos   139

Summary   139

12

Search   141

About the feature   141
Implementation   141
Frontend experience   142
Backend   144

Configuring search   145
Search pages   147

Extending Search   149
Facets   149

Third-party indexes   149
Autocomplete   149

Use cases   150
Querying for two different movie titles
simultaneously   150
Filter by sport   150
Restricting a specific content type
from search   150

Summary   150

13

Contact Forms   151

Contact forms in Drupal   151
Basic information   151
Form management   152

Form submissions   154

Configuring contact forms   154
User profile configuration   155

Permissions   155

Extending contact forms   **155**

Viewing and managing form submissions   155

Beyond just a page   156

More robust email notifications   156

Spam prevention   156

More advanced forms   156

Summary   **157**

Part 4: Using - Content Management

14

Basic Content Authoring Experience   161

Authoring content   **161**

Nodes   162

Menus and taxonomies   170

Authoring digital assets   **172**

Summary   **174**

15

Visual Content Management   175

Blocks and custom block types   **175**

Managing blocks   175

Custom block types   177

Layout Builder   **178**

Configuring a default layout   179

Node-specific layouts   182

Setting up Layout Builder   183

Contributed projects   **183**

Paragraphs   184

Gutenberg   184

Summary   **187**

16

Content Workflows   189

Configuring workflows   **189**

Managing states   189

Managing transitions   190

Managing workflows   190

Managing permissions   192

Using workflows   **193**

Use case   **195**

Summary   **195**

Part 5: Advanced Topics

17

Git, Drush, Composer, and DevOps   199

Technical requirements	199	Common commands	205
Git basics	200	**DevOps practices**	**205**
Setup	200	A developer pushes a new commit to a	
Common commands	201	development branch	206
Drush basics	**202**	Developer reviews and merges code	
Setup	202	into the main branch	206
Common commands	203	Tag-based deployments for release	
		candidates	207
Composer basics	**204**	Addressing production deployments	207
Setup	204	**Summary**	**208**

18

Module Development   209

Concepts	209	Drupal patterns	213
Early Drupal concepts	210	**Module definitions**	**214**
Modern Drupal concepts	210	Configuration	214
Common patterns	**211**	PHP code	215
PHP patterns	211	Templates	217
Symfony capabilities	212	**Summary**	**217**

19

Theme Development   219

Technical requirements	219	Setting up theme debugging and	
Setting up for theme		disabling caches	220
development	**220**	Turning on verbose error messages	223
Disabling CSS and JS aggregation	220	Creating a new theme using the theme	
		generator tool	223

Creating a new theme from scratch   223
Creating your dexter.info.yml   224
Creating your dexter.libraries.yml file   225
Creating your CSS directory and files   225
Creating your templates directory   225
Creating your JS directory   225

Creating a new theme from a base theme (subtheming)   **226**
Popular base themes   226

Working with Libraries API (and where to put CSS/JS)   **226**
Loading the library globally through your theme's *.info.yml file   226
Attaching the library through a Twig template   226
Loading the library programmatically through preprocess   227
Overriding another module's or theme's libraries   227
Managing dependencies   227
Notes on CSS grouping   228
Setting weights and other options   228

Working with templates   **228**
How to find and create templates   228
Twig basics   229
Twig filters   232
Twig functions   232
Working with the attributes object   234

Preprocessing data and PHP   **234**
Working with CSS   **235**
Working with JS   **236**
Drupal behaviors   236
Passing data from PHP into JS   237

Single Directory Components   **237**
Drupal accessibility tips   **238**
The visually hidden CSS class   238
Drupal announce JS API   238
Using buttons as menu items   238

Contributed modules that help with theming   **238**
Summary   **239**

20

Delivering Drupal Content through APIs   241

Web services primer   **241**
Web service APIs in Drupal   **242**
Concepts   242
Modules and configuration   243

Using web services   **247**

Basic JSON:API examples   248
Basic REST API examples   250
REST clients   251

Summary   **251**

21

Migrating Content into Drupal   253

Migration concepts	253	Custom events	256
The Migrate system	254	Operating migrations	256
Extract	255	Contributed modules	257
Transform	256	**Use cases**	257
Load	256	**Summary**	260

22

Multisite Management   261

The multisite feature	261	Automating deployments across	
Benefits	262	many sites	263
Drawbacks	262	Summary	263

Appendix A - Drupal Terminology   265

Index   269

Other Books You May Enjoy   280

Preface

Thank you for choosing this book. Digital experience is the broad set of ways users can engage through a website, online shopping, apps, and more. Drupal is an open source digital framework used to create digital experiences. Incepted as a content management system built on structured content models, Drupal's flexibility, extensibility, and evolution has positioned Drupal to serve the broader digital space. Drupal's interoperability allows it to work with other things like social media networks, CRM systems, technical capabilities, apps, and even internet-of-things connected devices. Drupal is known for its configuration layer that enables no-code modification through an administrative user interface. The extensibility allows Drupal to be customized both functionally and visually through a robust development framework that often appeals to enterprise use cases. The community maintains both the core of Drupal and a large series of modular projects that can be readily installed, if desired for a given installation.

There are many books on Drupal, several of which dive deep in a specific way. This doesn't reflect the experience I've had with Drupal, in which I have been asked to solve a large number of problems that have spanned every aspect of Drupal that have spanned various Drupal agencies and companies that build products supporting Drupal applications. My experience covers:

- Participating in the community
- Installing Drupal
- Evaluating/installing Drupal projects
- Configuring features
- Writing code through modules and themes
- Deploying updates
- Running/configuring Drupal's technology stack
- Dependent and complementary technologies
- Broader DevOps implementations, and more

Drupal continues to be one of the longest standing and largest open source communities. Community members are often in high demand to help companies advise, build, maintain, or upgrade Drupal. Drupal affords continuous opportunities to learn through its community, which is always at the ready to help find important work, coach new community members, and ultimately, help members grow as technologists.

Who this book is for

Such a broad and capable digital platform covers a large number of technologies and skillsets. This book aims to introduce as much of Drupal as possible to help gain exposure spanning several personas:

- **End user** : Elements of the book highlight the experience offered to website visitors or content authors who engage with Drupal but don't necessarily build it

- **Site builder** : A user who can install and configure Drupal without custom code

- **Backend developer** : A user who can customize Drupal functionality through its development framework with modules

- **Front-end developer** : A user who can customize Drupal's visual appearance through its development framework with themes

- **Systems administrator** : A user who needs to help maintain Drupal's technology stack and servers

The book is heavy in content for the site builder persona, given it is a foundational persona. Customization is not expected or desired until after a site builder has exhausted no-code configuration for a Drupal application. Several chapters then explore the more advanced topics around customized code through Drupal's framework, tooling, and deployment mechanisms.

What this book covers

Chapter 1, What is Drupal?, introducing content management fundamentals, basic Drupal concepts, and case studies.

Chapter 2, Drupal Core, Modules, and Themes, introduces the three major components of a Drupal application, their purpose, and project examples.

Chapter 3, Infrastructure and Overview of Technical Architecture, covers Drupal's hosting requirements, backend architecture, front-end architecture, and "trifecta" of code, database, and files.

Chapter 4, Drupal Community, describes how to engage with the Drupal community and why it is important to do so.

Chapter 5, What's New in Drupal 10, defines important new features and changes in Drupal 10 from earlier versions.

Chapter 6, Bootstrapping, Installing, and Configuring a New Drupal Project, walks through the experience of starting a new Drupal application from nothing.

Chapter 7, Maintaining Drupal, outlines the specific maintenance footprint for Drupal and its technical stack, including recommendations for best practices in maintenance.

Chapter 8, Content Structures and Multilingual, describes how people create models for content and how content stored in those models can support versions across multiple languages.

Chapter 9, Users, Roles, and Permissions, covers configuration capabilities that allow different users to perform different actions within the same Drupal application.

Chapter 10, Drupal Views and Display Modes, outlines how to create content displays and display configuration for standard content rendering and for different display formats like listings, feeds, and more.

Chapter 11, Files, Images, and Media, outlines digital asset features in Drupal that work with its underlying structured content and across other Drupal features.

Chapter 12, Search, gives an introduction on enabling and configuring search capabilities in Drupal with commentary on more advanced use cases.

Chapter 13, Contact Forms, provides an overview of user engagement through public forms including optional features like spam prevention and more advanced form building capabilities.

Chapter 14, Basic Content Authoring Experience, helps demonstrate various configuration options and their impact on the experience offered to content authors.

Chapter 15, Visual Content Management, introduces Drupal's block system and a visual layout capability known as Layout Builder for placing blocks within configured layouts.

Chapter 16, Content Workflows, gives an overview on moderated content configuration options that allow various user roles to be configured to create, review, and approve content before it gets published.

Chapter 17, Git, Drush, Composer, and DevOps, helps define underlying tooling, practices, and use cases that impact code development, deployment workflows, and maintenance.

Chapter 18, Module Development, provides concepts, patterns, and various code samples aimed at understanding how to customize Drupal's functionality through the backend framework.

Chapter 19, Theme Development, is an overview on everything theme-related in Drupal covering practices, examples, and concepts that span libraries, templates, CSS, JavaScript, and Drupal-related conventions.

Chapter 20, Delivering Drupal Content through APIs, introduces features for web services and interoperability with other systems interested in retrieving Drupal content or performing actions within Drupal.

Chapter 21, Migrating Content into Drupal, introduces tooling and a framework that maps content sources, transformations, and content destinations to move content into Drupal.

Chapter 22, Multisite Management, outlines how to run multiple Drupal applications from the same codebase, including the benefits and drawbacks of this capability.

Appendix A serves as a quick reference to help review terminology or "Drupal-isms

To get the most out of this book

You will need to have a basic understanding of web applications, general web technologies, and request/response models through a browser.

Software/Hardware covered in the book	OS Requirements
PHP	Windows, macOS, and Linux (Any)
JavaScript	Windows, macOS, and Linux (Any)
CSS	Windows, macOS, and Linux (Any)
HTML	Windows, macOS, and Linux (Any)
Server administration	Linux

Local tools, like DDEV (`https://ddev.com/`), help run a containerized application that hosts Drupal. There are active discussions on DDEV becoming the community standard. Such a tool provides a well documented experience and commands to run Drupal applications. Given this book has several hands-on examples, a local container-based tool brings automation and the ability to destroy and rebuild a Drupal application rapidly. DDEV is also supported across several operating systems.

This book tries to not be too opinionated. The Drupal community, like any community, often has more than one way to solve a problem and it has passionate, smart people that may not always agree. Efforts were made while writing this book to remain objective while trying to give readers as much context on topics as possible. It will be important to get informed on the basics from this book, form your own opinions, and be opportunistic in learning.

Conventions used

There are a number of text conventions used throughout this book.

`Code in text`: Indicates code words in text, database table names, folder names, filenames, file extensions, pathnames, dummy URLs, user input, and Twitter handles. Here is an example: "Create a `*.services.yml` file within the root directory of the module."

A block of code is set as follows:

```
use Drupal\user\Entity\User;
$user = User::load(\Drupal::currentUser()->id());
```

When we wish to draw your attention to a particular part of a code block, the relevant lines or items are set in bold:

```
namespace Drupal\my_module\Service;
```

Any command-line input or output is written as follows:

```
$ mkdir css
$ cd css
```

> **Tips or important notes**
> Appear like this.

Sections

In this book, you will find several headings that appear frequently (Concepts, Use cases, Community Projects, etc).

To give clear instructions on how to complete a recipe, use these sections as follows:

Concepts

This section tells you about the purpose behind a feature or tool.

Use cases

This section often walks through a common way a feature or tool is used.

Community Projects

This section expands beyond what is offered in Drupal core through community-related efforts or projects.

Get in touch

Feedback from our readers is always welcome.

General feedback: If you have questions about any aspect of this book, email us at customercare@packtpub.com and mention the book title in the subject of your message.

Errata: Although we have taken every care to ensure the accuracy of our content, mistakes do happen. If you have found a mistake in this book, we would be grateful if you would report this to us. Please visit www.packtpub.com/support/errata and fill in the form.

Piracy: If you come across any illegal copies of our works in any form on the internet, we would be grateful if you would provide us with the location address or website name. Please contact us at copyright@packt.com with a link to the material.

If you are interested in becoming an author: If there is a topic that you have expertise in and you are interested in either writing or contributing to a book, please visit authors.packtpub.com.

Share your thoughts

Once you've read *Drupal 10 Masterclass*, we'd love to hear your thoughts! Scan the QR code below to go straight to the Amazon review page for this book and share your feedback.

https://packt.link/r/1-837-63310-X

Your review is important to us and the tech community and will help us make sure we're delivering excellent quality content.

Download a free PDF copy of this book

Thanks for purchasing this book!

Do you like to read on the go but are unable to carry your print books everywhere?

Is your eBook purchase not compatible with the device of your choice?

Don't worry, now with every Packt book you get a DRM-free PDF version of that book at no cost.

Read anywhere, any place, on any device. Search, copy, and paste code from your favorite technical books directly into your application.

The perks don't stop there, you can get exclusive access to discounts, newsletters, and great free content in your inbox daily

Follow these simple steps to get the benefits:

1. Scan the QR code or visit the link below

https://packt.link/free-ebook/9781837633104

2. Submit your proof of purchase
3. That's it! We'll send your free PDF and other benefits to your email directly

Part 1: Foundational Concepts

This part covers all of the basics for Drupal. You will get an overview on what Drupal does at a high level followed by understanding the differences between core, modules, and themes. A review of the supporting infrastructure and Drupal's primary architectural components are covered. The open source community and their practices are reviewed. And, the part finishes by reviewing the new features of Drupal 10.

This part has the following chapters:

- *Chapter 1, What is Drupal?*
- *Chapter 2, Drupal Core, Modules, and Themes*
- *Chapter 3, Infrastructure and Overview of Technical Architecture*
- *Chapter 4, Drupal Community*
- *Chapter 5, What's New in Drupal 10*

1

What is Drupal?

Drupal is a popular **content management system** (**CMS**) for building websites, web applications, and digital experiences. With such flexibility, it can be difficult to define exactly what Drupal is. This chapter explores that question in depth to clarify its identity, purpose, and objective.

The goal of this chapter is to provide a solid foundation that we will build upon in the more practical, hands-on chapters found later in this book. Learning basic concepts and understanding the community are essential for anyone who wants to work with Drupal.

In this chapter, we will explore the following topics:

- What is a CMS?
- Framework and extensibility
- Basic concepts
- Popular case studies

What is a CMS?

A **CMS**, in its simplest form, is a tool to create, update, maintain, and present content. This was historically for websites, but now, they're commonly used for digital experiences given the rise of omnichannel content delivery. The foundations of the web started with servers delivering static HTML files over the internet. Tools that abstracted technical complexities in building HTML, such as Macromedia Dreamweaver, allowed non-technical audiences to author websites without knowing how to code. HTML files would be modified on someone's personal computer and subsequently pushed up to a web server through protocols such as FTP or SFTP. A CMS abstracts both the coding and the file-based operations to enhance the capabilities of a system. Many CMSs also handle content delivery given that managing content has evolved to address more complex use cases with specific access controls, editorial reviews, and more.

The modern CMS has evolved to serve several popular use cases. Many eCommerce websites manage products, pricing, and promotions through a CMS where the system manages shopping carts, users, and payment transactions. Social networks, such as Twitter and Facebook, harness content management capabilities to deliver user-specific, innovative digital experiences.

Enterprise CMS systems must account for much more than just browser-based content delivery, which explains Drupal's evolution. Omnichannel capabilities often allow a CMS to serve as a central content store while allowing the same content to be served across any channel from a website, app on your phone, a notification stream, and more. A CMS is now viewed as a major enabler for an effective digital strategy spanning simple websites for small businesses to a highly integrated content store for major corporations. Over time, Drupal has added the features and extensibility necessary to be a platform that enterprises adopt.

CMS systems began by managing content published on basic websites. Today, applications such as Drupal have evolved to be able to dynamically deliver content through many channels and manage data across a vast amount of enterprise capabilities. Recognizing this evolution helps explain Drupal's position in the space of CMS solutions as an enabler not just for simple website use cases, but far more.

Frameworks and extensibility

I once heard Drupal described as analogous to Lego building blocks in that Lego blocks of all shapes and sizes; what can be created is limited only by your imagination. Many people have attempted to define what Drupal is. While a clear definition may help people understand when and how to adopt Drupal, if Drupal is of interest to them, or if Drupal can help them deliver a specific solution effectively, this is not a constructive way to understand what Drupal is.

Drupal is a tool. What is delivered with the tool can vary drastically. That is why the Lego analogy works. With Lego blocks, you can build a house, a car, a Star Wars figure… practically anything. Lego blocks empower a builder to create what they want to create. Often, people want a clear definition of Drupal. Is it a house, a car, or a Star Wars figure? No – it is a tool that helps you create the digital experiences you want to build. While I understand a desire to define what Drupal can be used for, looking at Drupal in this manner can be significantly limiting.

Drupal grew in popularity as a CMS. Drupal empowered site builders by offering a user interface for configuring structured content and serving that structured content as rendered HTML. Imagine a system that can be used to both create and deliver websites. Drupal offers that. Content is stored persistently by authors and then rendered for site visitors dynamically. Drupal is an application developed in PHP that leverages a database storage backend. Older CMSs simply managed static files, whereas Drupal is a functional system that can be programmed to manage content. Page requests do not correspond to static files; instead, they are dynamically processed by Drupal. The system interprets a URL, parameters, and sessions to deliver a unique, generated result back to the browser at the time the request was made. Some requests get content, others serve the user interface to manage content. Drupal handles all of that.

However, Drupal can do much more than basic content management. Out of the box, the core of Drupal delivers many features that allow it to be configured for conventional content management. This includes structured content, WYSIWYG, media/static file management, caching, rendering content displays, API-based content delivery, and more. However, Drupal also comes with a highly extensible framework that allows for it to be customized. Given Drupal is open source, community members have contributed their customizations back to the open-source community as projects that can be downloaded and installed on any Drupal application.

The goal of this book is to show how Drupal, its out-of-the-box features, and contributed projects can be built and configured to deliver amazing digital experiences. Like a large box of Lego blocks, the aim of this book is not to define exactly what can be built but to show you how to use the tool to accomplish a large number of potential outcomes. What you do is only bound by your imagination.

Basic Drupal concepts

Drupal's core delivers two fundamental parts of the application: a frontend web application and a backend administrative system. Both are delivered through the Drupal application, which can be accessed from a web browser differentiated based on the request. Common backend paths, such as the user login page "user" and administrative console "admin," help Drupal differentiate requests.

Drupal's administrative backend

Conceptually, Drupal's backend performs tasks and retrieves information about the Drupal system. Tasks change based on the access granted to the user. However, common tasks include performing content updates, configuring Drupal system settings, and managing modules. Useful information, such as Drupal's system status page, access to Drupal logs, and help pages, can also be accessed from Drupal's backend. It is useful for content editors and those managing the Drupal system.

The following figure demonstrates Drupal's administrative backend, which can be found at /admin after logging in:

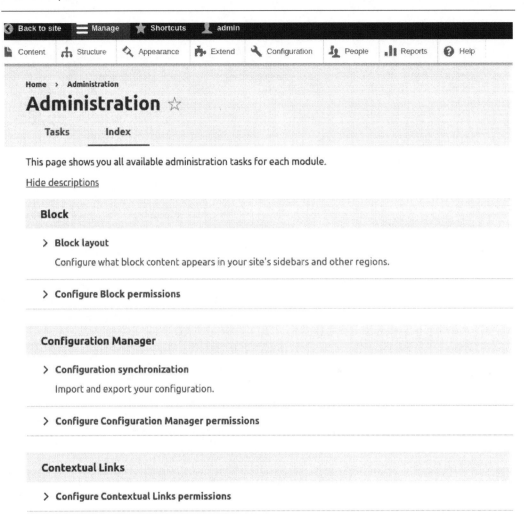

Figure 1.1 – Drupal's administrative home page

At the top, Drupal has an administrative menu that helps navigate the entirety of Drupal's administrative backend. This figure demonstrates the initial, primary administrative page that lists links within Drupal's backend. Each category has a gray background that represents a core feature or subsystem. Under each category are links to pages that perform administrative actions or configure the behavior of that subsystem.

Drupal's frontend presentation layer

Since the backend configures Drupal and manages content, the frontend is responsible for serving content. Drupal's render subsystem is used to correlate a page request to the corresponding response, which is dynamically returned by Drupal. While there is far more complexity, a high-level request flow interprets the path, gathers the relevant structured content from Drupal's backend, maps the content to HTML templates found in the enabled Drupal theme, and returns rendered markup.

The following figure shows Drupal 10's default home page rendered by the frontend presentation layer:

Welcome!

You haven't created any frontpage content yet.

Congratulations and welcome to the Drupal community.

Drupal is an open source platform for building amazing digital experiences. It's made, used, taught, documented, and marketed by the Drupal community. Our community is made up of people from around the world with a shared set of values, collaborating together

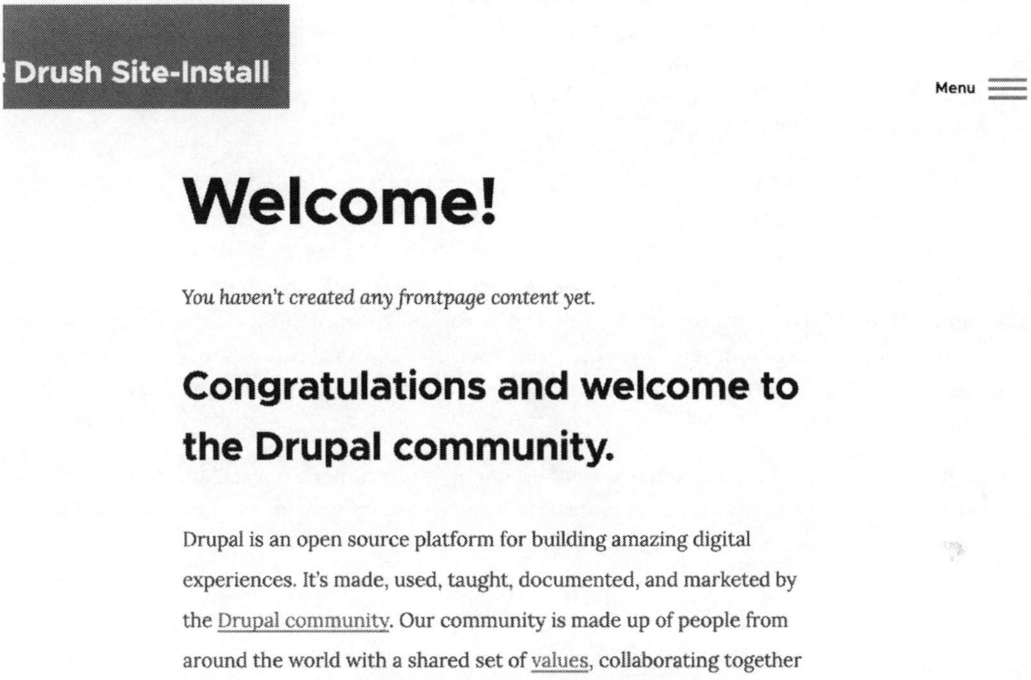

Figure 1.2 – Drupal's default home page

While this shows simple, basic placeholder content, it differs drastically from *Figure 1.1*, given that it is presenting content and not configuring Drupal.

Consider authenticated users while using Drupal's frontend and backend. Drupal can deliver content, but not just for anonymous visitors who visit a Drupal website. During frontend processing, Drupal can render content specific for the user who's being authenticated. Such a capability allows you to leverage Drupal features to build dashboards with individualized content, create personalized experiences, and even deliver content moderation workflows that pair with Drupal's frontend. The most common use case for authenticated users is still accessing and using the administrative backend of Drupal, but a user can be configured without permission to access the backend. Given users have an expanded role in Drupal, a user can log into Drupal with no backend access and get content that's specific and relevant to them. Imagine building a social network where every user only sees content they subscribe to. Drupal can do that.

Popular Drupal case studies

Drupal case studies start with their fundamental content management features, which build off of structured data. Drupal has been commonly used for blogs, websites, or news. Stanford University offers a web content management program that delivers Drupal and various content management features as a service through their IT department. The State of Georgia offers a similar web platform built with Drupal. Other popular Drupal websites include London.gov.uk, home.cern, unicef.org, the Syfy network, the State of Massachusetts, The Weather Channel, Tesla, Entertainment Weekly, NCAA, the Emmy Awards, and NASA.

Distributions in Drupal often represent popular use cases for Drupal, reducing the time and cost of creating multiple sites that have similar requirements. Websites built with the Open Social distribution (getopensocial.com) help create community-based websites with groups, events, private messaging, and enhanced user profiles. Case studies include Local Gov Drupal (drupal.org/project/localgov), The United Nations, The Salvation Army, and The European Commission. Drupal Commerce is a distribution tailored for eCommerce websites, with a series of optional features for payment gateway integrations, promotions/coupons, analytics, shipping, and fulfillment. Case studies include EuroCentres, Open Sesame, and Artellite.

Drupal has countless published case studies and even more undocumented installations that highlight its wide adoption. These case studies demonstrate Drupal's ability to be used in different industries and verticals, as well as for different implementations.

Summary

This chapter covered introductory concepts regarding CMSs and highlighted how Drupal built a CMS through its high-level features. First, we introduced Drupal's framework and extensibility value proposition, which enables both its vibrant community and enterprise-level customizations. Next, we reviewed Drupal.org, which introduced you to how to engage with the community, work with community projects, and the purpose of the Drupal Association. Finally, we looked at some case studies that demonstrate Drupal's capabilities. The next chapter dives deeper into projects by reviewing core, contributed, and custom projects.

2

Drupal Core, Modules, and Themes

Drupal starts with a powerful, foundational core that all Drupal applications build from. This chapter describes what *core* is, how it was conceptually created, how to harness it to create a Drupal application, and how an application can be extended beyond just core. Learning how to create Drupal applications starts with enabling and configuring Drupal core features. It is only after leveraging core that the application should be extended through contributed and/or custom projects. This chapter serves as the foundation for configuring applications, understanding high-level architecture, and then solving additional problems through extended projects.

In this chapter, we're going to cover the following main topics:

- Drupal core
- Overview of Drupal projects
- Drupal modules
- Drupal themes
- Contribution

Drupal core

Drupal core is the foundation of every Drupal application. It represents all out-of-the-box Drupal features and contains the framework every Drupal application is built on. It has the most rigorous contribution process while having the largest amount of contribution activity.

While Drupal itself, as an open source project, is free, it should be viewed more through the perspective of "free like a puppy." Drupal code is freely available, and there is a vast community helping to maintain and support it. However, Drupal applications require ongoing maintenance. Major and minor upgrades need to be performed to update the code. The underlying servers and platform need to be maintained as core evolves its platform dependencies. The community helps promote efforts to more seamlessly and automatically perform code updates, but adopters are still largely responsible for running their own platforms or picking a commercial PaaS offering. This takes ongoing work and investment as it requires a conscious decision from those selecting Drupal as their digital experience framework. But Drupal and the framework that core provides can be extensible and address complex, enterprise digital needs that can deliver value in ways other platforms simply cannot. While it can complicate upgrades with the added complexity of custom code, these capabilities position Drupal as a powerful tool capable of addressing enterprise needs. Even with efforts that simplify the maintenance work required, adopters still need to understand Drupal and the systems required to run it. Small businesses that cannot make this investment may not be in a position to effectively get the same value out of Drupal as an enterprise would. Professionals should advocate for the right tool for the right job.

What is core?

Every house has a foundation. Every car has a frame. And every Drupal application has a core. It is the basis of all Drupal applications.

Drupal core is an out-of-the-box Drupal application. When the core is first downloaded, the application loads Drupal's core installer. After installation, the application renders Drupal's content and affords access to Drupal's core user login feature. Logged-in users can access Drupal's administrative systems and content management tools. All of this is facilitated by Drupal's core.

Drupal core is built to be modular. In this definition, there are a series of independent parts that encompass all of Drupal's core. This modularity is incredibly useful to afford Drupal developers the ability to enable or disable parts independently based on their use case, and many of the parts of Drupal core are extensible through configuration and the framework. The core of Drupal and its modularity serve as an underlying design principle that has allowed Drupal to solve countless problems in the digital space and be able to deliver on a wide array of various use cases.

Drupal's core also helps drive some governance aspects of Drupal. As an example, Drupal core sets the various system requirements needed for running the Drupal application. Drupal core has explicit open-source licensing that influences all other Drupal communities and projects. Developing core often sets the highest standard for contribution to a Drupal project through processes, tooling, quality standards, and more.

Core features

Drupal core also has a set of common features. The features deliver Drupal's out-of-the-box value and help to differentiate Drupal from other digital content management applications.

Content management features help deliver on Drupal's promise as a **content management system** (**CMS**). Such examples include the following:

- **Structured content**: Nodes, content types, blocks, fields, field types (dates, phone numbers, links), and taxonomy

- **Content features**: WYSIWYG, comments, moderation/workflows, layout builder, API feeds/web services, multilingual, Drupal views, statistics/analytics, forums, books, and blocks

- **Digital assets**: Files (PDFs, Word documents), media (images and videos), and responsive image management

- **Migration**: Methods to import and export content within Drupal

- **Engagement**: Contact forms and search

Administrative features help provide the content management experience, manage Drupal features, or change Drupal's settings. These include the following:

- **Authorization/authentication**: User roles and permissions

- **Configuration**: Changing settings of the Drupal application, and managing the state of the application's Drupal configuration

- **Logging**: Accessing and managing Drupal logs

- **Documentation**: Help pages, inline help, and tours

Important note

It is always important to leverage Drupal core's out-of-the-box features before performing custom development or installing other projects. Drupal core itself is feature-rich, and it is the most established aspect of Drupal. The core should be leveraged before extending it.

If some of the terminology or concepts are new to you, don't fear this. These features are covered in depth in future chapters.

Core systems

Drupal core is built on subsystems. Some subsystems can be considered features of Drupal, while others are low-level, fundamental capabilities that a feature can leverage. Some pragmatic examples of features include the "node" system, which is common for structured content, and the "media" system used for file asset management. Low-level subsystems include the module subsystem, which allows Drupal to be modular, and the database subsystem, which allows for persistent Drupal storage (not assets). The combination of these subsystems provides both the framework and the features offered by the core out of the box.

Some examples of these core systems include the following:

- **User**
- **Cron**
- **Theme**

- **Cache**

- **Entity**

- **Batch**

- **Queue**

- **Database**

- **Installer**

- **Locale**

- **Mail**

- **Plugin**

- **Test**

Core development

Drupal is a PHP application that has harnessed modern PHP development practices. Drupal core is built on Symfony components that, in essence, offer low-level capabilities that Drupal adopted. Earlier versions of Drupal had their specific systems built into core that overlapped with widely adopted open-source capabilities offered throughout the PHP ecosystem. Drupal 8 introduced this change, which was a significant architectural shift from a more procedural legacy PHP application into more of an **object-oriented** (**OO**), modern PHP approach. Composer, a popular PHP-based command-line tool, is used to manage Drupal's dependencies to pull projects and versions based on the core's provided directives. Both the use of Symfony components and Composer represent common practices of modern PHP applications and allow Drupal to more effectively focus effort on its value proposition. It also allows Drupal community members to contribute to and influence the broader PHP ecosystem.

Overview of Drupal projects

Drupal core leverages projects as the construct for its modularity. Projects are built with code and harness Drupal core's framework to customize Drupal. Community members have contributed their projects on `drupal.org`. Projects created for the specific needs of a Drupal application are known as custom. Custom projects are intended to add specific business logic that may be unique to an organization, integrate internal enterprise systems, or add specific company branding.

> **Important note**
>
> Before creating custom projects, evaluate the contributed projects on `drupal.org`. Given the maturity of the Drupal project and the vast number of contributions, it is common to find a contributed project that can help address the desired use case. This all assumes the feature is not provided by the core itself.

Projects are managed by Drupal core for the application. Core can install, enable, and disable projects. Each version of the project is managed so that the core can check for updates. Core also has the concept of update hooks, which allow for new versions of a project to perform specific tasks once new code exists.

Drupal modules

The first type of project is known as a module.

What is a module?

A module is a code that leverages Drupal's framework for backend customization. This often modifies the Drupal application and is processed within the server. The core itself organizes its features by leveraging modules. This way, each application can control which core modules are installed based on the desired needs of the application.

Modules have compatibility with the core. Every major version of the core modifies its framework. Given the framework changes, modules must provide metadata that defines their compatibility with major core versions. It should not be assumed that every module found on `drupal.org` is compatible with the version of Drupal on the application. In fact, given that Drupal now has 10 major versions, basic searches for modules can find modules dating back to early versions of Drupal. Popular modules from earlier versions may have even been moved into core in later versions (for example, Views). The **Content Construction Kit** (**CCK**) module served as the basis for what later became Drupal's Entity system.

Popular community modules

Given the number of Drupal applications in the world, community members have created a large number of modules aimed at solving specific problems. It is best to check on `drupal.org` before investing time in coding something someone else contributed.

Some popular module examples include the following:

- **Webform**: A robust and extensible form-building solution
- **Redirect**: Creates manual and automatic path redirection, especially useful to have old content point to new content
- **Pathauto**: Provides automatic path generation for content managers
- **Google Analytics**: Enables integration with Google Analytics
- **Taxonomy Menu**: Allows for a hierarchical taxonomy to be rendered as a menu
- **Antibot**: Spam protection for form submissions

- **Sitewide Alerts**: A solution that posts a banner message at the top of every page
- **Metatag**: Delivers more metadata for content toward better **search engine optimization (SEO)**

Before diving into code, harness what the community has already provided.

Drupal themes

The second type of project is a theme.

What is a theme?

Drupal themes are front-end development projects that leverage the core's visual system to control the look and feel of the Drupal application. A theme can be the visual presentation of content for end users. It can also be the theme used for the administrative experience of the Drupal application, known as an admin theme.

Themes control the HTML, CSS, and JavaScript used for the Drupal application. HTML is created through the use of templates. Based on the enabled features, content-related features define expected templates that map variables provided by the backend to the corresponding HTML. Templates leverage the Twig framework for functionality and syntax. A theme registers the templates, CSS, and JavaScript, which can then be subsequently enabled in Drupal.

Core themes

The most well-known themes are provided by Core. Core themes provide useful examples for integrating with all core-related features, demonstrate web accessibility standards, and often leverage modern frontend practices.

The following examples are the core themes provided by Drupal 10:

- **Olivero**: The default theme for content
- **Claro**: The default admin theme

More information about themes will be provided in the next chapter and as a common theme throughout the book.

Contribution

Drupal core, modules, and themes are not even possible without developers contributing their efforts. As an open-source project, Drupal has managed to attract a large number of contributors throughout the globe. These community members provide complementary ideas, build new Drupal projects, create bugs, submit fixes, write documentation, give talks at events, and more. These contributions have helped Drupal become one of the most established open-source projects—a project with longevity and one that continues to be relevant. Without the community, there would be no Drupal. It also emphasizes the importance of Drupal adopters finding ways to give back.

Community contributions will be covered in much greater detail in *Chapter 4*.

Summary

Drupal core provides both foundational features and an extensible framework that can be used for building the application and customization. Projects provide modularity built into Drupal core. Drupal has projects for both frontend and backend development through its themes and modules. The community and contributions to Drupal core help to continually evolve and improve this foundation, and extending Drupal can often yield useful community contributions and address the needs of enterprise integrations. The next chapter covers the infrastructure needed to run Drupal and more about Drupal's technical architecture.

Infrastructure and Overview of Technical Architecture

This chapter focuses on many technical aspects of Drupal. It begins by covering the required infrastructure to host Drupal applications. Then, the three primary components of Drupal's application architecture are reviewed. After that, Drupal's code architecture is explored from both the backend and the frontend, covering the programming languages, tools, and practices used to develop Drupal. The chapter concludes with a high-level overview of how to effectively maintain a Drupal site and perform standard operations, such as code updates.

In this chapter, we're going to cover the following main topics:

- Hosting Drupal and platform requirements
- Drupal architecture
- Drupal management and operations

Hosting Drupal and platform requirements

Drupal requires a hosted platform to run any Drupal application. Drupal runs as a server-side rendered PHP application accessible from a web browser. The hosting platform must be able to process requests made through its web server to execute the Drupal application. Drupal is not stateless. To be able to make configurations and store content, Drupal requires the hosting platform to persistently store files and structured content in a database. The context of each request helps the application determine how to process the request. Drupal loads its configuration, queries relevant information from the database, and leverages PHP to do the processing.

The following figure shows an example **LAMP (Linux, Apache, MySQL, and PHP)** stack with a Drupal application:

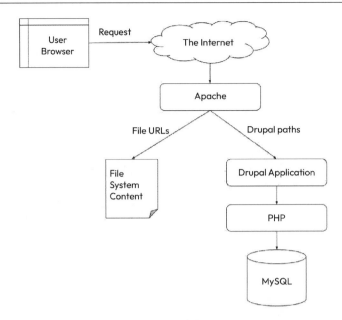

Figure 3.1 – High-level LAMP stack and request flow

Each version of Drupal sets its own platform requirements. Platform requirements are published on `drupal.org` and are updated upon the release of each major version. They often correlate with planned releases of dependent projects and are communicated well in advance of new Drupal releases. At a high level, Drupal observes semantic versioning that follows a convention of major, minor, and patch versions. This is formatted as `major.minor.patch` and has explicit definitions. With major versions, it is important to consider platform requirements given that they span developers working on their systems, code deployments, and more. Platform requirements span web servers, database servers, supported programming languages, enabling libraries, and system configuration. Details on the servers and their purpose are covered in the next section of this chapter.

The platform should not be viewed as static. The underlying platform must evolve as Drupal evolves. While Drupal is built on PHP and comprises a lot of the code in Drupal's application, each PHP version introduces new programming language conventions and the deprecation of old ones. It cannot be assumed that a hosting environment will just work if it is not running Drupal's specified version of PHP. This is especially important when upgrading Drupal applications. Major versions of Drupal update platform requirements that commonly include the latest stable version of PHP at the time of the major release. This practice is in line with dependent projects, such as Symfony, which require Drupal to foundationally run its application. Drupal's dependencies are detailed in the next section.

Drupal architecture

Drupal's architecture is both broad and deep; there are many technical aspects of Drupal, and each typically requires some level of specialized knowledge to understand. It starts with the infrastructure that runs the Drupal application, which has a specific stack and knowledge of system administration. The application itself has three main architectural components, which are detailed shortly. The most complex is code. Backend development and frontend development leverage different programming languages and best practices. This section will not provide a deep dive into any specific subject matter, but rather an overview of high-level knowledge for all of Drupal.

Infrastructure technical stack

Drupal spans many layers of a technical stack, as shown by its platform requirements. Drupal is an application that is commonly associated with the LAMP stack. At the lowest level, Drupal dependencies run on operating systems. Given the free and open-source nature of Drupal, Linux is the most common operating system. It offers administrators a more polished and documented experience for running Drupal. While it is technically possible to use Windows, this is less common and may result in unexpected edge cases.

On top of the operating system runs various servers and capabilities, including the web server, PHP, and database server. Apache is a widely adopted web server, but alternatives, such as Nginx, can be used effectively. PHP is installed on the system and also integrated with the web server through various mechanisms (normally Apache mods or PHP FPM). MySQL and Percona (a variation of MySQL) are common database options, but Drupal offers support for PostgreSQL and other databases. Pay careful attention to system firewalls that may block traffic between services or not allow a public interface to the web server.

At the top of the stack is the end user's browser, which Drupal defines as explicit browser and version support. This is most common for Drupal's frontend given that browsers have different support for features in CSS and Drupal's commitment to accessibility. This was shown previously in *Figure 3.1*.

With any technical infrastructure, each component has its own maintenance needs. As an example, PHP routinely releases new versions. A major version release adds new functionality and deprecates the old. Upgrading even one component in the infrastructure requires it to correspond to the version of the Drupal application and its platform requirements. Note that each infrastructure component has a specific configuration (MySQL and PHP in settings), extensions (PHP and Apache mods), and options that need to be set up to effectively run Drupal. Specifics can be found on `drupal.org` and are detailed in the release notes of each major version.

Application architecture

Drupal's application architecture has three primary components:

- **Code**: The files that define Drupal's application executed by the server
- **Database**: Persistent structured data for Drupal's content, configuration, and more
- **Files**: Assets, such as images or documents, that are stored on the server's filesystem

Starting with Drupal 8, a fourth component for the configuration was established. However, the configuration is built upon the three primary components, as configuration files are most often versioned with the code but can optionally be stored in files. The three primary components must be in sync with one another for the Drupal application to maintain parity. It is incredibly important to understand the purpose and value of each component.

The code runs the Drupal application and maintains the connection to the database and file components. It is also responsible for exporting, importing, and synchronizing the configuration between the code/files and the database. Code is often versioned in a code versioning system (usually Git), so it has a persistent log of changes (commits) and tags for releases. Both the database and file components maintain persistent content. The database stores the structured content and state of the Drupal application using a history called schema versions. Both core and Drupal projects maintain a record of schema versions within code that can afford changes to the database defined within the code updates. The file's component is responsible for content-based file assets, such as a JPEG image managed by Drupal's media system or a PDF file attached to a Drupal node. All of the metadata for the file assets are stored in the database with the content itself.

The following figure shows a request being made to Drupal that has code deployed from Git:

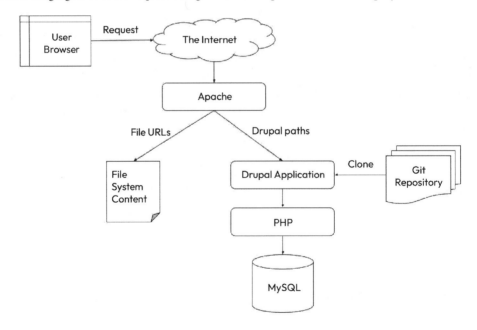

Figure 3.2 – LAMP stack with a cloned Drupal application

Drupal harnesses projects for its modular architecture. As previously mentioned, Drupal resembles building blocks. Some applications may want some projects enabled, while others may not. Drupal affords four types of projects: core, modules, themes, and distributions. As of now, Drupal only has one core project, but it overlaps with project contribution processes on drupal.org. Modules are changes to Drupal's backend application that add new features or extend existing features of Drupal's subsystems. Themes extend Drupal's frontend application. Both modules and themes are stored in code and have static metadata in YAML that allow Drupal to effectively articulate what is in the project and what its basic Drupal settings are. Distributions offer opinionated starting points that integrate into Drupal's installation process. A distribution defines its corresponding modules, themes, and default configuration to allow a brand-new Drupal application to have specific features and configurations set up during installation. It is unclear whether distributions will exist beyond Drupal 10, as a new feature called **recipes** will be built in Drupal 10. The primary benefit of recipes is that distributions complicate code updates because the entire distribution must be maintained as a whole. Recipes allow for one-time installation without the maintenance burden of a distribution. A recipe can also be installed at any point in the lifecycle of a Drupal application. More details on recipes can be found in the *What's new in Drupal 10?* section of *Chapter 4*.

Backend architecture

Drupal's backend code architecture is a combination of standard projects in the PHP ecosystem (akin to upstream projects) and its code built on top of the projects. This was a significant difference between Drupal 7 and Drupal 8. The Drupal community claimed the new architecture *got off of the island*, meaning it adopted more modern PHP development practices that harnessed and contributed to a broad ecosystem of PHP projects in favor of implementing application-specific solutions that other projects already solved. Upstream projects are stable, well-tested, highly adopted, and integrated by countless projects outside of Drupal. To realize this benefit, Drupal needed to support Composer (getcomposer.org) to have thoughtful dependency management for its code and dependencies in the PHP community. The adoption of Symfony components was one notable change that helped Drupal adopt PSR standards and leverage widely adopted capabilities such as Symfony's HTTP kernel, filesystem, routing, and dependency injection. Drupal then proceeded to build subsystems and features, such as modules, media, and logging, on top of the foundational components pulled from the upstream ecosystem. Drupal core is delivered with a composer.json file that defines the foundational components, but Drupal projects can have their composer.json file to bring in other PHP libraries from the upstream community. A drupal core often still abstracts the use of specific libraries or projects through its APIs to minimize reliance on specific projects and to abstract supported capabilities through Drupal's framework. Should another project be better in the future, Drupal can readily adopt it while not breaking backward compatibility in its framework. It is strongly recommended to use Drupal's provided framework within custom and contributed code for these reasons.

The following figure shows the code workflow, from cloning code in Git, through building code in Composer, to deploying built code on a web server:

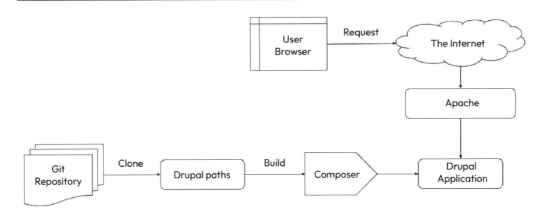

Figure 3.3 – Drupal code deployment workflow

Modules have a specific composition. Basic metadata, such as the project name, category, and dependencies, is stored in a [module-name].info.yml file. Various other YAML files exist for registering services and managing libraries. A composer.json file also exists with packaging metadata and dependencies on both drupal.org and the broader PHP ecosystem. Historical *hook-based* code, introduced in earlier versions of Drupal, is found in the [module-name].module file. However, PSR standards were introduced that use new object-oriented conventions aligned with the Symfony projects Drupal depends on. Under the src directory, a series of subdirectories and PHP classes exist that the underlying systems automatically register and process. Under the tests directory is where all PHPUnit tests exist, tied to a specific module's functionality. Finally, schema versions are managed with a [module-name].install file. Modules may also deliver submodules, commonly found in the modules directory. This pattern is used for tightly coupled, optional capabilities for the base module.

Automated testing is another critical aspect of Drupal's code architecture. Drupal core delivers various types of tests built off of the PHPUnit framework: unit, kernel, functional, browser, and functional JavaScript. Each type of test is intended to cover different test cases found within module or theme projects and is well documented on drupal.org. Drupal also leverages the backstage project for the frontend testing framework. Effective Drupal projects harness automated testing for predictable and reliable changes to code. In fact, Drupal core has a gated process that requires test changes and passing tests before committing a change. Great community contributions and effective project maintainership can often be measured by the existence of tests. Tests can also be created for custom Drupal projects. A high-quality and change-friendly Drupal application has high test coverage for both contributed and custom code.

Frontend architecture

While Drupal's backend manages the foundational application, Drupal has a robust frontend architecture as well. Drupal's frontend architecture spans CSS, JavaScript, and HTML markup. Drupal leverages themes for the frontend. Themes can be built for delivering Drupal content or for styling Drupal's administration system (often referred to as *themes* and *admin themes*). Out of the box, Drupal core delivers several themes:

- **Claro**: The default admin theme
- **Olivero**: The default theme
- **Stark**: A theme with minimal styling and features commonly used for debugging
- **Starter Kit**: A theme used as a launch point for custom Drupal theming

Both Claro and Olivero were deemed stable shortly before the release of Drupal 10, replacing Bartik and Seven found in earlier versions. Starter Kit is a unique type of theme, as it offers a framework for creating default custom themes from a defined starting point and has a command-line tool to create new themes from a starter kit. This is a useful feature when you want an opinionated starting point for a theme but need to perform specific customization for one or more Drupal sites.

The following command creates a new theme from the default StarterKit:

```
$ php core/scripts/drupal generate-theme my_new_theme
```

Themes have a specific architectural composition. First, a theme has various metadata defined as YAML in an `info.yml` file. Common settings, such as name and category, exist. Other settings register Twig templates/CSS files, project dependencies, logo, supported core versions, and registered regions that the theme provides. Libraries are defined in a `libraries.yml` file to give instructions on what CSS or JavaScript libraries need to be loaded in the Drupal application for the theme to work properly. A theme can also provide a base theme setting for a theme to only provide overrides from an inherited theme. A theme also contains directories for Twig templates to render HTML markup and is commonly used to organize CSS and JavaScript files (assumed to be generated given that Drupal does not have an opinionated CSS generation tool). Twig files follow specific naming conventions that expose templates to themes for specific Drupal features, such as blocks, views, and node-based templates. All out-of-the-box Drupal themes maintain explicit support for browsers as per the policies defined at `drupal.org`. Developers that use out-of-the-box themes as base themes should be mindful of the policy tied to each major version of Drupal, as there may be unintended consequences supporting certain browsers or versions of a browser (such as older versions of Internet Explorer).

This section reviewed the infrastructure required to run Drupal and Drupal's application architecture. It is critically important to know what is required to run Drupal and to be aware of Drupal's backend and frontend aspects when creating applications. The modularity of Drupal affords developers flexibility in enabling or disabling features based on the use cases required for the application. Understanding the technology behind Drupal helps developers with training, making open-source contributions, and understanding Drupal's approach to solving specific problems.

Drupal management and operations

Often people joke that Drupal is free "like a puppy." While the software is made available for free through the open-source community, it takes work to build your application and subsequently maintain and operate it. It can be as basic as performing routine code updates, or it may involve complex concepts, such as staged code workflows and automated deployment processes. This section provides approaches and considerations for maintenance and operations for a Drupal application.

Maintenance

Drupal runs at the top of a technology stack, but thoughtful maintenance includes keeping the full stack up to date. Updates apply at all levels of the **operating system (OS)**, packages running on the OS, the web server, the database server, and more. PHP commonly runs as a package of the OS and is configured on the web server. Any update in the stack can introduce new or updated configurations that should be carefully managed because they may not be supported by the Drupal application. PHP updates can directly impair Drupal's application code if left unmanaged. While many of the projects found in a LAMP stack have mature update processes and routine maintenance rarely breaks Drupal, it is important to note that a thoughtful maintenance strategy should at least have measures in place to upgrade and test safely. There is also value in using established tools.

Adopters need to consider maintenance for Drupal as well. The most notable is code updates. Drupal only offers support for specific major and minor versions of Drupal core. Doing more would put a substantial burden on a community largely made up of volunteers who maintain the software. This policy includes supported versions of Drupal's dependencies, such as Symfony projects. The most notable impact of supported versions is a policy tied to security releases. Drupal will only offer security coverage for code that falls within the supported versions. It is prudent to keep code running on a Drupal application up to date. Given that a security update can come at any time and during any project that an application adopts, it is best practice to update your application when releases come out. Making a larger number of releases within a code update has a higher risk of introducing unintended changes or bugs that require adequate time to test against the specific capabilities of your application. Security updates should be applied in a timely fashion to mitigate the risk of your application getting compromised. Keeping an application up to date when a security release comes out provides more confidence that a smaller change will not break a Drupal application. The Drupal Steward service offered by the Drupal Association is a web application firewall that protects your application from malicious requests. Any request that attempts to exploit a vulnerability is filtered by the firewall. This can save you time and lower the urgency of performing security updates.

Drupal also has a deprecation policy where minor versions will mark deprecations that get removed from the next major release. It is best practice for applications to remediate deprecations when they become known in minor versions as opposed to when they get delivered by major releases. Application developers need to pay close attention to deprecations found in custom projects, but developers have an opportunity to contribute deprecation remediation back to projects on `drupal.org`. This can help make progress for projects that an application may depend on upstream on `drupal.org`. Be mindful that custom code may leverage deprecated capabilities in PHP that may also need remediation.

Drupal code updates may also drive changes to the stack. As mentioned, major versions of Drupal have defined platform requirements. When upgrading, it is implied that the platform requirements are in place, including versions of PHP, database servers, and web servers.

Operations

This section covers what is required for the effective operation of a Drupal application. Heavy emphasis is placed on keeping Drupal code up to date and employing practices that help deploy code responsibly. Best practices harness DevOps philosophies, which emphasize the automation of processes over manual efforts.

We start with the concept of a deployment. A deployment is the act of updating code on the servers that execute the code. It is highly recommended to update code early and frequently because a deployment creates a change. The smaller the change deployed, the easier it is to ensure that the deployment is successful. In Drupal, the code provided by the community is updated all the time. It can be as simple as a contributed module addressing a bug or a minor update to Drupal core. Alternatively, it can be far more significant, such as a major Drupal version update that has deprecations or a new major version of a module that may break the API for other modules that depend on it.

Environments are a critical concept to modern code deployment workflows. Deployment workflows operate in stages, where code is tested in an earlier stage and eventually promoted to a production environment in the final stage. An environment represents the infrastructure needed for one stage of a code deployment. Each environment should be a close replica of the production infrastructure to have parity. Earlier-stage environments should be used for testing changes. This concept applies to any code update, including routine updates to community-sponsored projects or new projects created for new features in your Drupal application.

Drupal applications have common deployment approaches and stages. It is common for Drupal developers to harness their local systems to perform initial code updates and high-level testing. Code is then deployed into environments accessible via the web by non-developers. Many Drupal applications harness development, stage, and production (dev, stage, prod) stages within a deployment workflow. This model affords effective single-stream development, meaning one change increment can be tested at a time and promoted through dev, stage, and prod environments. Dev, stage, and prod represent static environments where various stakeholders test changes as they get promoted. It is common for a quality assurance team to test in dev and a business team to test in stage. Prod should only be promoted after rigorous testing. However, single-stream development models are losing favor to multi-stream models made popular by **continuous integration/continuous delivery (CI/CD)**. This model creates an environment for every change. Each change gets promoted into one static staging environment for stakeholder validation and is then more rapidly deployed to production. This workflow can be faster, enables concurrent development across one or more developer/development teams, and does not package a series of changes that dev, stage, or prod testing may demand if multiple changes are being worked on at a time.

Drupal is not just code. As mentioned in *Chapter 1*, Drupal maintains code, a database, and a filesystem, where configuration is often stored in code and the state resides in the database. Deployment should be viewed as a point in time that maps specific code, a specific database backup, and a specific archive of the filesystem. Performing any stage-based development workflow needs to observe a *code up, content down* promotion model. Code is promoted from earlier-stage environments up to production. However, production is *the source of truth* for Drupal's persistent content. A snapshot of the content found in the production database and filesystem should be created at the point at which a deployment occurs and then be staged down to the environment where the code deployment happens. This ensures the deployed environment has the most up-to-date state of production to effectively perform testing. A stale database and files in an environment may not allow effective testing or help mirror a production deployment. As such, code is promoted up through stages to production, and content is pushed down in stages from production. It is best practice to do this for each deployment.

The following figure demonstrates a code deployment workflow with dev, stage, and prod environments with a *code up, content down* model:

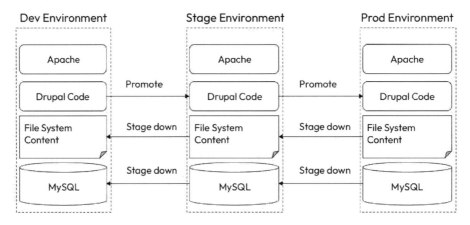

Figure 3.4 – Drupal code deployment workflow with environments

Given Drupal's extensibility and the freedom afforded to open-source maintainers, it cannot be assumed that pulling updated code from the community can be done simply and without issue. Custom projects that harness Drupal's APIs do not have the benefit of engagement from the broader open-source community. Some level of testing needs to be in place, and it is ideal for this testing to occur before the code is launched into a production environment. The best Drupal applications harness automated testing to ensure there is effective continuity for updating code. The importance of small deployments done frequently cannot be overstated. A small deployment makes it far easier to isolate issues and ensure that there is less code to roll back until the issue is addressed. Given that core and contributed projects are open source, any issue should be reported back to the respective project.

Administrators need to be prepared for something to go wrong, even with well-tested code deployments. At the time of a production deployment, a backup needs to be created for the database and file assets.

Ideally, code should be managed in a code versioning system. All `Drupal.org` projects use Git, as Git has become a well-adopted community standard for code versioning. Git has built-in revisioning with its commit log. Rolling back code on a failed deployment is as simple as checking out an earlier commit. It is important to not store logs in the database (Drupal's `dblog` module), as this can cause the size of your database to grow significantly. Any restoration would also both take longer and lose log data between the backup and restoration. The restoration process should involve loading the SQL, loading the file archive, and reverting to the last commit. Please note that restoration is a destructive operation and should be used as a last resort, as any content or file assets created between the code deployment and restoration will be lost. A failed release should be identified and restored as soon as possible to avoid loss of data. Leveraging tags in a code repository per release can ensure that you can more easily see what was released and when.

The code that gets deployed must be a fully built code artifact. Given that Drupal uses Composer, it is common for a code repo to contain custom code and the packaging metadata to assemble the code. This packaging definition is stored in a `composer.json` file, which defines the version of Drupal core and the projects with their desired installed versions from `drupal.org`. Each Composer update modifies the `composer.lock` file, which should also be versioned. The code assembly can happen on a server after the code is updated, but it is extremely important to load code from a specific, tested deployment defined in `composer.lock` and not install the code from `composer.json` directly. Many Drupal themes also generate frontend code using tools such as **npm**. A fully built code base needs to load both backend and frontend code.

Once the new code is deployed, a few steps need to be executed to load the changes. First, the database schema needs to be updated. Second, the configuration needs to be loaded, as this is often maintained with code within the Git repository. Third, Drupal's cache needs to be cleared. It is common to see both updates and deployments automated with Drupal's command-line tool, Drush. More advanced DevOps and automation are shared in *Chapter 17, Git, Drush, Composer, CLI, and DevOps*.

Maintaining and operating Drupal is critical to keeping the application running, effectively loading updates, keeping your application secure, and having practices that enable testing and predictability. Understanding tools such as Composer, Git, and Drush is a core skill that any Drupal developer needs. Harnessing concepts such as environments and automation in deployment workflows helps promote consistency in the process and ensures that the web server, database, and files respect Drupal's code and content differences.

Summary

In this chapter, we covered aspects of Drupal's high-level architecture, including its backend application and its frontend presentation layer. The three main components of Drupal, code, files, and the database, were highlighted. Various hosting platform requirements were defined and high-level deployment strategies were shared, covering each of the three main components. Finally, the chapter explained maintenance considerations regarding Drupal architecture to help you effectively run Drupal applications. The next chapter will explore the Drupal community.

4
Drupal Community

While Drupal itself is an extensible enterprise digital technology, the community behind Drupal is its true superpower. Effectively harnessing the community, its tools, and its practices helps any developer become better at Drupal. The community builds Drupal and contributes its experience and code to make Drupal better. Without a vast and healthy community, Drupal wouldn't be what it is today. This chapter aims to help you better understand the community while stressing the importance of everyone contributing their experience to sustain and shape the Drupal project.

In this chapter, we're going to cover the following main topics:

- Understanding the open source community
- Projects on Drupal.org

Understanding the open-source community

Drupal's biggest strength is the community behind it. Unlike proprietary software, which has developers paid to build and maintain it, Drupal leverages its active, open-source community. Understanding how to work with the community is critical to working with Drupal and to keeping it vibrant.

Drupal.org basics

Drupal.org is one of the primary places where the community engages. The following figure shows the initial Drupal.org landing page, which provides a high-level direction for those interested in Drupal:

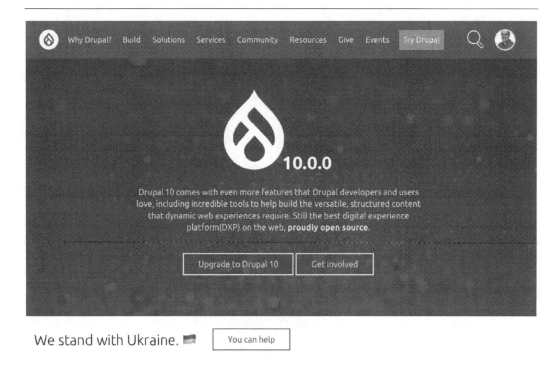

Figure 4.1 – Drupal.org home page

The figure shows a lot of relevant information, starting with the top menu, which can help direct you to useful starting points. **Why Drupal?** and **Solutions** capture useful marketing material for different types of users in the community. **Build** helps direct community members toward projects and issue queues that help create Drupal applications. Community information is found in **Community Resources**, **Give**, and **Events**. One can also find useful links in the footer and throughout Drupal. org, such as security advisories, licensing information, jobs, and more. Drupal.org is a fairly complete resource for the community to collaborate with maintainers, suggest improvements, surface issues, find help, and contribute. Becoming familiar with this tool is imperative to learning Drupal. It can take time to learn the Drupal concepts and terminology that are important to how the community engages. However, harnessing Drupal.org is the single biggest tool for self-help, as you can readily find solutions to issues and benefit from others who are also using Drupal. If you get stuck, go to Drupal.org, as there is a high likelihood that others have encountered the same issue. Also, create an account on Drupal.org so you can join in and participate.

Core on Drupal.org

A project is how Drupal organizes its open-source code, documentation, issues, and more. Core is a special type of project that differentiates between contributed modules, themes, distributions, and community projects. While Drupal core is the foundation of all Drupal applications, it still shares elements of all projects for consistency.

The following figure shows Drupal core's project page:

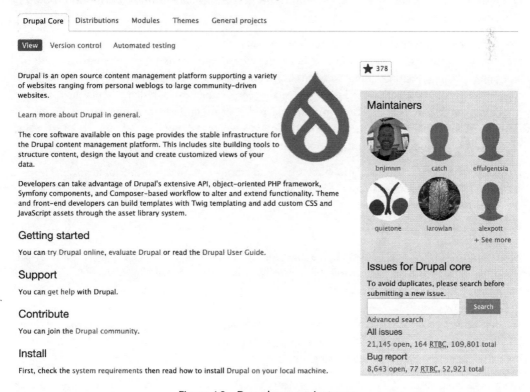

Figure 4.2 – Drupal core project page

Like other project pages, this one features core maintainers, issue queues, releases, and more. This consistency with other projects, as demonstrated in the example project in *Chapter 1*, helps the community to collaborate and engage in the same way across core and contributed projects.

Core contribution

Core has something for all community members to contribute to. For beginners, issues in the core often have the most visibility and support from other community members and subsequently can be a great tool for learning. The technical core contribution goes through the most rigor, given that the core is foundational for every Drupal install and that changes must be managed carefully. While this may seem more difficult, it is the best way to get acclimated to Drupal's contribution. Processes are in place to ensure that automated testing coverage exists and that all tests pass. While this requires more care and may seem overly rigorous, it helps Drupal adopters avoid introducing bugs that could be caused even by simple changes. The significant positive impact of this contribution should be welcomed by all contributors.

However, Drupal core has established processes to evolve thoughtfully. Minor versions often maintain the same platform requirements and core dependencies while releasing ongoing improvements and additional planned features. Major versions are for larger changes. Applications can often expect a clean and easy upgrade path for minor core updates. Major updates often demand platform changes, upgrade Drupal core's dependent components, and commit code-level framework deprecations introduced from the previous minor version. This is a larger task but one that affords added value, new features, continued community support, and more.

Drupal core provides the foundational features and framework that run the application. The next sections will highlight more about the purpose of these features and how to build applications.

Projects on Drupal.org

Understanding projects on Drupal.org is a must for anyone developing with Drupal. The next chapter will go into great depth on what a project is; basically, projects extend Drupal's out-of-the-box behavior for explicit use cases. Drupal core, which is its out-of-the-box foundation, is also a project on Drupal.org. Harnessing contributed projects is one of the most valuable aspects of Drupal, and learning how to discover projects is critical to realizing the value of the open-source community instead of just diving into development. This approach harnesses the collective talent and excellence of the community (also known as "standing on the shoulders of giants").

Drupal.org is the home of all community projects and is perpetually evolving. Projects are routinely created or updated, as are the documentation (content), features, and experience found on Drupal.org. Some of the figures shared may routinely change through updates or changes to Drupal itself, but the core principles outlined in this chapter, and the book more generally, remain true. The following figure demonstrates a project page:

Password Policy

`View`   Version control   Automated testing

This module provides a way to enforce restrictions on user passwords by defining password policies.

Overview

A password policy can be defined with a set of constraints which must be met before a user password change will be accepted. Each constraint has a parameter allowing for the minimum number of valid conditions which must be met before the constraint is satisfied.

Example: an uppercase constraint (with a parameter of 2) and a digit constraint (with a parameter of 4) means that a user password must have at least 2 uppercase letters and at least 4 digits for it to be accepted.

8.x-3.x released

A version for Drupal 8 has been released for feedback. Constraints are now plugins. Please see the example constraints bundled as submodules to this release. Formal documentation will soon follow.

Features

Current constraints include:

- Character types
- Digit
- Letter
- Letter/Digit (Alphanumeric)
- Length
- Uppercase
- Lowercase
- Punctuation
- Delay
- Username

Maintainers

AohRveTPV   deekayen   miglius

nerdstein   shrop   paulocs
+ See more

Issues for Password Policy

To avoid duplicates, please search before submitting a new issue.

[   ] Search
Advanced search
All issues
234 open, 18 RTBC, 969 total
Bug report
99 open, 10 RTBC, 551 total
Statistics

Figure 4.3 – Project pages on Drupal.org

The figure shows one example project page, which features the primary content as well as the content in the sidebar. The primary content has the project title (**Password Policy**) and description (text under the title) to summarize the purpose of the project. This description is often the starting point for evaluating whether a project will or won't solve a specific problem. Project releases are found at the bottom of the page. The sidebar shows the maintainers and offers links to the documentation, source code, and issue queues. Maintainers are listed as the points of contact for the project.

Every project has an issue queue, as shown in the following figure, for community engagement and the organization of planned work:

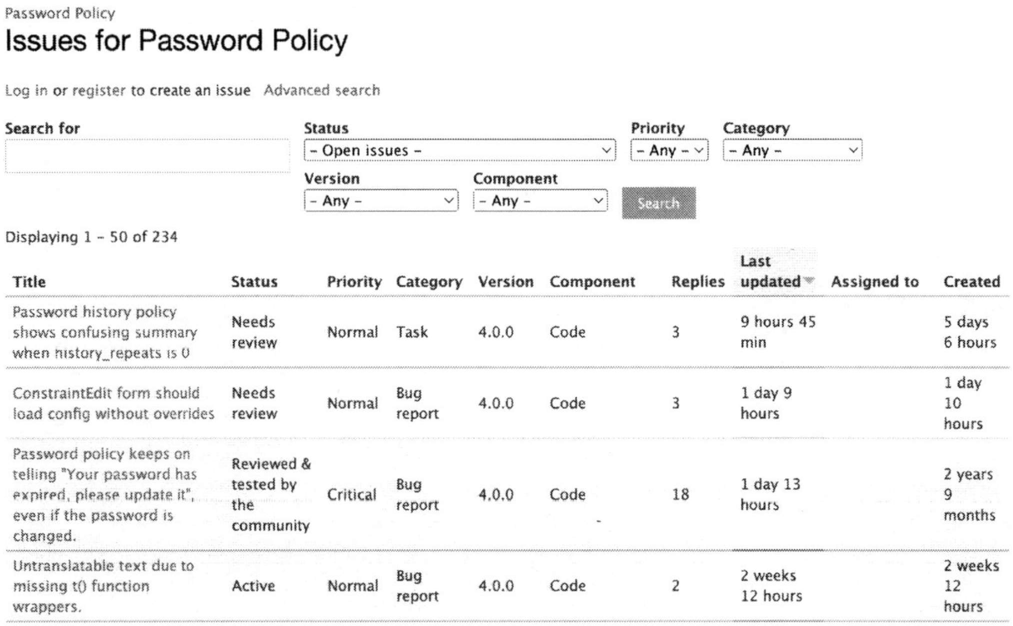

Password Policy
Issues for Password Policy

Log in or register to create an issue   Advanced search

Search for

Status
– Open issues –

Priority
– Any – ∨

Category
– Any – ∨

Version
– Any –

Component
– Any –

Search

Displaying 1 – 50 of 234

Title	Status	Priority	Category	Version	Component	Replies	Last updated▼	Assigned to	Created
Password history policy shows confusing summary when history_repeats is 0	Needs review	Normal	Task	4.0.0	Code	3	9 hours 45 min		5 days 6 hours
ConstraintEdit form should load config without overrides	Needs review	Normal	Bug report	4.0.0	Code	3	1 day 9 hours		1 day 10 hours
Password policy keeps on telling "Your password has expired, please update it", even if the password is changed.	Reviewed & tested by the community	Critical	Bug report	4.0.0	Code	18	1 day 13 hours		2 years 9 months
Untranslatable text due to missing t() function wrappers.	Active	Normal	Bug report	4.0.0	Code	2	2 weeks 12 hours		2 weeks 12 hours

Figure 4.4 – Project issue queues on Drupal.org

The figure demonstrates the basics of a project's issue queue for a specific project, **Password Policy**. Filters at the top of the issue queue are helpful, as each filter can differentiate the status of the issue, compatibility with the major version of Drupal, the type of issue, and more. The issue queues are searchable and sortable to help look for keywords and order by priority. If you have a problem using a project, check the queue. For widely used projects, there is a high likelihood that an issue may already exist for a challenge you face.

The next figure shows an example of a Drupal issue where community members help manage project code, collaborate on specific requests, and more:

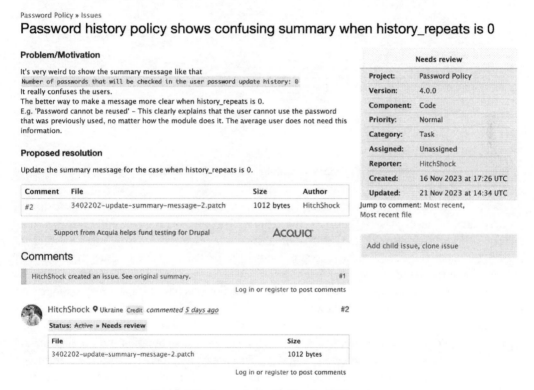

Figure 4.5 – A sample project issue on Drupal.org

After logging in, community members can both update an issue and engage in comments at the bottom of an issue, as seen in the following figure:

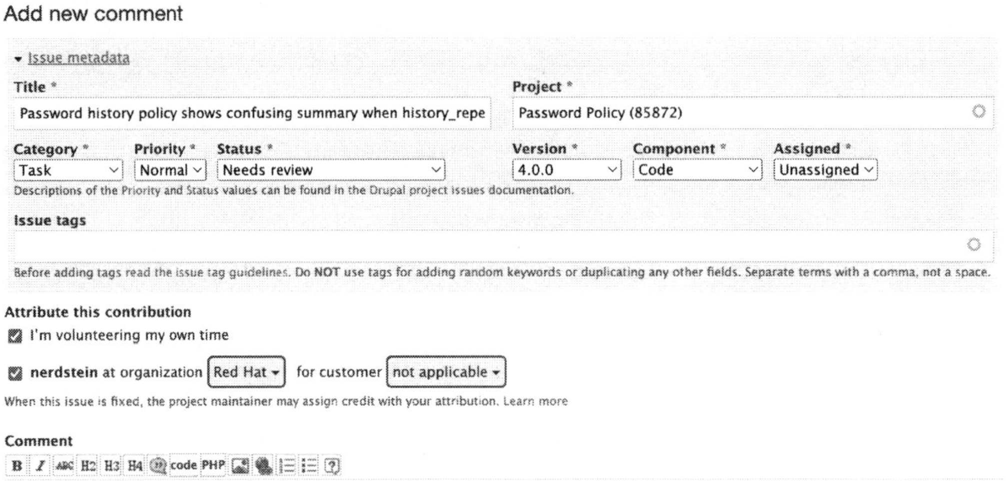

Figure 4.6 – Collaborating within a project issue on Drupal.org

Issues are composed of titles, summaries, metadata, and comments. An accordion exists for the primary-issue metadata. The categories of **Bug report**, **Plan**, **Support request**, and **Feature request** all have different semantics that categorize the intent of the issue filed. Dropdowns exist for the priority, the status of the issue, the user assigned, and the impacted component. Issue summaries help describe the purpose and context of an issue and comments are used for discussion. Issues also offer instructions for contributing code to fix the issue. Some projects have Drupal.org's merge request workflows enabled. If not, they will show standard commands to propose changes. Finally, users can link related issues that are helpful for historical conversations or dependent work. Project maintainers are the stewards of issues and their projects and are often active in collaboration and decision-making when considering an issue filed. A crediting system exists where maintainers can credit contributors for their efforts. Community members can gain greater exposure for individuals and their supporting organizations, gaining direct results from contributing to the benefit of all.

Contribution impact

Drupal developers often have to address unique requirements in their created applications. In building the application, developers may run into new use cases, find bugs, or find limitations based on their experience. This experience serves as an opportunity for contribution, and every project on Drupal. org has an issue queue that allows people to contribute based on their experience.

The impact can be noteworthy. Take Drupal Commerce as one example. Built on top of Drupal, Commerce is a set of fundamental features, such as a cart and products, combined with a highly extensible framework. The framework was designed to offer third-party integration with different payment processors, the ability to satisfy additional optional use cases such as fulfillment, and more. Community members have not only submitted fixes to bugs with Commerce itself but have contributed integrations for over 132 different payment gateways, such as Stripe, PayPal, Amazon Pay, and more. Community members also built complementary features for subscription management (recurring payment models), coupons (promotions), managing taxes, and shipping capabilities. The net result of these contributions has yielded a robust ecosystem of Commerce capabilities built on Drupal and its content management capabilities to deliver effective digital storefronts.

Contributions provide opportunities to help the Drupal ecosystem. Even the smallest of changes can make a material impact across a significant range of installed Drupal applications or benefit the vast Drupal community. Each community member has the chance to share their experience and to use that experience to improve Drupal.

Other community resources and tools

The Drupal community engages in other ways that help foster collaboration. Discussion commonly happens on Drupal Slack (`drupal.org/slack`). General and specific channels exist that are tied to getting help, specific projects, or specific topics that span both professional and social subjects. Drupal camps and conferences, most prominently the global conference known as DrupalCon, bring the community together through sessions, supported contributions, and social events. Some regions hold local events and meetups. Finally, community members routinely write blogs, engage in social networks, and join podcasts.

The Drupal Association is a US-based non-profit organization tasked with "uniting the global open source community to build, secure, and promote Drupal." They run Drupal.org, maintain the project's infrastructure, host DrupalCon, and lead strategic programs. While their responsibilities do not overlap with the vision of the Drupal project or hands-on contributions to the project itself, the Drupal Association is a critical enabler. As a resource for the community, they serve in other ways, such as governance, oversight of the code of conduct, and executing improvements to the infrastructure that aids in contribution or testing.

The broader community surrounding Drupal is both vast and inspiring. Between Drupal.org content, projects, issues, events, Slack, and the Drupal Association, there are endless resources available to community members to engage, learn, grow, and contribute. The community and resources that enable this are why Drupal stands out as one of the largest and longest-standing open-source projects. The community has engaged to collaborate on building Drupal, identifying and fixing issues, contributing meaningful add-ons that extend Drupal, and helping others become technical professionals.

Summary

This chapter covered a review of Drupal.org and provided an introduction to engaging with the community, working with community projects, and the purpose of the Drupal Association. All of these are important to effectively harness one of Drupal's best assets: its community. The next chapter covers what is new in Drupal 10.

5

What's New in Drupal 10

Drupal 10 is the latest release in the long-time open source project. Drupal 10 launched with a series of improvements, features, and modernization. And, Drupal 11 is built in Drupal 10. Deprecations will be proposed, but not removed until Drupal 11 is launched. Features desired for Drupal 11 will be built during Drupal 10's life cycle. This chapter covers everything about Drupal 10, from its platform requirements to its features to its maintenance considerations.

In this chapter, we're going to cover the following main topics:

- Release methodology
- New to Drupal 10
- Built in Drupal 10

Release methodology

Drupal 10's initiatives and requirements were defined before Drupal 10 was launched. This was based on several factors.

Drupal 10 has a defined life cycle with roughly 6 months of minor releases. There is no explicit number of minor releases before a major release is announced. However, major releases, starting with Drupal 8, have been on an approximate 2-to-3-year cadence. After this cadence, a new major version is released and the previous major version reaches its end of life. The only exception is Drupal 7, which has extended end-of-life support. Details can be found on drupal.org by searching for *Core Release Cycles*.

Drupal applications inherit life cycle considerations of Drupal's dependencies. Infrastructure, such as PHP and MySQL, have explicit supported versions at the time a major version is supported. As an example, Drupal would not explicitly support an end-of-life version of PHP. Application-level dependencies, such as Symfony components or JavaScript libraries, often help define the specific PHP versions or set browser compatibility. Dependencies drive a lot of the logic around major releases. Drupal's major release cadence often overlaps with major releases of Symfony. And, major releases are remediated and tested against the supported requirements only. The supportability of other requirements may vary but should not be assumed.

Platform requirements

Drupal 10's platform requirements were defined roughly 6 months before its release. Drupal 10 requires at least PHP 8.1 and an explicit set of PHP extensions defined on drupal.org. MySQL requires at least 5.7.8 and MariaDB at least 10.3.7. Support for PostgreSQL 12 and SQLite 3.26 exists but with specific extensions enabled.

Upgrade considerations

As mentioned previously, Drupal applications are "free like a puppy." Major release upgrades are no different. While the code is open, it takes work to maintain. The infrastructure must be updated first, which helps split a major upgrade into a logical sequence of events. Like previous versions, Drupal 10 was built in Drupal 9. When preparing for Drupal 9, it is best to upgrade the platform and infrastructure with the last minor version of Drupal 9. All of the platform-level support is already in the last Drupal 9 release and ready for the upcoming Drupal 10 deprecations. Deprecation scanning can be used to remediate code-level issues, after which the application code can be upgraded to Drupal 10. Each part of the infrastructure has an upgrade process. It is best practice to harness environments where a development environment can be updated safely for testing and remediation before a production release.

Major releases

Major releases demand more maintenance effort than minor releases, but a careful and methodical approach to upgrading both the platform and the code helps ensure a smooth and thoughtful execution. Note the relevance of semantic versioning (semver.org) for the conceptual differences between major and minor releases. Note that Drupal's life cycle can help with planning for when to release both major and minor versions. New features and changes to Drupal's underlying APIs are built into earlier minor releases before being officially released as a new major release. It is only in the new major release that changes get fully implemented and new features are supported.

Understanding how Drupal defines releases is critical to the infrastructure required to run Drupal, how Drupal manages dependencies, and the nuances of upgrading from earlier releases. Next, we will cover the new features and capabilities of Drupal 10.

New to Drupal 10

Many new features and updates to Drupal were delivered when Drupal 10 launched.

Symfony 6.2

While this is not necessarily a user-facing feature, Drupal 10 upgraded the underlying Symfony components to version 6.2. This version is the current, stable release of Symfony at the time of Drupal 10's launch. Drupal core leverages Symfony as a framework for underlying capabilities such as routing, services, dependency injection, events, kernels, and processes. Drupal also adopts utilities for serialization, validators, YAML, and translation. This helps Drupal leverage a well-adopted framework instead of creating its own code to achieve the same outcomes as exemplified by other PHP projects, such as Laravel and Joomla. Symfony components also helped define the platform requirements of Drupal, given Symfony 6.2 required at least PHP 8.1 and must maintain parity with the Drupal application.

Upgrading Symfony incorporates improvements such as bug fixing and stability, all of which were brought in from the Symfony community. Given that Drupal 9 was pinned to Symfony 4.4 components, this was a significant upgrade and, subsequently, a lot of updates. Symfony 5 released new components, performance improvements, and a significant reduction in the code base. Symfony 6 incorporated newer PHP development patterns, various improvements, and improved debugging.

CKEditor 5

CKEditor was upgraded to version 5 in Drupal 10. CKEditor was already the de facto WYSIWYG adopted by Drupal for long text, free-form field widgets. However, CKEditor5 delivered significant user experience improvements, modernized JavaScript for smoother integrations with frameworks such as ReactJS and VueJS, provided a large library of useful plugins, and more.

CKEditor's release was a significant architectural change from previous releases. The Drupal community members needed to work closely with contributors of CKEditor to overhaul Drupal's CKEditor integration. This spanned Drupal core's native WYSIWYG feature to plugins for things such as Drupal's media integration. Contributed plugins needed to be rebuilt for CKEditor 5. Drupal also had to replace its backend processing and serialization to properly support the new CKEditor 5 data format. This was no trivial effort but helped Drupal deliver a modernized, feature-rich WYSIWYG.

Olivero

Drupal replaced its long-time default theme, Bartik, with a new and improved theme, Olivero. Olivero, named after the late Rachel Olivero, was a blind Drupal community member and champion for inclusivity. Rachel's influence helped steer Drupal to become an open source leader in web accessibility and community member inclusion.

The new Olivero theme is a fitting tribute to Rachel's legacy. Olivero is more than just a refreshed, modernized look and feel. It delivers on WCAG AA compliance, a stringent web accessibility standard that demonstrates Drupal's commitment to building a platform for all. Olivero also delivers revamped support for some of the newer Drupal features, such as media, a layout builder, and more.

The following figure shows Drupal's home page with the Olivero theme:

Figure 5.1 - Drupal's out-of-the-box front page with Olivero

This figure demonstrates the fresh new look and feel of Drupal 10's new default theme. The previous theme, Bartik, was the default through the Drupal 7, 8, and 9 major releases, which spanned over 12 years from Drupal 10's release.

Claro

Seven, Drupal's longtime default administrative theme, was replaced by Claro. Claro brings a fresh look and feel to Drupal's backend administration. Like Olivero, it delivers improvements for web accessibility standards. Claro also incorporates modern JavaScript techniques and improved administrative usability.

The following figure shows a screenshot of Claro:

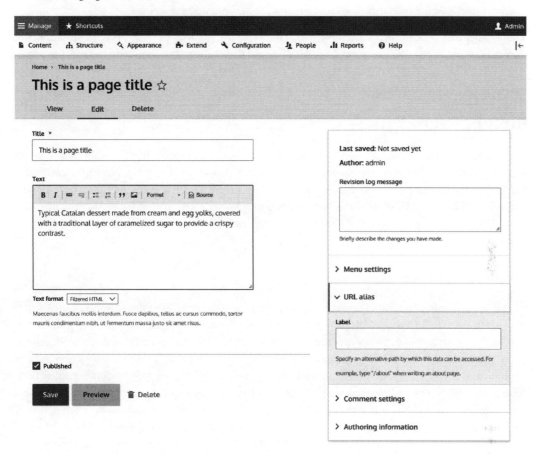

Figure 5.2 - Drupal's out-of-the-box node authoring page in Claro

As we can see, the delivery of Claro helped ensure that Drupal's administrative experience was modernized and delivered on updated standards.

Starter kit themes

Natively, Drupal has a feature for base themes, where a theme can inherit templates and styles from another theme to override them. Drupal 10 launched with a similar concept to create a new feature called starter kit themes. This feature annotates specific themes as starter kits and works with a command-line utility that generates themes from these starter kits. Drupal 10 core has one starter kit theme and the command-line utility. Generated themes do not maintain the inheritance of the original starter kit. This lack of inheritance allows for a generated theme to be fully customized while changes can still be tracked through Git. Developers can create their own starter kits to have a consistent starting point.

This is useful for agencies or teams that may incorporate consistent, opinionated frontend development practices into a theme but wish to generate themes independently for websites.

These new features of Drupal 10 not only use the latest and greatest of Drupal's dependencies, but they deliver net new value from previous versions of Drupal to enable new use cases and empower developers. This may not be exhaustive of what gets delivered in Drupal 10, however, as many features will be worked on and may be delivered during Drupal 10's life cycle.

Built in Drupal 10

Dries, the founder of Drupal, announced strategic initiatives that are actively being built in Drupal 10. It is common for strategic initiatives to deliver in the next major version of Drupal, but occasionally, these efforts will get merged into minor releases of the current major version. As such, the following strategic initiatives will be created in Drupal 10 and may be delivered in a minor version of Drupal 10 should they finish. And, adopters of Drupal 10 can try out work-in-progress initiatives and contribute to them.

Automatic updates

As this book mentions multiple times, Drupal requires ongoing maintenance. Complex Drupal sites with a large number of installed projects may have updates routinely as new releases span both Drupal core and its projects. Security updates are especially important to prevent a Drupal application from being compromised. Performing updates today is a largely technical task that requires knowledge of Composer, Git, and more. This can require a large investment and knowledge of technical skills. Tools such as Wordpress offer native features to perform automatic code updates that help non-developers adopt WordPress. This effort aims to automatically install updates in Drupal without the need to do any development work. Drupal checks for updates to its application and securely loads updates, all while providing the ability to roll back. Features like this allow Drupal to become more competitive outside of enterprise environments as small businesses are less likely to pay developers to maintain a website.

Recipes

One common pain point in Drupal is its distribution feature. Distributions are installable packages of projects and configurations that allow for a new Drupal installation to be set up in a specific way from the start. However, distributions do not allow for more fine-grained updates. The distribution must be updated all at once and maintainers must provide updates to the distribution before an application can perform the update. This is a heavy burden for maintainers of distributions who subsequently need to update their distribution every time a project updates, including Drupal core. Applications need to wait, which is not ideal when security updates are announced. A new feature called Recipes aims to offer an alternative.

Recipes allow you to perform a one-time configuration of a Drupal application. Recipes are declarative, not functional. Each recipe defines what to set up. Drupal offers a command-line tool to load this recipe. Recipes can come in a bundle, allowing for one recipe to package multiple recipes. And, Drupal will be augmenting its installation process to allow for one or more recipes to be loaded. In contrast to distributions, recipes have no persistence in Drupal after setup and they can be loaded at any point in the application's life cycle. Recipes have already been created for Drupal's standard installation profile. While it is undecided, recipes may eventually deprecate distributions.

Decoupled menus

Drupal natively offers features for web services through its JSON API capabilities. Also, Drupal is an appealing structured content backend for modern JavaScript frameworks such as ReactJS and VueJS. Decoupled menus is an initiative aimed at providing a reference architecture for Drupal menus. It provides a JSON-based web service that exposes menu-related data and a JavaScript-based library to parse the web service. Future efforts will move beyond just menus into other entities such as nodes, taxonomies, and even customs.

Project browser

It can be difficult to understand Drupal's terminology, especially when evaluating projects. The project browser initiative aims to help showcase some of Drupal's most adopted projects with easy-to-understand language and a user interface to readily browse and install projects. This effort helps non-technical evaluators more readily discover, access, and install prominent contributed features. The project browser will be a step during installation and a standalone catalog. It will handle downloading the code without leveraging Composer. And, future efforts will integrate recipes beyond just projects.

Summary

Drupal has established a methodical release process for both major and minor releases and a definition of platform requirements. Major and minor releases differ in expectations for performing updates. Drupal 10 delivered the latest major release of Drupal with notable features, improvements, and updates. It shipped with new default themes, a CKEditor upgrade, and updates for underlying Symfony components. New strategic initiatives are expected to deliver even more features during Drupal 10's life cycle.

The next chapter will teach you how to load a new Drupal application, perform an installation, and review common upfront configuration use cases.

Part 2: Setting up - Installing and Maintaining

This part starts hands-on exercises for starting a new Drupal application. You will gain an understanding of Drupal's installation methods and recommendations to configure a brand new Drupal application. Finally, a review of how to maintain both Drupal and its technical stack is covered.

This part has the following chapters:

- *Chapter 6, Bootstrapping, Installing, and Configuring a New Drupal Project*
- *Chapter 7, Maintaining Drupal*

6

Bootstrapping, Installing, and Configuring a New Drupal Project

All Drupal developers must have the fundamental skills to create Drupal applications, install them, and perform configuration. This would be considered all of the best practices to getting started with building Drupal. Drupal 10 has various practices to start new projects. A new codebase must be established, which requires understanding the basics of Composer, starting a Drupal project, and a series of commands frequently used to manage code. Next will be reviewing Drupal's installation options, including use of Drush and recipes which are new in Drupal 10. The results of the installer will be reviewed that includes settings.php, a sites directory, a writable files directory, and more. The reader will then learn about how to change out-of-the-box Drupal settings like site, notification, caching, logging, regional, cron, and filesystem. Finally, the user will be introduced to the help section and status pages.

In this chapter we're going to cover the following main topics:

- Establishing a new codebase
- Installing Drupal
- Out-of-the-box Drupal building
- Basic configuration
- Help, logs, and reporting

Establishing a new codebase

The first step of creating a new Drupal application is creating the codebase. And, Drupal leverages Composer to manage its code, including provisioning a new codebase.

What is Composer?

Composer is a command-line tool used to manage code in a Drupal application. Composer is not just for Drupal. Drupal adopted Composer because it is used to manage code across many PHP-based projects. This is especially helpful to manage Drupal dependencies, like Symfony projects. And, it works natively with projects hosted on Drupal.org and thus can readily manage core and community projects.

Composer requires two primary constructs to function, a "composer.json" file and a "composer.lock" file. Applications are composed of various projects and those projects are, typically, managed by Git. A built application is basically a series of projects cloned at a specific commit. The project and commit-level metadata is stored in the composer.lock file, to best understand what is currently installed in an application. Alternatively, composer.json helps maintain the logic for what code gets built when you update the codebase. This defines which projects are loaded and what versions are acceptable to download. Acceptance is determined through Composer's native constraints which adds logic for specifying which code to download when an application is built. As an example, a release "10.0.2" can be hardcoded for Drupal core. But, to automatically pull in all Drupal 10 minor updates, a constraint like "^10" would allow for any core update in Drupal 10 but not Drupal 11. Understanding constraints and being intentional with what releases are loaded can help provide a responsible maintenance strategy that does not unintentionally load code that could break a Drupal application.

Drupal has a slightly unique implementation with Composer to ensure it works with the architecture of core, contributed, and custom projects. Every project, including core, can define its own dependencies. This means that Composer has to cascade and resolve dependencies across all of the provided projects and their dependencies. At the root of an application, a fundamental composer.json exists for the entire Drupal application. When built, code is loaded into a subdirectory (commonly web or docroot) that should be bootstrapped by the web server. Dependencies are also loaded into a vendor directory, which is bootstrapped by Drupal. This setup is incredibly useful for projects to load dependencies throughout the PHP ecosystem, of which projects exist for countless system integrations or specific problems that someone may want to incorporate into their Drupal application.

Drupal 10 and Composer are tightly coupled. Understanding how to effectively use Composer is time well spent.

Composer projects

Composer has built in capabilities to provision new applications through its project template functionality. This is what Drupal harnesses for creating the initial codebase for an application.

A very simple Drupal 10 application can be provisioned with the following command:

```
$ composer create-project drupal/recommended-project
```

The command will load the most recent Drupal core release and in a default directory.

The command can be extended in a number of ways. The following command loads a specific version of Drupal core, 10.0.2, and into a specific directory, my_directory.

```
$ composer create-project drupal/recommended-project:10.0.2 my_
directory
```

Be mindful that Composer can run on different systems, including a local system and hosted environments. The version of PHP should be the same across all of these. To enforce this, the following command can be run exemplified by PHP 8.0.7:

```
$ cd my_directory

$composer config platform.php 8.0.7
```

Composer.json can also be manually updated with the following code exemplified by PHP 8.0.7 below.

```
"config": {
    "platform": {
        "php": "8.0.7"
    }
}
```

Note that any environment that runs Composer commands must not only have parity with the PHP version, it must also have various PHP extensions installed. Composer has native capabilities to check for PHP-based platform requirements when commands are executed.

Common commands

Once a Drupal application has been bootstrapped from Composer's project template, there are a series of common commands used.

Most Drupal applications are managed by Git repositories. Once a Drupal application codebase has been established, it can be pushed to a Git repository. The following commands extend the earlier create-project command show to initialize a Git repository, sync it to a fake "upstream" repository, and push code to a "main" branch.

```
$ cd my_directory
$ git init
$ git remote add upstream https://git.com/my-drupal-project.git

$ git checkout main
$ git add *

$ git commit -a -m "Initial commit"
$ git push upstream main
```

There is some discretion on what is committed to a Git repository. Environments that harness Composer to build code do not require built code to be committed to Git. The metadata found in composer.lock effectively means an environment can pull down the desired code from Git and build the application within the environment. As such, it is best practice to leverage .gitignore to not commit the code downloaded by Composer if an environment is able to build the codebase. In fact, one ships with some defaults found with Drupal core to exclude files related to caching, image styles, and more. New projects may need their own .gitignore tailored to application-specific needs.

Applications that have a composer.lock can build a codebase by running Composer's install command:

```
$ cd my_directory

$ composer install
```

Alternately, updates to Drupal applications can be performed with the following command:

```
$ cd my_directory

$ composer update
```

This rebuilds the Drupal codebase based on the logic provided in the composer.json file. The rebuild then updates the composer.lock file with any changes, which should be committed in any commit to a Git repository.

Projects can be loaded into a Drupal application by leveraging Composer's require command, as exemplified by the "password_policy" project:

```
$ cd my_directory

$ composer require drupal/password_policy
```

Require commands can be found on every project page on Drupal.org.

Drush can also be loaded by Composer. Drush versions must match the corresponding Drupal application. As such, it is best practice to use "vendored Drush" which means that Drush is managed through Composer and associated with the specific version of Drupal running within the application codebase.

```
$ cd my_directory
$ composer require -dev drush/drush
```

The use of "--dev" highlights Drush as a development dependency. This is a Composer construct designed to allow Drush to be run on different environments.

Finally, Composer supports Drupal's patching strategy with a utility called Composer Patches. This approach uses patches to ensure Drupal core and projects are not manually overridden in a project (also known as the "don't hack core" mantra). The public projects downloaded are pristine and there is a deliberate patch-based strategy implemented with Composer to manage any desired changes. The following demonstrates how to load the utility:

```
$ cd my_directory

$ composer global config --no-interaction allow-plugins.cweagans/
composer-patches true
$ composer require cweagans/composer-patches
```

Patches for Drupal can then be managed through composer.json and loaded when executing the update command. An example composer.json with a Drupal core patch enabled looks like the following as exemplified by a fake drupal.org patch:

```
"extra": {
    "patches": {
      "drupal/core": {
        "Address a bug found in installation": "https://www.drupal.
org/files/issues/installation_bug-199658-66.patch"
      }
    }
  }
```

A second utility can be used to load patches from the command line, which is exemplified by the same bogus patch noted above:

```
$ cd my_directory

$ composer global config --no-interaction allow-plugins.szeidler/
composer-patches-cli true
$ composer require szeidler/composer-patches-cli

$ composer patch-add drupal/core "Address a bug found in installation"
"https://www.drupal.org/files/issues/installation_bug-199658-66.patch"
```

Many of the common commands highlighted have additional parameters that can be used to address different or advanced behaviors. Such parameters can be found through Drush's documentation found online at drush.org.

Composer is the tool required to establish a new Drupal 10 codebase and management of projects within a Drupal application. Git repositories can be an archive for the code and perform version control necessary for history and rollback of failed releases. Now that a codebase is established, the Drupal application can be installed.

Installing Drupal

Once the codebase exists, it is time to install Drupal. Drupal is installed on every environment, including local systems. Drupal has two primary means of installation: through the UI, and through the command-line with Drush. Installation requires a few key requirements. And, after installation, the Drupal application can effectively bootstrap. It is only then can the application be configured.

Installation preparation

An environment should be prepared to install Drupal. It requires a database and a web server that has the proper platform requirements loaded.

Users have the option to specify which installation profile or distribution is loaded. By default, the "standard" installation profile is used that is delivered with core. This installs the most set of common features and themes. Developers commonly leverage the "testing" installation profile for a more minimal, but refined set of features aimed at creating an ideal testing installation. And, custom distributions can be installed if loaded into the codebase during installation.

UI-based installation

When accessing Drupal for the first time before an install, it will prompt the UI-based installer. This runs a series of installation steps with various options a user can configure Drupal. Please note that some installation steps will be auto populated if a settings.php file exists and has provided values.

Follow these instructions to perform a UI-based installation:

1. The installer prompts the user for the language in the following figure:

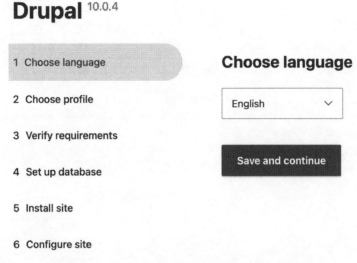

Figure 6.1 - First installation step of language selection

2. The installer prompts the selection of the profile in the next figure:

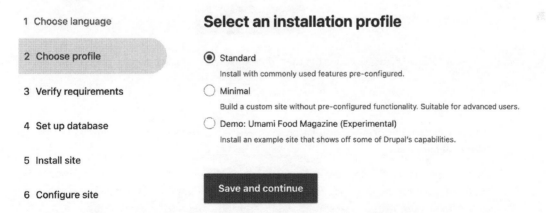

Figure 6.2 - Second installation step of install profile selection

If the codebase has a distribution loaded, it will prompt on that screen with the installation profiles.

3. Drupal will verify the platform requirements. It will only show the third step when or if there is an issue with the verification. Otherwise, it moves forward.

4. The installer prompts the database setup as demonstrated by the following figure:

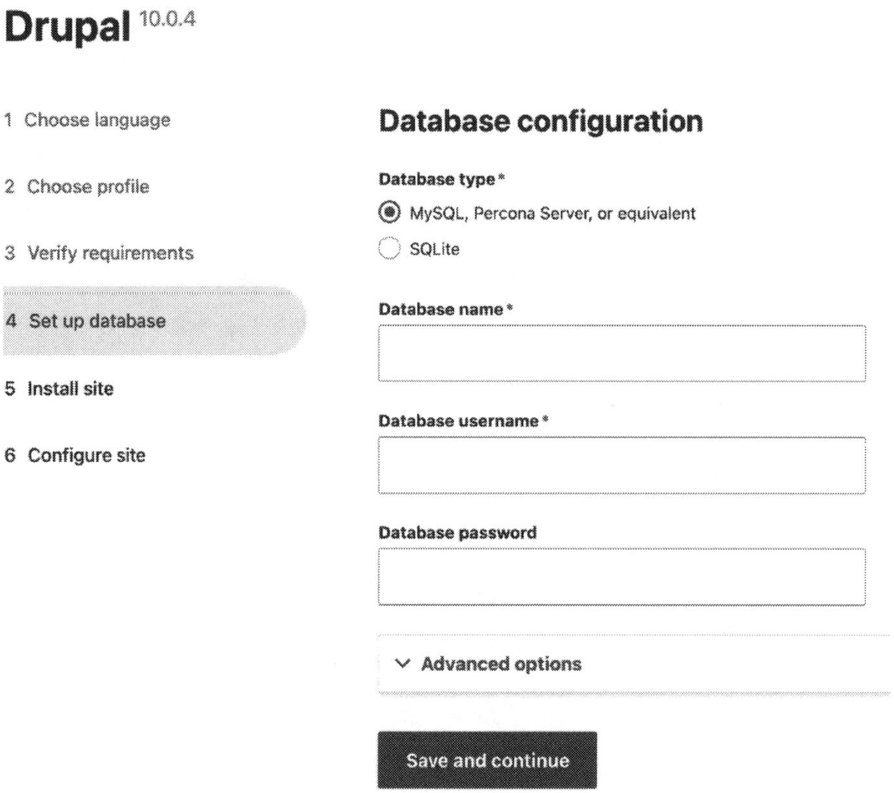

Drupal 10.0.4

1 Choose language

2 Choose profile

3 Verify requirements

4 Set up database

5 Install site

6 Configure site

Database configuration

Database type*

⦿ MySQL, Percona Server, or equivalent

◯ SQLite

Database name*

Database username*

Database password

⌄ Advanced options

Save and continue

Figure 6.3 - Fourth installation step of database setup

Parameters for the database name, username, password, server, and port will all be required in this step.

Drupal will then perform its installation. A progress bar and sequence of steps will display as the install happens.

5. Once the installation finishes, the installer prompts for the initial configuration for the minimal settings needed for the Drupal application. The following figure shows the configuration of the site name, an administrative account, regional settings, and notification settings:

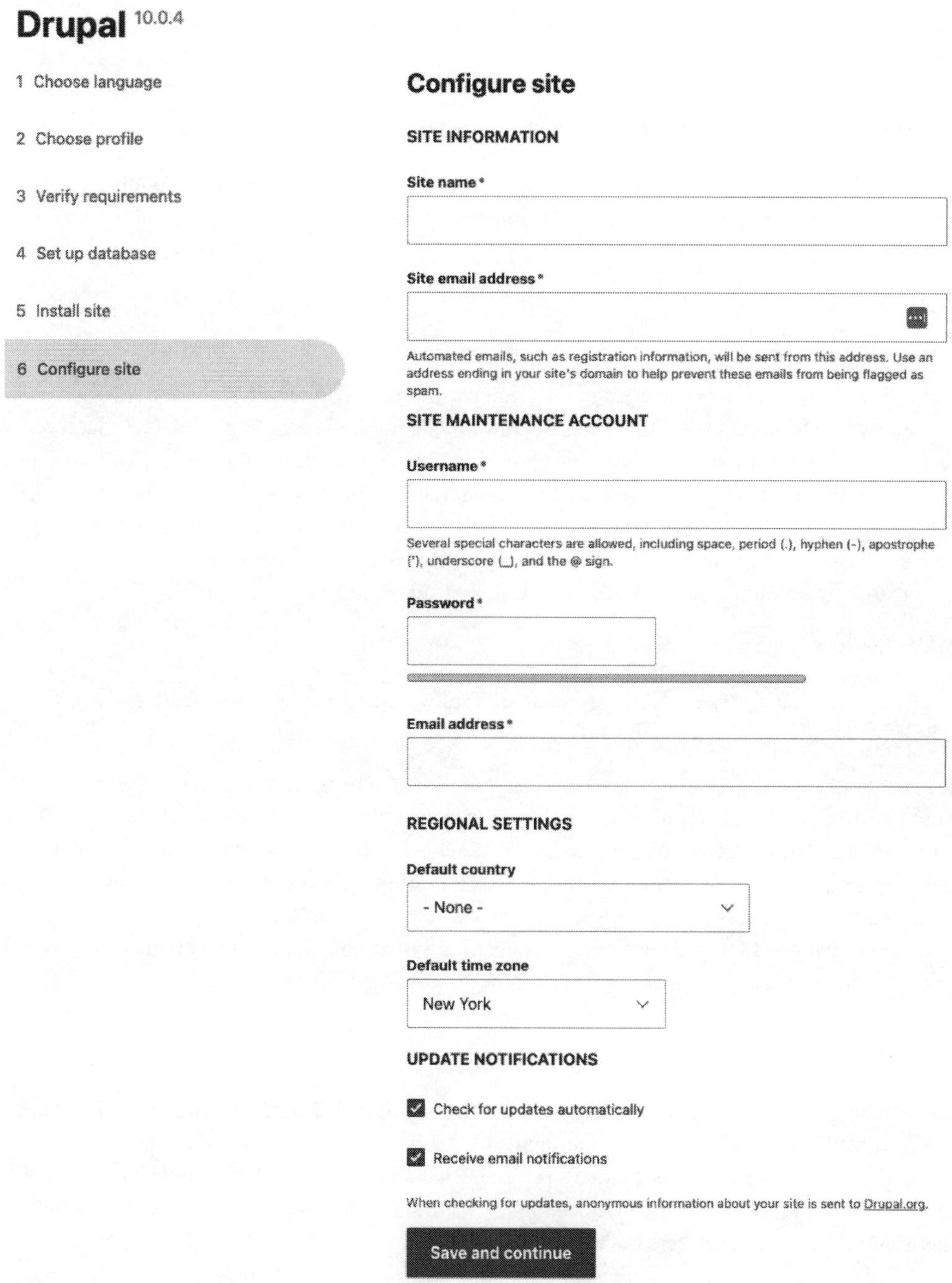

Drupal 10.0.4

1 Choose language

2 Choose profile

3 Verify requirements

4 Set up database

5 Install site

6 Configure site

Configure site

SITE INFORMATION

Site name *

Site email address *

Automated emails, such as registration information, will be sent from this address. Use an address ending in your site's domain to help prevent these emails from being flagged as spam.

SITE MAINTENANCE ACCOUNT

Username *

Several special characters are allowed, including space, period (.), hyphen (-), apostrophe ('), underscore (_), and the @ sign.

Password *

Email address *

REGIONAL SETTINGS

Default country

- None -

Default time zone

New York

UPDATE NOTIFICATIONS

☑ Check for updates automatically

☑ Receive email notifications

When checking for updates, anonymous information about your site is sent to Drupal.org.

Save and continue

Figure 6.4 - Sixth installation step of the minimal configuration

Once configured, the installer redirects back to Drupal's homepage authenticated with the administrative account configured in the final step.

Performing an installation with Drush

Drupal is able to be installed through the command line on an environment through Drush. The following example extends the earlier created Composer project and shows how to install the "standard" installation profile:

```
$ cd my_directory/web
$ ../vendor/bin/drush site:install standard
```

The site install command has a series of optional parameters that can be provided for each of the UI-based steps. The previous example was the minimal command without parameters that leverage default values for parameters like account name (admin) and locale/region (en). It will randomly generate an administrative password. Database credentials, if not provided, will attempt to load from settings.php or will throw an error if not provided. The following example demonstrates a more common Drush-based installation without a settings.php file present that sets bogus information for the database information, administrative account, and site name:

```
$ cd my_directory/web
$ ../vendor/bin/drush site:install standard -db-url=mysql://tugboat@
tugboat:3306/tugboat -account-name=admin -account-pass=rAndOM -site-
name="Cool Site"
```

One key difference with Drush is that a Drupal application can be re-installed. The UI-based installer cannot be invoked after an application is already installed and tables in the database exist. Drush can run its installation at any point in the life cycle. This is especially helpful for developers testing installation routines or for expected results of a distribution after installation. For most use cases, especially a production system, it is not necessary or even desirable to reinstall as it destroys the application's database, files, and configuration. Thankfully, Drush will prompt a confirmation double checking if the command should execute if it finds an existing database in place.

Post-installation

Once installed, the Drupal application can then be bootstrapped. The UI no longer redirects to the installer. A settings.php file exists that maintains hardcoded settings, like the database information. A writable filesystem directory is created to store Drupal's file content. Drupal now has its installed configuration. An initial administrative account exists to start site building and content management activities. And, visitors can access the front-end of Drupal.

Out-of-the-box Drupal Building

Drupal gained popularity as a low/no-code tool given its backend could readily be configured to meet a large number of common cases. A third persona of Drupal developer, beyond a backend or frontend developer, is known as a site builder. The site building activity is the combination of Drupal configuration and selection of community-provided modules to achieve the goals of an application. Modules often come with their own configuration as well. This is not an exercise of developing code but assembling existing capabilities that have been built by the community culminating in the desired intent of the Drupal application.

Developer Classification

Drupal system concepts of front-end and backend have corresponding development practices. Front-end development is considered working on Drupal themes (CSS, Twig templates, lightweight PHP) or building JavaScript-based integrations. Backend development typically refers to PHP and harnessing Drupal's framework through module development. Drupal developers commonly self-identify as having backend or front-end expertise.

Site Building Concept

Site building is a third classification of development and a foundational skill all Drupalists, including developers, must learn. It starts by understanding how to configure Drupal's out of the box subsystems and modules. Learning the terminology, experimenting with the functionality, and getting comfortable understanding the subsystems are critical. Thankfully community modules harness the same capabilities as core modules so the impact of site building extends well beyond just the out-of-the-box subsystems. Configuration requires authenticated access and proper permissions for users. Accessing the administrative area is most commonly found at "/admin". Be mindful that one pattern adopted by Drupal community members is known as "UI modules" where the user interface and functionality can be enabled independently. In core, the Views capability is a common example of this, where the feature can be turned on but the site building user interfaces can be enabled or disabled as needed. It is common for local or non-production Drupal sites to have UI-modules enabled.

Requirements Gathering

The most critical aspect of developing an application is having clear requirements. Understanding Drupal capabilities can help inform the kinds of questions to ask to get requirements. But, good requirements lead to good implementation choices and less rework later. Given that Drupal is so extensible, it's important to get good direction upfront. With great power comes great responsibility. And, the old saying of "measure twice, cut once" applies for Drupal development as well.

Beyond core features

Drupal core delivers many common features for conventional content management capabilities but this is only one aspect of Drupal's value proposition. Many competitors to Drupal offer similar features (both SaaS and PaaS products, both open source and proprietary). But, Drupal stands out and is often adopted because of its extensibility that appeals to the enterprise. Extending core features often spans site building exercises geared around community-provided modules and developing custom code with Drupal's framework. Conventionally, I've found the "80/20 rule" to apply when developing applications. Site building often comprises about 80% of the work to build a site. You can get really far, fairly quickly configuring core and various modules. Unique requirements like third party systems integration or specific business processes implementations, make the remaining 20% time consuming. Theming is also common, as it allows a Drupal application to be styled to match the branding of the organization it's being created for. While Drupal is up to task, it is the last mile that often requires the largest investment.

One of the most evergreen Drupal best practices is not "hacking core." Drupal projects, like core and contrib, can be fully downloaded into an application's repo and altered within the repo only. An alternate approach is leveraging patches, which keep the public projects pristine and apply changes systematically. More information on patching can be found on drupal.org (`https://www.drupal.org/docs/develop/git/using-git-to-contribute-to-drupal/working-with-patches`). Drupal is already configurable, extensible, and flexible. Hacking core creates a major issue in maintenance and can have unpredictable results. Given the number of subsystems and expectation of interoperability between those systems, even simple one-off changes may seem trivial but can create problems. Plus, it is a red flag to hack core when it is already extensible and has a framework intended for that purpose. It is far more likely someone did not do something correctly. The most notable issue is around Drupal core upgrades. Without a thoughtful patching strategy, a core hack basically creates a change management issue where the same change needs applied for every update. Again, it is far better to create your own modules, themes, or patches.

Learning how to extend core features can be daunting when evaluating the vast ecosystem of community projects. A tip is to select well adopted, actively maintained, and popular projects. This helps avoid surprises because the community is actively using it, submitting fixes to bugs, and making improvements to code, documentation, and more. This speaks to Drupal's value. Adoption grows contribution and projects mature because of it. The next person to use a project subsequently benefits and the ecosystem remains vibrant. It may seem obvious, but if you adopt projects that are not well maintained but address a more specific niche you need to solve, you may run into more challenges. It is even better if you can contribute to making the project better from that experience. But, the most adopted path is often the safest path that affords the least number of surprises.

Basic configuration

Site builders are often afforded robust configuration options that allow Drupal to be extensible while not having to get into code.

Post-installation configuration

During Drupal's installation, the administrator is asked to select an installation profile during one of the steps. This profile enables a pre-defined set of modules and loads a default configuration. It is common to change the default configuration, especially for common use cases, like:

- Application notifications email address, like who gets notified when updates exist

- Enabling caching of pages

- User registration settings, like open registration, invite-only, and closed

- Updating the default logging mechanism

- Enabling or disabling of core modules, like translation, web services, or various field types for your content structures

- Enabling or disabling of comments on out-of-the-box content types

Another useful starting point is the module listing page found at admin/modules. The codebase installed contains Drupal core and potentially projects that were added. Reviewing the projects found on the listing page can more rapidly enable or disable projects required for your application. Many modules still may have their own configuration that may need attention, even if the module is enabled. Common examples include disabling the Comment module for websites without user comments. Most Drupal installations disable the DbLog module in favor of the Syslog module, which allows for Drupal to write logs to the system in favor of the database. Doing so helps with a multi-environment workflow, as it's desirable to only store content in the database and keep the logs relevant only for the environment. Synchronizing a production database with logs to another environment would subsequently remove the logs from another environment. And, logs stored in the system often natively work with enterprise log platforms.

Common configuration changes

Again, configuration will change based on the specific and desired use cases. But, reviewing the defaults is important to not unintentionally miss more desirable configuration.

Drupal is intended to be configurable for the desired needs of the application, but there are some common configurations performed on most Drupal applications right after installation. Common use cases may vary depending on the specific requirements needed for the application, but it is useful to review common configuration regardless. And, configuration of Drupal is only possible when a user is authenticated and with a user account granted the correct permissions.

A helpful starting point is the high level configuration page found at `admin/config`. Reviewing this page can help evaluate all of the potential configuration options. It is common to review some of the default behaviors:

- `admin/config/people/accounts`: contains user registration settings that are often disabled if visitors cannot create an account and maintains configuration for user-based contact forms that are only needed if there is engagement with Drupal users

- `admin/config/search/pages`: helps define which entities are searchable and has settings for the interfaces provided to end users

- `admin/config/system/site-information`: contains settings found in the installer, but adds the ability to specify paths to content for error pages

- `admin/config/development/logging`: configures log-related settings and verbosity, which is important for production and non-production environments (often non-production should make errors visible for testing and include log backtracking for context)

- `admin/config/development/configuration`: helps identify which configuration only exists in the database and has not been pushed to the filesystem. This typically suggests the configuration has not been committed or pushed to Git for deployment purposes or for other developers to pull down and load in their Drupal applications.

- `admin/config/development/performance`: settings that help manage Drupal's caching behaviors. It is common to enable caching and for site builders to use this page when needing to clear the cache through the UI.

While the aforementioned configurations are not exhaustive, they represent typical cases a site builder can expect to review when starting a new Drupal build.

Help, logs, and reporting

Drupal core natively offers inline documentation to help guide users and features to report system logs and insights.

Help

Authenticated users can be granted access to Drupal's native documentation found at admin/help. This is designed for multiple audiences. Help defined as a "tour" is designed to help with using Drupal. This can be as simple as editing page content or managing Drupal blocks. It also offers overviews for Drupal modules to help provide site builders more context about a module. All projects, even custom ones, are able to furnish their own documentation through Drupal's help feature.

Logs and Reporting

Drupal maintains a robust logging and reporting system that can be helpful for administrators. All logging and reporting capabilities are found at admin/reports. This can be specific to projects, like reporting on the frequency of search terms or Views-specific usage. Or, it can be helpful in getting insights for the system.

The most useful page for insights is known as the status page, found at `admin/reports/status`. This page is an excellent overview of checks, warnings, and errors found that Drupal can self-report. The following image shows an example status page:

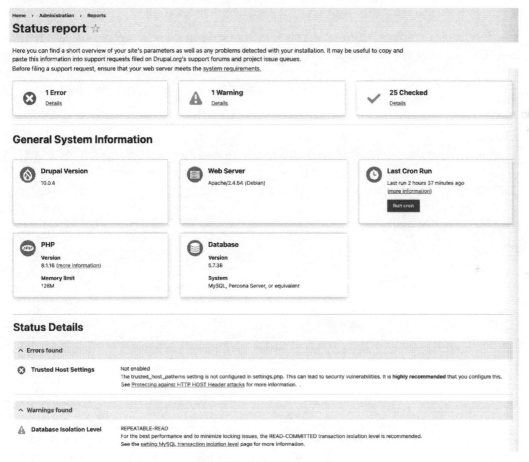

Figure 6.5 - Drupal status page

The status page is able to analyze your Drupal applications for specific issues. The figure demonstrates a Drupal application where the trusted host settings were not added to settings.php. The figure also demonstrates a warning where one of the recommended platform configurations was not observed in MySQL. This can be extremely useful for ensuring your Drupal configuration is correct. It is also a helpful overview for seeing what platform requirements are running on the environment.

Drupal can self-report available updates by checking the metadata found in the codebase and referencing information found on drupal.org. The report can be found on `admin/reports/updates`. Checking for updates can be run manually or can happen through CRON, a Unix-based job scheduler, over a defined period of time. Users can be emailed when the system discovers updates, which can be configured at `admin/reports/updates/settings`.

Logs for Drupal are exposed through the UI at `admin/reports/dblog` when leveraging the `DbLog` module. The following figure demonstrates this interface:

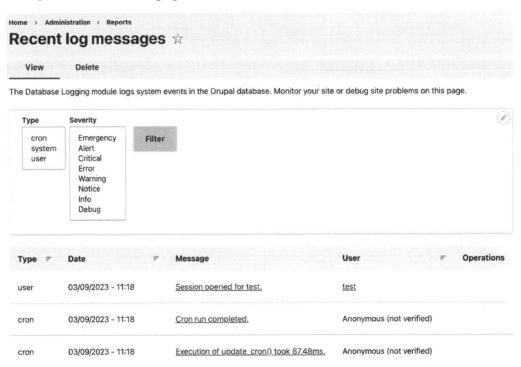

Figure 6.6 - User interface for Drupal generated logs

The figure demonstrates a paginated list of logs, starting with the most recent. Several columns, like the user, type, and date can be both filtered and sorted to drill down into specific types. Severity filters are very common when trying to debug a behavior in Drupal or to get context for a critical error.

Drupal's logging system also goes by the name *watchdog*, which dates back to earlier versions of Drupal. Watchdog motivated a series of Drush commands related to Drupal's log. The following example demonstrates an interactive log message listing through Drush:

```
$ cd my_directory/web
$ ../vendor/drush watchdog:list
```

Drush also has a useful command for searching logs, as the following example shows for checking for new user sessions:

```
$ cd my_directory/web
$ ../vendor/drush watchdog:search "session opened for"
```

All watchdog commands in Drush have parameters that can be useful to tailor the results for specific needs. Such examples include the number of messages, search parameters, severity filters, and more.

Summary

This chapter covered how to leverage Composer to create a new Drupal application and build its code. Setting this up properly ensures Drupal can be installed and maintained effectively. Installing Drupal through the UI or through Drush happens after the codebase is built to provide a functional Drupal application. Finally, a review of help pages, common post-install Drupal configuration, and system reporting capabilities were presented. Next chapter, readers will gain more knowledge on how to maintain Drupal.

7

Maintaining Drupal

Every Drupal application requires maintenance. Those who adopt Drupal must understand common maintenance activities, including how to check for updates. Earlier chapters discussed code deployment workflows, environments, Composer, and more. This chapter brings these concepts together for a more comprehensive view of maintaining Drupal. This may propose practices that help automate the maintenance of Drupal new to some. Next, the book will discuss how to apply updates after the code is deployed. Finally, we share best practices when performing updates.

In this chapter, we're going to cover the following main topics:

- Types of maintenance
- Code maintenance process
- Best practices

Types of maintenance

Maintaining a Drupal site can take many forms. Drupal itself is always evolving. Changes can be very frequent because they span releases in all projects of a Drupal application, including core and contributed projects. Releases can even happen based on project dependencies, so changes to Drupal application code can be very frequent. Drupal also runs on a platform stack with physical infrastructure built on software that also evolves. It is also common for content to require maintenance, such as when new staff is hired at a company and the staff listing is no longer up to date. Content management activities are covered in *Chapter 14*. This chapter covers how to effectively maintain a Drupal application.

Code-related maintenance

Drupal projects often put out new releases, and those managing Drupal applications need a strategy for this. Releases can come in the form of major and minor releases. The semantics around major and minor are intentional. Major implies a significant architectural change without assumed backward compatibility. Minor assumes updates that may add features and fix bugs but maintain backward compatibility. It is often safe to assume minor updates can be loaded without something breaking. However, maintainers of projects are not perfect, and manual testing can be error-prone. Achieving a high percentage of coverage for automated tests requires significant, ongoing effort for complex projects. Don't assume perfection even if it's rare a minor update will break things.

Major updates often require investment. This is intentional. A major update signifies a major change. It also brings some discretion as a major version does not suggest the previous major version will not continue to have minor version updates. Application maintainers have discretion on what is maintained. Previous major versions may also have maintenance for some defined period to afford a longer upgrade window. An older major version may continue to get releases for bug fixes or routine maintenance for a period of time or even indefinitely. Application maintainers need to review each project and major release specific to their application. If possible, upgrade.

Drupal core has the most significance for major updates. Drupal applications harness other Drupal projects, as this is a major part of its extensibility value-add. Projects, much as with custom Drupal projects, are required to remediate any code deprecations found in major versions. Some community projects may not have yet been ported to the next version of Drupal. Application maintainers can submit patches to the community and help project maintainers with this effort.

Project updates also come in the form of routine updates and security updates. Routine updates are normal for bug fixes or requests from the community. Application maintainers have some discretion on when to apply these updates, but security updates are time-critical to ensure a Drupal application is not vulnerable to attack. Releases are sequential, and a security release can come at any time. As such, to address the security release, application maintainers may also have to install several routine updates if the application is leveraging an earlier release of a project.

Themes can be another source of code-related maintenance. Some maintenance can be discretional based on how a developer builds a theme and which dependencies are used for development. Most Drupal applications have their custom theme. Themes have Drupal-related standards, such as Twig, CSS, libraries, and more, but there is no broader standard for other frontend technologies. It is common for frontend developers to use popular tools found in frontend communities to build themes in Drupal. Tools such as npm and the Node ecosystem can often be used to compile CSS, develop responsive functionality, and more. This is largely outside of Drupal and discretional for those working on themes. But, as Drupal, Node projects have their maintenance with releases, security updates, and more. Given how common this practice is, Drupal applications often have to maintain both Drupal- and Node-related projects.

Infrastructure platform maintenance

Platforms also evolve. Drupal conventionally runs on a LAMP stack. Linux, Apache, MySQL, and PHP all have their releases and are tightly coupled with Drupal's platform requirements. Lower-end hosting providers commonly sell raw infrastructure with a high degree of discretion on what is configured and installed on the host. While the flexibility is good, this leaves a heavy burden on operators. Those managing their infrastructure would then subsequently be responsible for keeping each component of the LAMP stack maintained and in concert with Drupal's major releases found in the application. Package managers, such as `apt` and `yum`, can help perform routine system updates, often with minimal downtime. However, maintainers must be mindful that system updates can sometimes alter configuration and restore specific services back to defaults. A manual review may be required to ensure security settings and usage-based configuration are intact.

In an ideal world, the infrastructure of a Drupal application can handle anything. However, this is rarely the case. Traffic spikes can flood logs, use up significant system resources, and expose bottlenecks. Often, this goes back to the infrastructure and platform running a Drupal application.

Storage is one potential but common bottleneck. Storage applies to both the web server and the database. The web server often manages Drupal's code, file content, and logs. The database has its storage considerations. Effective platform oversight ensures that storage is managed. Storage goes up with heavy Drupal usage. Issues can happen suddenly, whereby storage can fill up quickly. Monitoring storage periodically is one way to mitigate risk. Affording Drupal adequate storage to grow can effectively afford time before an outage.

Finally, do not forget about SaaS products. Outages or planned maintenance of third-party SaaS products can impair Drupal applications. This is common with analytical tools, third-party search, or even the infrastructure running Drupal.

When running a Drupal application, it is important to understand what needs to be maintained. From the infrastructure to the code, each element of the stack is different but requires maintenance. Given the complexity of the Drupal application and the frequency of updates, the next section dives deep into the code maintenance process.

Code maintenance process

One of the technical and more frequent types of maintenance is around code updates. The community is already making efforts to lessen the technical burden of code updates through the Automatic Updates initiative worked on throughout Drupal 10 and, hopefully, in preparation for Drupal 11.

Reviewing code management and deployment concepts

Earlier chapters covered useful concepts when considering maintenance. A brief review of these concepts is important when considering code maintenance.

Chapter 6 covered the creation of a Drupal application through the Composer project template and common Composer commands. Every Drupal 10 application should have a corresponding and accurate `composer.json` and `composer.lock` file. Those files help understand what code is currently built in an application and which constraints the update logic should follow for installed projects.

Chapter 3 covered the concept of environments and code deployment workflows. Production environments should only have well-tested deployments promoted from non-production environments. Production content should be staged down and sanitized to lower environments to properly test a code deployment. Recall *Figure 3.4*, which shows a potential environment-based code deployment workflow.

Awareness and update checking was also covered in *Chapter 6*. Drupal natively offers an email notification of updates based on its routine update checking. This can be configured to send to an email address and on a specified cadence. Pending updates can also be seen on Drupal's status page, with special attention afforded to security releases. The Drupal community also offers specific feeds for project updates, a Slack channel with releases, and Twitter accounts that publish tweets when security updates come out, and there is documentation on `Drupal.org`. Application maintainers can pick the best channel that serves them.

Typical code maintenance process

Code maintenance largely follows standard code deployment procedures, but with specific code that is built through Composer.

It is best to prepare updates on a local environment to help resolve errors and perform initial testing. A local environment should be prepared with the latest code in Git and production content staged down.

> **Important note**
>
> Staging down can be performed in automated ways by using Drush. Drush has a native Drush aliases feature that can be used to perform remote operations. This book routinely references the use of environments. Each environment for a Drupal application can have its alias. Application maintainers with access to the environment infrastructure can leverage SSH to execute commands remotely with Drush through aliases. An alias can be widely used for remote operations from code deployments, clearing of cache, and more.

The following example leverages a `mydrupal` bogus alias with a `prod` bogus environment that shows how to prepare a local system for code updates:

```
$ cd my_directory
$ git fetch -all  # pulls updates from remote repositories
$ git reset -hard upstream/main  # resets local git to latest main
branch
$ cd web # switch to Drupal root
$ drush @mydrupal.prod sql:dump > prod.sql # export database locally
```

```
$ drush sql:drop # remove local database
$ drush sql:cli < prod.sql # load prod database
$ rm prod.sql # removes export
$ drush config:import # imports config from code
$ drush cr # clears cache
```

The result of the example effectively rebuilds a local system with the most recent production content and code pulled down from a Git repository.

> **Important note**
>
> Drupal developers do not have to stage down file content. The Drupal community has created tools such as *Stage File Proxy* that allow for files to be served remotely. Large Drupal applications can often have gigabytes of files. Allowing a local or non-production system to reference files from a production system can often save significant time and storage space from manual synchronization.

Once the local environment is prepared, it is time to perform code updates. It is best practice to review the composer.json file ahead of time to ensure the update logic is correct. The following example shows how to load updates with Composer:

```
$ cd my_directory
$ composer update
```

The following screenshot demonstrates a sample of output from the Composer update command:

```
> DrupalProject\composer\ScriptHandler::checkComposerVersion
Loading composer repositories with package information
Updating dependencies (including require-dev)
Package operations: 0 installs, 3 updates, 1 removal
  - Removing pear/console_table (v1.3.1)
  - Updating phpunit/phpunit (6.5.7 => 6.5.8): Downloading (100%)
  - Updating zendframework/zend-stdlib (3.1.0 => 3.1.1): Downloading (100%)
  - Updating drupal/material_admin dev-1.x (25c5889 => c859faa):  Checking out c859faad86
Writing lock file
Generating autoload files
Removing packages services cache file:
/private/var/www/sites/d8_webform/vendor/drupal/console/extend.console.uninstall.services.yml
Creating packages services cache file:
/private/var/www/sites/d8_webform/vendor/drupal/console/extend.console.uninstall.services.yml
> DrupalProject\composer\ScriptHandler::createRequiredFiles
```

Figure 7.1 – Output of Composer's update command

The output of the Composer update command shows some useful information. First, it demonstrates which projects were updated and to which version. If projects were removed from the application's composer.json file or any project dependencies were found in a project's composer.json file, they would get removed from the code.. Finally, it updates the composer.lock file with the updated versions.

> **Important note**
>
> Composer's changelog can help identify a testing strategy. Some updates may only be dependencies and not the actual projects loaded in the Drupal application. Dependencies can be mapped back to their project by running the why command in Composer.

Now, it is time to deploy the changes and test the updated code on the local system. The following example shows how to leverage Drush to do the deployment:

```
$ cd my_directory/web
$ drush updb            # runs database updates
$ drush cr              # clears cache
$ drush config:import   # imports configuration
$ drush cr              # another cache clear
```

After Drush 10.3, a new command was added to consolidate the preceding commands and standardize deployments:

```
$ cd my_directory/web
$ drush deploy          # runs commands above
```

Once testing has been performed, changes must be committed and pushed up to the Git repository. The following example creates a new branch, commits the code, and pushes the new branch to the remote upstream repository:

```
$ cd my_directory
$ git checkout -b code-update      # creates code update branch
$ git add *
$ git commit -a -m "Code updates"
$ git push upstream code-update
```

The upstream Git repository should now have a new branch with the local code changes.

> **Important note**
>
> Developers often do not push code directly to a main branch. Code review workflows often harness separate branches and features such as pull or merge requests. Pull or merge requests allow other developers to review the code, and these requests often work with **Continuous Integration (CI)** systems that execute automated testing, code scanning, and more. This is a recommended gate before outright deploying code to any environment.

Effective code maintenance helps keep applications routinely up to date. Observing deployment best practices helps avoid issues and perform updates effectively.

Best practices

Maintaining Drupal has several best practices that can help promote efficacy and ease maintenance.

Backups

Before performing any maintenance, ensure environments are effectively backed up. While the aforementioned Drush commands are capable of exporting databases or downloading files, backups are often offered by platform hosting providers. Some providers have policies to perform automated backups periodically. Doing so can help ensure quick and effective restoration should there be an issue.

Restoring Drupal can be performed with a series of commands. Releases of a specific Drupal application often correspond to tags in Git. As an example, suppose there was an issue with the deployment of the application's 1.1.20 release. The following example restores Git tag 1.1.19 and loads the database from a `backup.sql` file:

```
$ cd my_directory
$ git fetch -all
$ git reset -hard 1.1.19
$ cd web
$ ../vendor/bin/drush sql:cli < backup.sql
$ ../vendor/bin/drush cr
```

The example reverts the code to an earlier release and restores the database backup. A complete restore may also include file content, which can happen through the selected hosting platform.

Environment differences

Code deployments are not the same across environments. Production environments do not have database or file imports. Performing an import would be destructive and effectively remove the live production content when it should be pristine. The following example is an altered code deployment process for production that releases a 1.1.20 release and does not include altering the database:

```
$ cd my_directory
$ git fetch -all
$ git reset -hard 1.1.20
$ cd web
$ ../vendor/bin/drush deploy
```

The example releases code in a production environment but differs from non-production environments which must stage down content from production.

> **Important note**
>
> Drupal configuration can change per environment. As a basic example, it is common to uninstall UI-based modules, such as Views UI, on production systems. Drupal maintains enabled extensions through its `core.extensions.yml` configuration. Leverage Drupal's Configuration Split module.
>
> A split represents any logical category of configuration. Configuration often resides in a standard configuration directory and is synchronized to the database. Each split has its directory with overridden or added configuration. It is common for production environments to have their configuration split with only specific production configurations.
>
> There are Drush commands for Configuration Split import that can be run during deployments on specific environments. Drush commands also exist for config split export to help generate configuration in splits.
>
> While every split adds maintenance overhead in ensuring configuration updates apply to every split, this allows for any environment, including local, to maintain its configuration.

Managed platforms

Several vendors sell managed platforms for Drupal. Many offer environments and native code deployment tooling that helps stage up code and stage down content. Each vendor offers different features that can help save time, perform automation, and more. This book does not offer any opinions or bias toward managed platforms, just that they often aim to reduce maintenance-related needs for Drupal applications.

One primary benefit of managed platforms is platform-level updates. Their products often offer and automate the upgrades of platform services, such as PHP, MySQL, and the underlying operating system. Also, the infrastructure is managed. This can help application maintainers just focus on the application.

SaaS services

It is very common for developers to leverage SaaS services. For Git, both GitHub and GitLab are popular managed Git services. Both offer CI tools that can invoke automated testing or even run Composer commands to build the code base. Managed Git services also offer dependency checkers capable of submitting pull or merge requests for updates. This is a helpful way to automate theme-level Node dependencies in a Drupal application. Tools such as Violinist (`https://violinist.io/`) can work with a managed Git offering to check a `composer.lock` file for Drupal-related updates and submit pull or merge requests with the updates. Such services help discover and submit code changes relatively easily.

Update frequency

Performing routine updates over " time helps stay on top of releases. All of the ease-of-use recommendations previously mentioned can help both find and release smaller changes more frequently. Performing smaller releases means it's easier to identify breaking changes with less to roll back and generally helps perform more targeted testing.

Security updates need to be applied as soon as possible.

Product life cycles

Understanding product life cycles can help plan ahead. Drupal often publishes its major and minor releases, including its end-of-life events. The same can be said for Symfony-, PHP-, MySQL-, and Node-based projects. Major and minor releases are often planned and published well in advance. Security updates, however, can come at any point in time.

System monitoring and tools

For those not using a managed service, consider leveraging system alerting and thresholds. No one wants to get paged in the middle of the night to swap storage that fills up or address a server that goes down. System alerts can help proactively raise awareness when an issue may be looming. As an example, proactive alerts can be sent if CPU usage peaks, storage is rising at an unreasonable pace, or storage crosses a desired threshold. Addressing potential issues before they become issues helps offer higher-quality service and avoids outages.

Log rotation is a common way to manage Drupal storage. Heavy-traffic Drupal applications can generate a lot of logs. Log retention policies that rotate, move older logs to other storage, and prune active storage help manage one of the biggest risks to storage. Managed enterprise logging capabilities can also be integrated and then offload logging from system storage altogether.

Edge systems

Enterprise Drupal applications commonly leverage a **content delivery network** (**CDN**) as a **web application firewall** (**WAF**). This has both performance and security benefits. CDNs often easily integrate with Drupal's native caching system to minimize direct web requests to the running Drupal hosting platform. Direct requests can be scanned and rejected if the request mimics an attack on the Drupal application. For maintenance and outages, CDNs can often serve a cached version of Drupal while updates run. This is helpful for end-user continuity even if an outage or a maintenance event is happening on the backend of Drupal.

Harnessing best practices helps Drupal developers learn from the experience of others to effectively maintain Drupal. Leveraging backups, maintaining different environments for code deployment, and leveraging third-party services such as managed platforms and edge systems all help mitigate risks of code deployments common with Drupal maintenance. Maintaining awareness of life cycles helps with planning, and effective monitoring provides transparency into how maintenance runs on your infrastructure.

Summary

Successful Drupal practitioners know how to effectively maintain Drupal applications. Performing maintenance with best practices and doing so routinely helps ensure Drupal applications continue to run well, are secure, and get the benefit of ongoing features and fixes furnished by the community. Applications must run on a well-maintained platform as well, which includes updates to PHP, MySQL, and operating systems. Maintenance of Drupal requires an effective code deployment strategy and an understanding of all parts of Drupal's architecture (code, content, files, and configuration). Leveraging tools such as Composer and Drush provides code-base management and helps to perform automation. Finally, best practices exist by reviewing product life cycles, having backup strategies, harnessing managed services for hosting, Git, CDN, and update checkers, and adhering to environment-level differences. The next chapter explores Drupal features around content structures and language-level support.

Part 3:
Building - Features
and Configuration

This part highlights many of Drupal's fundamental features that all developers need to understand. Each feature has its own configuration and use cases that can be set up per Drupal application. Readers will understand content structures, adding support for multiple languages, users, roles, permissions, and search. Configuring engagement through contact forms will be covered. And, dynamic displays with Drupal Views and Display Modes promote content reuse and build upon the structured content covered.

This part has the following chapters:

- *Chapter 8, Content Structures and Multilingual*
- *Chapter 9, Users, Roles, and Permissions*
- *Chapter 10, Drupal Views and Display Modes*
- *Chapter 11, Files, Images, and Media*
- *Chapter 12, Search*
- *Chapter 13, Contact Forms*

8

Content Structures and Multilingual

One of Drupal's core strengths is its ability to model and structure content. Structured data serves as a foundation of **content management systems (CMSs)** and is arguably one of the most important features of Drupal. Drupal's implementation is built on the concept of entities, fields, and bundles. Drupal has created features such as **Nodes**, **Content Types**, **Menus**, and **Taxonomy** from entities. Leveraging these capabilities is fundamental for any Drupal developer. Drupal extends the entity system to support multiple language translations per entity. This chapter reviews the structured content as a concept, with several examples in Drupal.

In this chapter, we're going to cover the following main topics:

- Importance of structured content
- Structured content in Drupal
- Multilingual features

Importance of structured content

Drupal has long been viewed favorably for its structured content capabilities offered to site builders. So, why is this so important?

Content management went through a bit of an evolution, starting around 1995 when programming languages such as ASP and PHP were introduced. Earlier CMSs ran software that annotated, scanned, and managed content through flat files. Those flat files were either HTML or software-generated HTML. HTML would still require uploads to web servers. While this was fine for simple content updates, content would end up being duplicated.

Take a news article, for instance.. That same news article may be featured on a listing found on every page and have its page with the full article. The listing likely lists the title of the news article and maybe a teaser to lead readers in. However, the title ends up being duplicated on basically any page where the listing is displayed and on the full article. Now, imagine this at scale where updating one news article title could end up updating a large number of pages on the site. It would be difficult to even track the pages manually, let alone perform changes.

Now, consider modern websites. A search feature returns dynamic results based on search terms. Attempting to extend the news article example for every possible search term would be impossible. Imagine trying to create, by hand, search results that accompany terms from content managed on multiple pages. This would be overwhelmingly labor-intensive. And, as with any technology, this forced the next phase of content management.

Relational database best practices

Content management solved the aforementioned scale problem by harnessing relational databases. Relational databases maintain one **source of truth** (**SOT**) for content. The same content is then linked where it is related, and querying systems allow for content to be returned that includes linked information.

Understanding the theory behind relational databases is necessary to comprehend structured content. It starts with a concept called **database normalization**. **First normal form** (**1NF**) states that every field in a database table must only contain one value and not multiple values. For example, a *color* field can only contain *red* and not *red and blue*. This would require *color1* with a value of *red* and *color2* with a value of *blue*. **Second normal form** (**2NF**) suggests you need a primary key that identifies table rows. **Third normal form** (**3NF**) suggests that, in favor of repeating information between tables, a field in one table should store the value of a primary key to relate and link it to the other data. The three normal forms promote atomic data principles aimed at stronger data integrity.

Structured content borrows all of these concepts. Back to the previous news article search example. A content structure could exist for news articles. News articles could be split into atomic fields, such as key, title, teaser, author, and body. Each row could be a unique article with a unique value for the key. A news article page could display the results of querying against the key, and a search feature could be implemented by querying against the fields in news articles to find matching rows for search terms. All of this extends onto the earlier concepts of content management where the same content was repeated page by page.

The notion of incorporating a relational database to manage content solved the scale problem by avoiding content repetition. Data integrity is then promoted, even if there is still discretion in how content is structured. Relational databases that avoid content replication also promote a clear SOT where one table maintains all of the related, atomic attributes. Other tables can link to the key of the SSOT in contrast to copying the same data from the table.

Structured content in Drupal

Drupal harnesses structured content as one of its foundational features. Several Drupal features rely on its structured data, such as rendering variables to specific field values in theme templates and being able to configure search behaviors for content-related fields.

Entities, types, and bundles

Drupal harnesses its Entity subsystem for the management of structured content, metadata, and data. This subsystem unifies operations around all entities for consistency. As an example, Drupal's subsystem manages all CRUD operations for entities. Such operations properly log transactions in Drupal's watchdog, clean up Drupal's cache, and more. Drupal features are largely interoperable and harness several entities, and that is a critical part of Drupal's value proposition.

Harnessing the subsystem receives the benefit of its features. Developers have access to the entity storage system, which abstracts the underlying implementation details for how entities are persistently stored. An access system exists to bridge permissions to entities.

An **entity** can be considered one content structure. The implementation details are managed by Drupal. Entities manage both their properties (metadata) and their fields. To extend the relational database analogy, an entity is similar to a database table. The rows of the table would be the instances of the entity.

Entity types help create different structures with their own properties and fields. This differentiation allows for both a logical categorization and functional or behavioral changes to exist between different types of entities. Each entity type would be its database table, where an entity type can manage its specific structured data.

Entities harness a UUID to uniquely identify instances of the entity. Similar to the concept of a key, this allows an instance of an entity to be referenced. Entities can then reference other entities by linking to their UUID within their content structure. This logic is abstracted through Drupal's UI for usability, where end users often can select from a list of human-readable attributes and not a machine-generated UUID. However, being able to build a relationship between an instance of one entity to another instance helps avoid duplication.

Fields and field types

Entities harness fields to structure content, but entities are not required to have fields. An entity that has fields is known as **fieldable**, and each field instance can be configured based on the entity, such as the name of the field, whether the field is required or not, the cardinality of the values, and more. Field settings associate back to the configuration of the entity.

Fields in Drupal go well beyond an atomic value in a relational database table. Drupal's framework offers various services that are extensible through module development. A summary of those is provided here:

- **Field storage**: Ability to change the underlying data model for how a field gets stored in Drupal's database
- **Field validators**: Specific logic that checks field values to promote data integrity
- **Field widgets**: Definitions of the UI experience for managing field data within a form
- **Field formatters**: Options and definitions for displaying field values
- **Field types**: The native selection of the type of data used for a field that has specific storage, validation, formatters, and widgets

Base entities

All entities have a base. A **base** helps define the fields and properties of that entity type that must be shared. Some entity types may only have a base, but a **bundle** allows for a base to be extended with its additional fields. This is a means of having parity between bundles of the same entity, given the bundles will all share the same base fields and properties.

Content entities

A content entity is a primary capability of the entity subsystem intended to create entity types that have complementary features and support tied to content management. This extends many of the base-level features of any entity but integrates effectively with other content-related features in Drupal. Such features include content rendering, revisioning, authoring-related properties, and more. Content entities also have translation support, which is discussed in greater length later in this chapter.

Entity example for Node

The concept of base and bundles is better understood with an example. A **node** is a type of entity in Drupal core that is one of the most used content entities. Every node starts with the same base that has the following information:

- Authoring properties, such as the user, date, and time
- Revisioning properties that enable tracking and reversion of changes
- Multilingual properties, such as the language of the node
- Path properties that allow Drupal to route to specific content
- Publishing properties, to enable or disable publishing
- Title and body fields, which are out-of-the-box fields applied to content types

However, nodes support bundles that allow for the fields to change by bundle. Those bundles are referred to as **content types**. This preserves the base functionality of nodes while allowing for each content type to provide its variation in the structured content.

This is helpful for use cases where the atomic structuring of data changes for different types of content. A simple page structure may be structured with out-of-the-box node title and body fields. A content structure for news articles may extend those fields by adding a featured image and a relevant section (news, sports, opinion, classifieds, and so on).

Example models

Modeling of a content type starts with the base, title, and body and then has fields configured per use case. A **use case** is often defined through requirements or design comps that inform how to structure the content type. Suppose a design comp shows a news article mockup with a featured image at the top. A news article content type can be configured to have a *featured image* field of type *image*. A comp may also show links to related articles. The content type can then be configured to have a *related articles* field of type *entity reference* to search and create an association from one article to others.

Configuration entities

Configuration entities represent a second primary capability for the entity subsystem. Configuration structures can be exported and imported into the system as YAML files known as **configuration schemas** found in Drupal projects. The entity subsystem is leveraged by Drupal's configuration to structure configuration through the configuration schemas and synchronize configuration between the filesystem and database (active and staged configuration). While it is a different use case compared to content entities, leveraging the entity system affords basic data structuring, data validation, and connectivity between other Drupal subsystems.

Under the hood

On the surface, many of the no-code site-building capabilities abstract what is happening within the underlying technical aspects of the Drupal application. It is important to understand these concepts for more advanced development and also for deploying changes.

Content entities, like nodes, are managed through the administrative interface. But what happens if you build a change locally and want to push the change through environments? Changes to content entity settings are tracked and managed by Drupal's configuration. For deployment, configuration can be synced back to the filesystem and subsequently committed to Git. This allows configuration changes to content entities to be deployed as with any code change. Note that the content itself, not the configuration, represents the SOT principle and must be maintained on a production system and staged down to lower environments for testing.

Drupal's core API allows a framework for extending out-of-the-box entity behavior through modules. Contributed modules exist that offer different types of fields, field storage, various widgets to manage fields and field validators. Custom use cases can be created through custom modules. This level of extensibility can address highly unique enterprise data integration needs while maintaining structured content.

Site building

One of the benefits of Drupal is that it offers no-code features through its administrative UI. This allows for site builders to create structured content without having to get into the code. The node example previously shared is fieldable and offers the ability to manage its fields and content types through Drupal's administrative experience.

The following screenshot shows the content-type listing found at **Administration | Structure | Content types**:

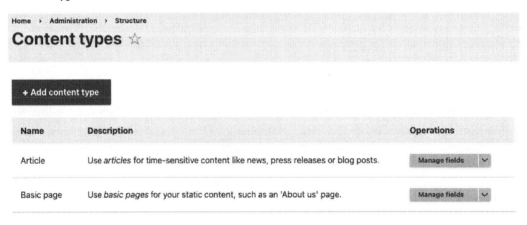

Figure 8.1 – Content-type listing page

Figure 8.1 not only shows the content types but also allows site builders to add their content types and configure existing content types. Adding a content type prompts an administrative form, as shown in *Figure 8.2*:

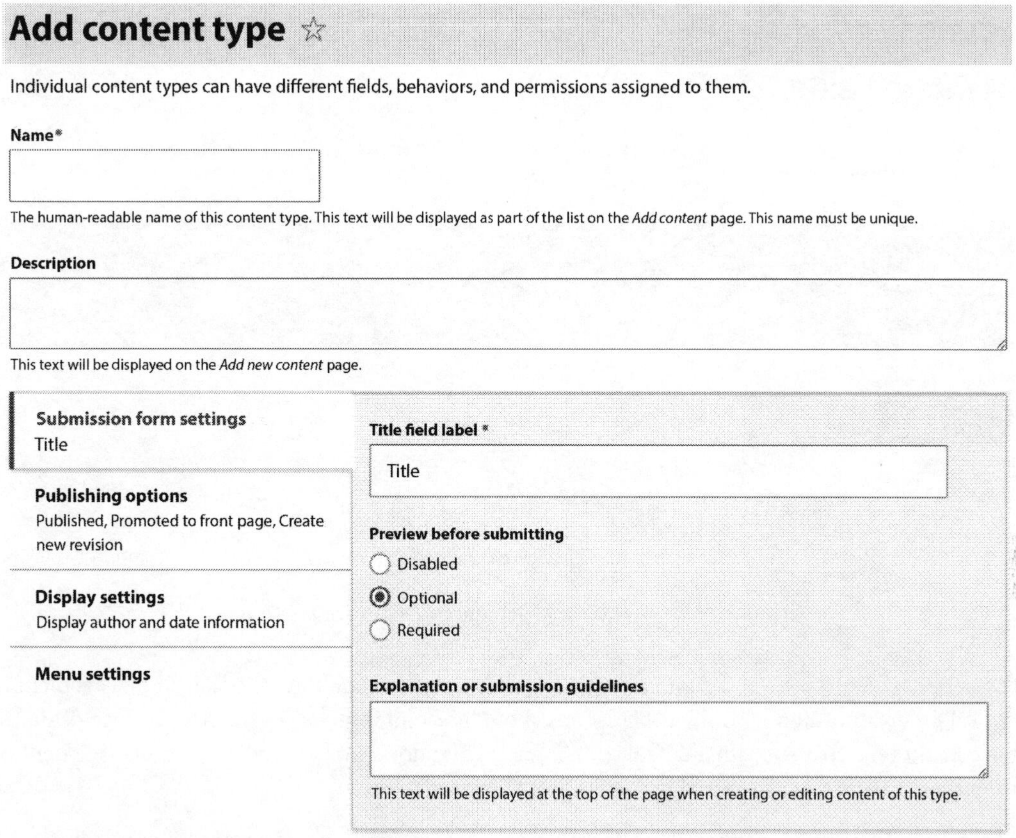

Add content type ☆

Individual content types can have different fields, behaviors, and permissions assigned to them.

Name*

The human-readable name of this content type. This text will be displayed as part of the list on the *Add content* page. This name must be unique.

Description

This text will be displayed on the *Add new content* page.

Submission form settings
Title

Publishing options
Published, Promoted to front page, Create
new revision

Display settings
Display author and date information

Menu settings

Title field label *

Title

Preview before submitting
○ Disabled
◉ Optional
○ Required

Explanation or submission guidelines

This text will be displayed at the top of the page when creating or editing content of this type.

Figure 8.2 – Step one of adding a content type

The form in *Figure 8.2* demonstrates the first step of adding a content type – a form for configuring metadata of a content type. The name and description of the content type help describe what it is. The sections on the left sidebar help perform basic configuration. **Submission form settings** help configure the experience for users entering content. **Publishing options** help set sane publishing defaults for when content authors manage content. **Display settings** control whether or not a node should display author and date information. **Menu settings** allow for the configuration of relevant menus that nodes of the content type can be added to.

The following screenshot shows the second step, which is the field management display:

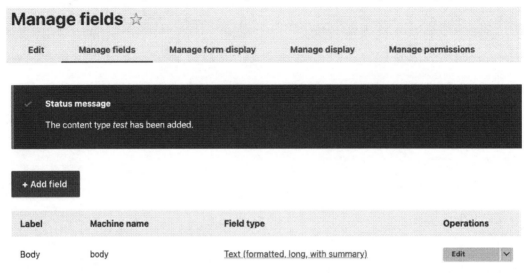

Figure 8.3 – Step two of managing fields in a content type

Given nodes are fieldable and content types (bundles) can maintain their fields, field management is critical for creating atomic content. This screenshot offers options to add fields and manage fields for the content type created, with a default body field. This allows for the creation and management of the structured content associated with the content type.

The **Add field** button prompts another multi-step process with various ways to configure fields. Modules can add the types of fields that can appear in this process. It starts with the screen shown in *Figure 8.4*, which prompts the user to select the type of a new field or associate an existing field to the content type:

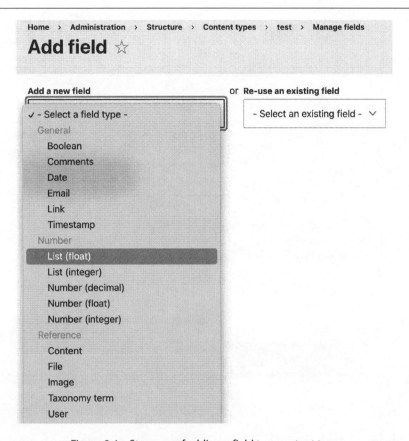

Figure 8.4 – Step one of adding a field to a content type

The selection of field type is important to promote data integrity. As an example, selecting a date type has corresponding field widgets and field validators that help content authors enter correct information. Reference field types extend on the relational database concepts by allowing a field in a content type to reference an instance of another entity. The following screenshot shows field settings after selecting the type and entering a label for the field:

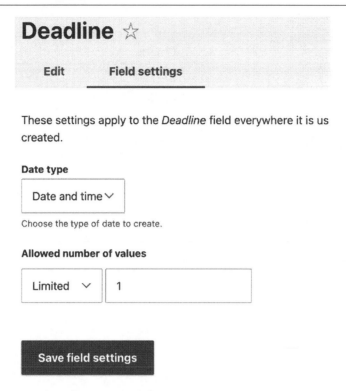

Figure 8.5 – Step two of adding a field to a content type

This form allows site builders to configure the settings for the field. Each field type can have its settings. *Figure 8.5* demonstrates the settings for a date field. The **Date type** option allows for picking a date only or a date and time. It also allows for setting the cardinality for the field to allow for one value or more. Under the hood, Drupal manages data integrity to avoid the concern of sets of values enforced by 2NF (`https://en.wikipedia.org/wiki/Second_normal_form`); it structures its database in a way that honors 2NF but offers the experience of managing a related set in a field for content authors.

Figure 8.3 allows for managing operations for created fields. The `body` field, created by default with a new content type, has operations for editing, storage, and deletion. **Edit** prompts the same configurable settings found in *Figure 8.5*, specific to the settings for the selected type of field.

There are more ways to configure content types. *Figure 8.3* has tabs at the top row for the following actions:

- **Edit**: This allows for changing the settings of the content type found in *Figure 8.2*.
- **Manage fields**: This manages fields for the content type found in *Figure 8.3*.
- **Manage form display**: This tab allows for customizing the content authoring experience around the content type's structured content (reorder form fields, change labels, and more).

- **Manage display**: This tab manages how a content type is rendered for view modes (detailed next).

- **Manage permissions**: These actions show a subset of Drupal's administrative permission management specific to the content type. It allows for associating user roles to specific actions for the content type, such as creating nodes of that content type, editing nodes of the content type, and deleting content (CRUD operations).

Manage display is a useful tool for site builders to control how content is rendered in different circumstances. The following screenshot, which can be modified by modules, shows the **Manage display** tab for a content type:

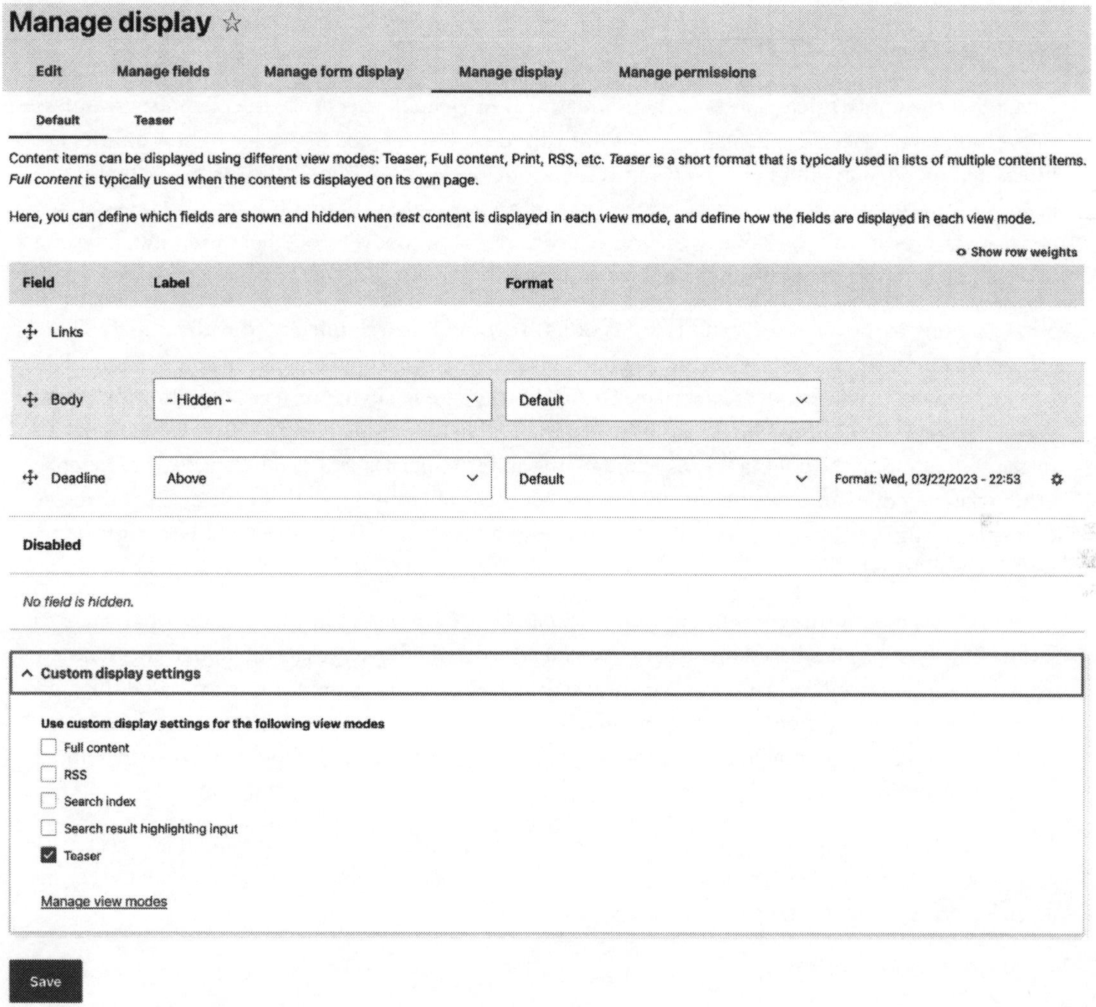

Manage display ☆

| Edit | Manage fields | Manage form display | **Manage display** | Manage permissions |

Default   Teaser

Content items can be displayed using different view modes: Teaser, Full content, Print, RSS, etc. *Teaser* is a short format that is typically used in lists of multiple content items. *Full content* is typically used when the content is displayed on its own page.

Here, you can define which fields are shown and hidden when *test* content is displayed in each view mode, and define how the fields are displayed in each view mode.

⟳ Show row weights

Field	Label	Format	
✛ Links			
✛ Body	– Hidden – ⌄	Default ⌄	
✛ Deadline	Above ⌄	Default ⌄	Format: Wed, 03/22/2023 - 22:53 ⚙

Disabled

No field is hidden.

⌃ **Custom display settings**

Use custom display settings for the following view modes
☐ Full content
☐ RSS
☐ Search index
☐ Search result highlighting input
☑ Teaser

Manage view modes

Save

Figure 8.6 – The Manage display tab of a content type

The top tabs list out enabled view modes. A view mode is nothing more than a type of display enabled for a content type that can have its settings to render the same content in different ways. Under **Custom display settings**, a site builder can associate which view modes are enabled for the content type, therefore creating a new tab on the top of the content type's **Manage display** page. Every view mode can configure the order of the fields, disable or enable which fields show up, and configure specific settings for the label and format of the data rendered. This allows for site builders to rapidly create different displays for the same content.

Nodes effectively demonstrate the features of entities, structured content, and the no-code value Drupal offers for site builders.

Applying to other features

Given that the entity subsystem is fairly foundational in Drupal, users can expect a fairly seamless integration with other Drupal features. It is difficult to capture an exhaustive list of how entities are integrated throughout all of Drupal's features, but one of the main benefits of Drupal is that it has been built to work across the core subsystems. There are no assurances that features and integrations between features are fully bug-free or that certain edge cases may not yet work, but the entity subsystem is largely an example of a well-integrated subsystem.

Views are one of the most powerful features of Drupal, and it is well integrated with entities. Views are covered in depth in *Chapter 10*, but it is best summarized by Drupal's querying and dynamic data retrieval capability. Views can create pages, Drupal blocks, or even dynamic feeds built from selecting specific fields from entities. Fields can have criteria and be filtered within the View to select entity instances that match the criteria. Views maintain the ability to harness entity relationships to reference other related entities and has support for view modes tied to entity types that have existing displays defined. The integration between entities and Views represents a nice example of two subsystems working well together.

User is also a ubiquitous content entity in Drupal. Users are fieldable, allowing Drupal users to build out robust profiles based on structured data. The user entity serves as the underlying data for authentication and authorization as part of the broader user subsystem. This is extended through Drupal's permission system, which ultimately maps configured roles back to users and performs authorization based on granted permission. Users are integrated in Drupal logs and relate to authors in the Node entity. Users will be covered in much greater depth in the next chapter.

Entities are deeply integrated in Drupal and generally work cohesively throughout all aspects of the application. Builders can expect a fairly seamless experience between the systems, with entities serving as one of the more foundational capabilities.

Multilingual features

Drupal has optional modules for enabling multilingual capabilities for entities. This effectively extends Drupal's native language capabilities with specific, related instances of the same entity. As an example, the same node can have different versions based on the language.

Modules

Drupal offers various modules that help enable or disable specific capabilities tied to multilingual needs. Site builders should understand the purpose of each module to get the intended result.

Language module

The language module must be enabled and configured to create general support for more than one language. The module can be enabled through Drush or the UI. The following screenshot demonstrates high-level language configuration found at **Administration | Configuration | Regional and language**:

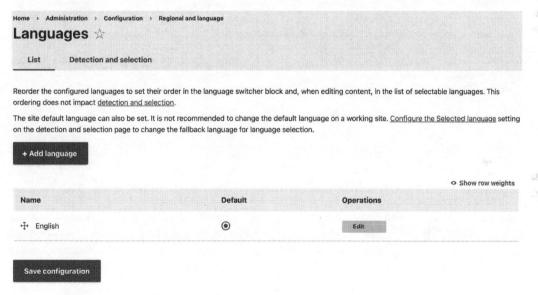

Figure 8.7 - The language management screen

The preceding screenshot demonstrates how to enable specific languages through the **Add language** workflow, change the default language for the application, and edit high-level settings for the language.

The screenshot also demonstrates a second tab, **Detection and selection**, which is shown in the following screenshot:

Interface text language detection

Order of language detection methods for interface text. If a translation of interface text is available in the detected language, it will be displayed.

⚙ Show row weights

Detection method	Description	Enabled	Operations
✛ **Account administration pages**	Account administration pages language setting.	☐	
✛ **URL**	Language from the URL (Path prefix or domain).	☑	Configure
✛ **Session**	Language from a request/session parameter.	☐	Configure
✛ **User**	Follow the user's language preference.	☐	
✛ **Browser**	Language from the browser's language settings.	☐	Configure
✛ **Selected language**	Language based on a selected language.	☑	Configure

Save settings

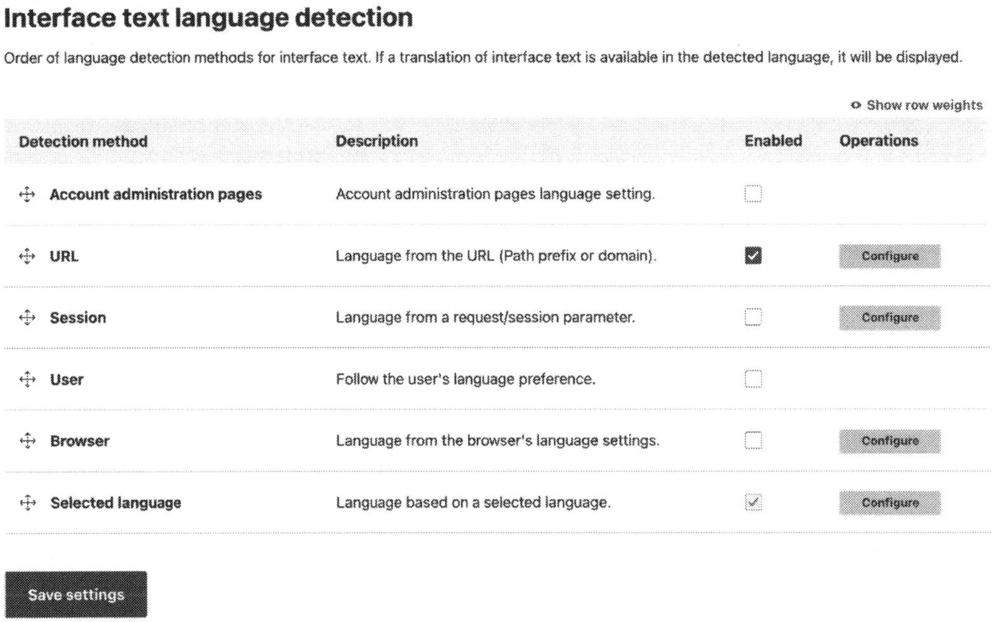

Figure 8.8 – The language detection screen

As the name implies, this configuration controls the logic of how the Drupal application determines which language to return. Specific logic can be enabled or disabled based on the intended behavior of what the application should use to determine language. There is an implied order of resolution, where a series of enabled checks can be performed if one check does not effectively resolve an enabled language. **URL** is common, where the path includes a language code, such as en/about-us for English and es/about-us for Spanish. Other resolvers can check the language of the user's browser and even default to letting users select which enabled language they want. Each detection mechanism can be configured for specific settings relevant to its resolution logic.

Content translation module

Content entities can have multilingual capabilities enabled through the content translation module. After enabling the module, the following screenshot demonstrates how to configure translation settings per entity type found at **Administration | Configuration | Regional and language | Content language**:

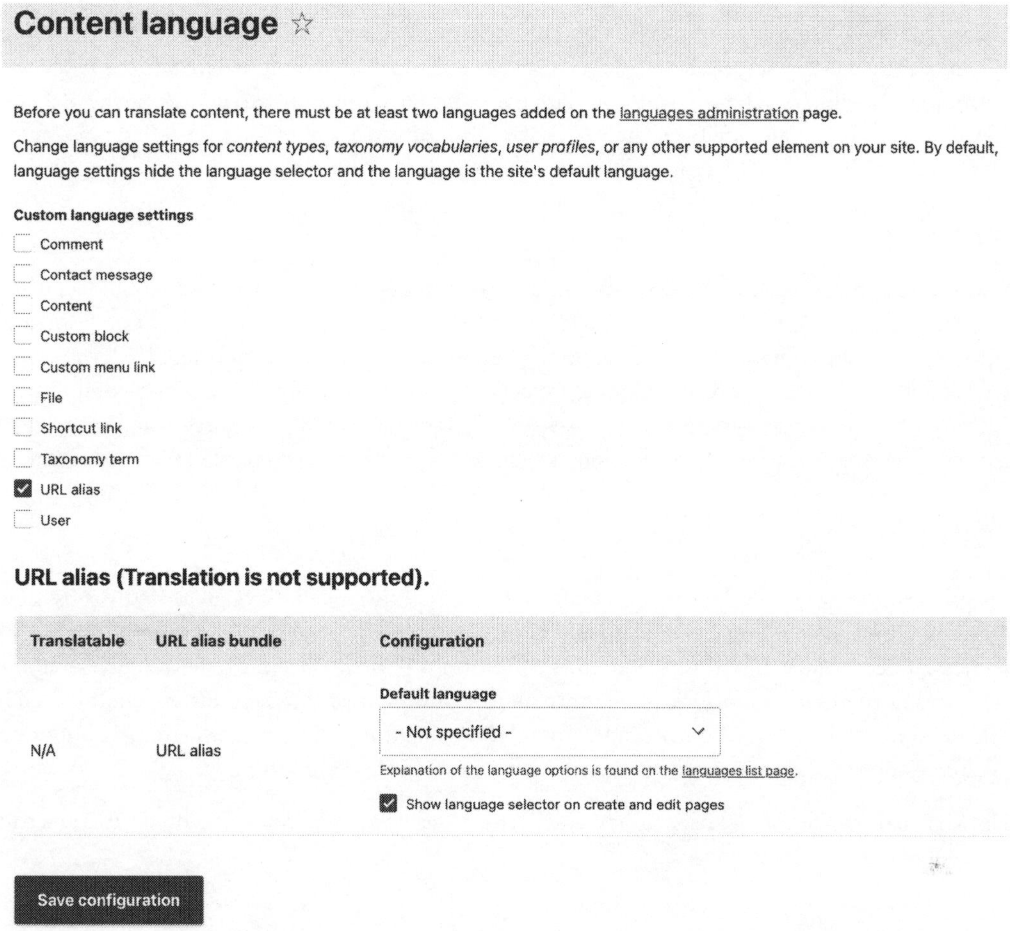

Content language ☆

Before you can translate content, there must be at least two languages added on the languages administration page.

Change language settings for *content types*, *taxonomy vocabularies*, *user profiles*, or any other supported element on your site. By default, language settings hide the language selector and the language is the site's default language.

Custom language settings

☐ Comment
☐ Contact message
☐ Content
☐ Custom block
☐ Custom menu link
☐ File
☐ Shortcut link
☐ Taxonomy term
☑ URL alias
☐ User

URL alias (Translation is not supported).

Translatable	URL alias bundle	Configuration
N/A	URL alias	**Default language** - Not specified - ⌄ Explanation of the language options is found on the languages list page. ☑ Show language selector on create and edit pages

Save configuration

Figure 8.9 – The content entity multilingual configuration screen

The preceding screenshot demonstrates the ability to select which entity types should have multilingual capabilities enabled. Each entity type may have the ability to select default languages by bundle if an entity type is translatable. These settings enable fine-grained controls for both entity type and bundle, given the intent of the application.

Locale module

The locale module performs interface translation of Drupal's administrative UI. This is especially helpful for site builders and content administrators who are able to have a UI in their native language. The module performs what is known as **string-based translation**, where specific terms (and plural versions of those terms) are converted from one language to another.

The community also offers pre-packaged translations through `localize.drupal.org`. Contributed by community members, specific translations have been uploaded and refined for various languages. Community members submit strings per language and have the ability to contribute new strings they discover are not already translated. This is useful for getting ongoing translation coverage of terminology to build a more native administrative experience with time.

Beyond core

Translatable content suggests you need authors capable of generating content across various languages. While manual efforts often afford a higher degree of accuracy, enterprises sometimes harness translation services where the content of one language can be submitted, translated, and sent back to Drupal. Services often have their own contributed projects that extend the core translation capabilities and interface with the service. Various vendors exist with their own strengths, weaknesses, and costs, which can vary application by application. Developers should pick what is most relevant to their needs, if at all.

Summary

Drupal harnesses relational database principles to help structure content through its Entity subsystem. This ubiquitous system impacts content and configuration and integrates with other features such as Views. Effective structured content follows conventions borrowed from databases, such as atomic fields and normalization. Entities are highly extensible through various settings, capabilities tied to fields, and multilingual features. Given the foundational nature of entities, it is extremely important to understand the system and how to leverage it properly throughout Drupal.

The next chapter will explore users, roles, and permissions, which allow for a tailored experience for different administrative purposes.

9

Users, Roles, and Permissions

Drupal can allow authenticated users to perform specific actions based on their granted permissions. This chapter presents Drupal's user system and **role-based access control (RBAC)** mechanisms. Drupal can model user profiles, create specific roles for those users, and grant users assigned permissions. In an enterprise setting, Drupal developers need to understand how to configure the same Drupal application to serve different user personas and manage the access of each persona accordingly. This chapter covers how to address these use cases through the user, role, and permissions capabilities.

In this chapter, we're going to cover the following main topics:

- Users
- Roles
- Permissions

Users

Drupal core has a subsystem for user management. The foundational feature serves as the tool in which users can access Drupal's backend systems. This is fundamental for site builders and content managers.

User entity

The user subsystem starts with the user entity. This entity, like others, is built on top of the entity system and is afforded structured data and management for Drupal users.

The user entity is fieldable. Enabling fields for users affords the ability for site builders to configure user profiles. By default, the user entity has a username, password, and email, all of which can't be modifiable but can be harnessed by the features in the user subsystem.

Features

The user subsystem has several features that are built on top of the user entity.

Users can log into Drupal to perform administrative actions and manage content, as well as site-building. This leverages the entity's username and password. The following figure shows Drupal's login form, which can be found at `/user/login` for those not already logged in:

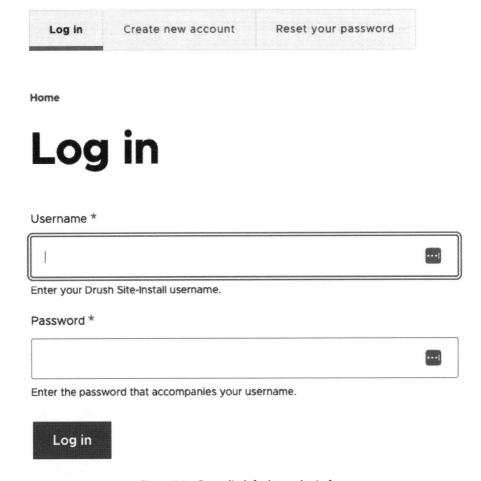

Figure 9.1 – Drupal's default user login form

Those with valid credentials to the Drupal application can enter their username and password to log in and gain access to Drupal's administrative backend. Also, note that Drupal can be configured to enable user registration, as shown in *Figure 9.1*. It is common to turn off open user registration if a Drupal application does not have a use case that engages any user that accesses Drupal (for example, allowing a site visitor to make an account to post comments).

Once a user is logged in, the user subsystem can perform authorization. This ensures that there are checks in place when a user tries to perform a specific action. This is different from authentication, which is tied to a user entering a valid username and password to log in. As one simple example, an authenticated user logs in with their username and password and then performs an action to manage other users. If the user is not granted access to manage users, the user will be blocked. Many Drupal features often respect user authorization. As an example, content types can have their permissions so that specific users can be assigned per content type.

A user is a critical aspect of Drupal watchdog, which is its auditing and logging capability. One day, a Drupal application may be working effectively, but the next day, it is not. Consider the use case of someone who incorrectly updated a configuration on the Drupal application. It is important to understand what actions a user performed and when those actions occurred. Drupal's user system is one of the underlying capabilities that helps surface this information and ultimately helps ensure Drupal activity can be audited.

Contact forms are another user-related feature of Drupal. A contact form allows a user to publish their form, which ultimately sends a notification to the user. Contact forms can be used by other users or even anonymous site visitors. Contact forms are separate core modules that can be enabled or disabled based on the desired use case, but they can be a useful way to engage with a user. Consider a publication with authors – if someone wishes to reach out to the author of an article, a contact form can be useful in those circumstances.

User management

During Drupal's installation, it creates the first administrative user. This user exists to afford full access to Drupal's backend system, which is required for all initial site building and content management. This user is often called "user 1" and is treated sensitively due to the full access the user is granted.

> **Important note**
>
> Do not remove user 1. This is often a safeguard for administrators to have an emergency account capable of addressing issues that arise. Access to the account should be reserved only for those with the greatest amount of access. This is similar to a *root user* on a Linux system. And, even those individuals should have their users so that they can effectively log and audit system activity.

Managing users is only afforded to those with a role that has been granted permission to access after logging in. This feature exists in Drupal's administrative backend at /admin/people, as seen in the following figure:

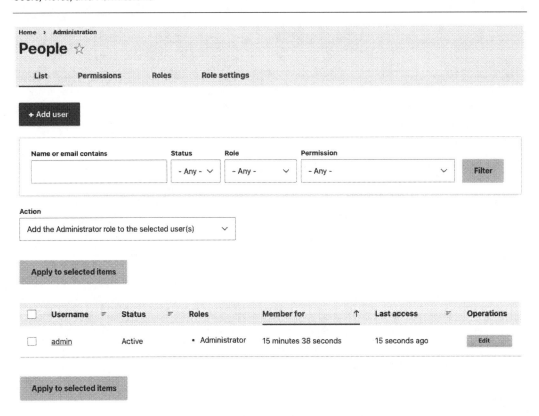

Figure 9.2 – Drupal's user management listing

There are many useful functions on the user management listing. Several useful filters can help you rapidly search for a user, find users of specific roles, or identify which users are granted specific permissions.

Figure 9.2 also shows how to add users, as demonstrated by the blue button at the top of the listing page. Clicking on this button prompts the following user management form, which can change based on the fields that have been configured for users:

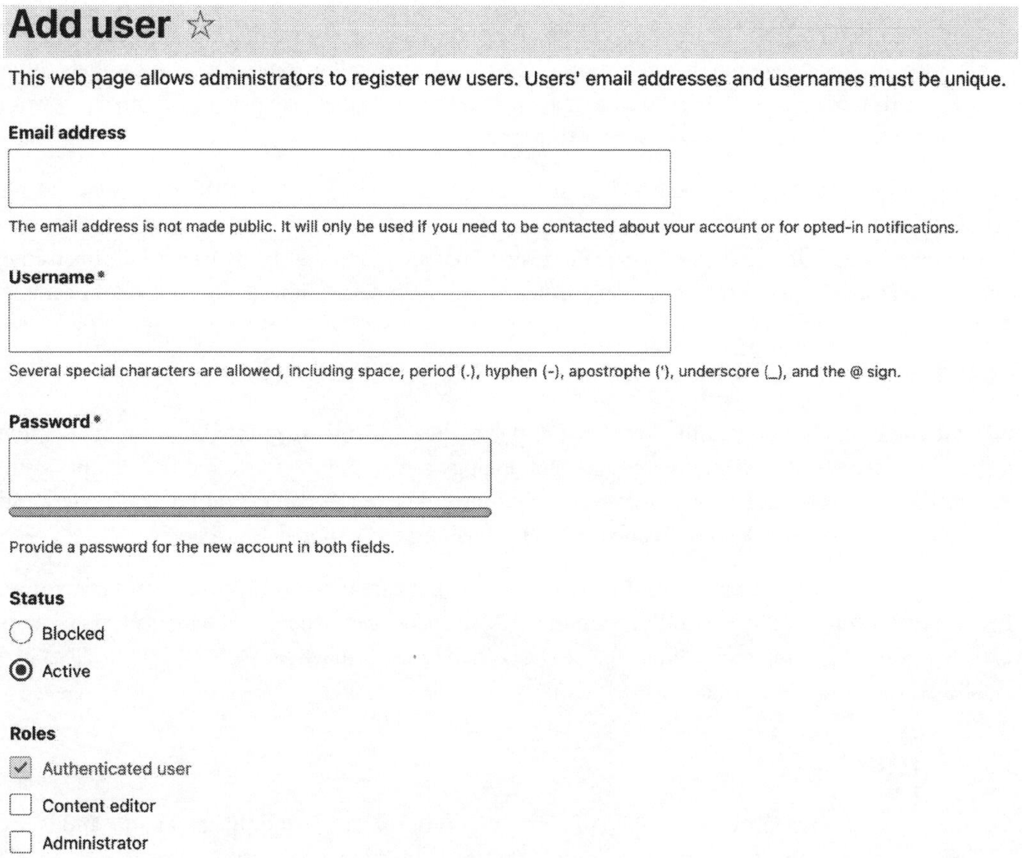

Add user ☆

This web page allows administrators to register new users. Users' email addresses and usernames must be unique.

Email address

[   ]

The email address is not made public. It will only be used if you need to be contacted about your account or for opted-in notifications.

Username *

[   ]

Several special characters are allowed, including space, period (.), hyphen (-), apostrophe ('), underscore (_), and the @ sign.

Password *

[   ]

Provide a password for the new account in both fields.

Status

◯ Blocked

◉ Active

Roles

☑ Authenticated user

☐ Content editor

☐ Administrator

Figure 9.3 – Drupal's user form

The user form has both profile-related fields, such as **Picture**, and functional fields, such as those for **Username**, **Password**, **Roles**, and **Status**. **Status** prevents a user from logging in if this is set to **Blocked**. **Roles** grant system access, and **Locale settings** allow you to set a time zone and language when certain language-based modules are enabled. Note that the form in *Figure 9.3* will change based on the fields that are configured on the user entity.

You may be concerned about a user being able to update the password of another user. It is conventional for a user to only be able to update their profile and must be explicitly granted access to update other users since this is often reserved for administrators. This capability can help perform manual password resets for administrative needs when a user forgets their password.

Users are foundational in Drupal as they help people log in and access parts of Drupal. A user can have their data beyond system credentials, such as their name, address, or other relevant parts of their profile. And, Drupal has specific conventions, such as user 1, that are granted very high-level administrative access upon installation. Next, we will cover roles, which help define different personas for users.

Roles

Roles are the different user personas for the Drupal application and are granted to users that match that persona. An effective content management analogy ties to publications that have authors and editors. The two personas have two different functions: one to write content and one to review and approve content. In Drupal, a role is effective at establishing different personas.

This goes beyond just content-related use cases as Drupal can also leverage roles for performing specific administrative actions. Consider a human resources use case where new joiners need accounts on the Drupal application or accounts need to be revoked for those who leave. A specific role can be established that is just able to manage accounts.

Role entity

Like a user, a role is an entity. It is a very simple configuration entity that only has a name and is not fieldable. Given that the entity system allows for relationships between entities, a user entity has a one-to-many relationship with the role entity. Roles are configured to their corresponding permissions.

Default roles

After a standard installation, Drupal has the following roles:

- **Anonymous**: A role that's automatically granted to those not authenticated
- **Authenticated**: A role that's automatically granted to any user
- **Content editor**: A role that can perform content management
- **Administrator**: A role with full control of the Drupal application

Authenticated and anonymous are fixed roles and cannot be deleted, while a content editor and administrator can.

Configuring roles

You can manage roles at `admin/people/roles`, as shown in the following figure:

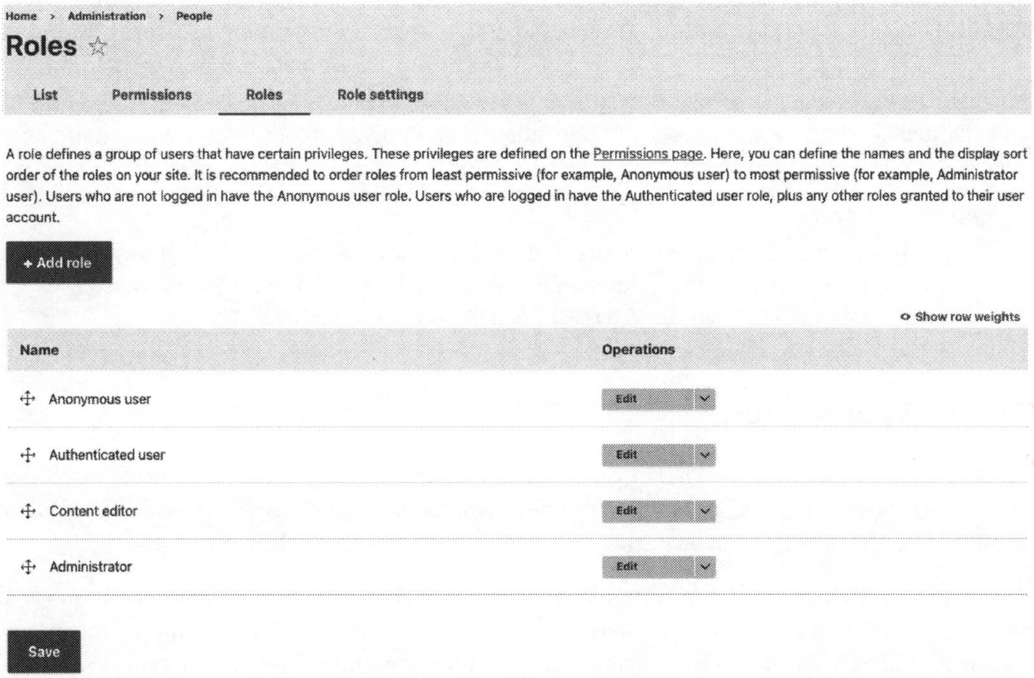

Figure 9.4 - Drupal's role listing

Clicking **Edit** on any of the roles allows you to change the name of the role. Clicking the + **Add role** button opens a form that allows you to create a new role. Adding roles can address the various personas found in the Drupal application.

Roles are the personas that are assigned to a user to help Drupal understand what that user can do. Drupal furnishes several out-of-the-box roles but allows any role to be configured. Next, we'll review permissions to help you understand how a role maps to specific actions in the Drupal system.

Permissions

A permission is an action that is granted to a role. Authorization happens when a user attempts to perform an action that is managed by permission. The role of that user is dereferenced and a set of aggregated permissions that have been granted to the user are checked.

Access control

Drupal leverages permissions as its means of access control. Users are assigned specific roles. Those roles have specific permissions assigned to them. Access control happens when a user attempts to act Drupal. Drupal will perform authorization based on the permissions granted to roles. As a simple example, the "manage users" permission can be granted to a role for **human resources** (**HR**), who are responsible for managing new hires or attrition. When one of the members of HR logs in and tries to go to Drupal's user management page, they are granted access where other Drupal users would not.

> **Important note**
>
> It is good practice to implement a "least privilege" model for user management. If a user does not need to access parts of Drupal, they should not. This helps limit the scope of what a user can do and subsequently manages the risk of making unintentional mistakes.

Types of permissions

Permissions can be for any action in Drupal. Given that Drupal has a significant amount of capabilities even out of the box, it has a large number of permissions, and their types are broad. This affords granular access control and can be helpful to address use cases that may be niche.

A common type of permission is content management. Drupal has granularity often by entity or even by bundle. In the case of content types, permissions exist for every content type (bundle). Operations can change for each entity as well, which impacts the type of permissions. Content types exemplify this with granular permissions for viewing or editing that specific content type.

Other types of permissions correlate to administrative functions. Each subsystem in Drupal has permissions that are tied to the functionality provided. One example that was covered in this chapter is permissions tied to user management. More examples include accessing Drupal logs, configuring features of Drupal, and enabling or disabling projects.

Managing permissions

Permission management happens through Drupal's backend user interface behind Drupal's user login. It is a site-building exercise, the results of which impact the configuration of a Drupal application. The following figure shows the user interface for this, which can be found at `admin/people/permissions`:

Permissions ☆

| List | Permissions | Roles | Role settings |

Permissions let you control what users can do and see on your site. You can define a specific set of permissions for each role. (See the Roles page to create a role.) Any permissions granted to the Authenticated user role will be given to any user who is logged in to your site. On the Role settings page, you can make any role into an Administrator role for the site, meaning that role will be granted all permissions. You should be careful to ensure that only trusted users are given this access and level of control of your site.

Hide descriptions

Permission	Anonymous user	Authenticated user	Content editor	Administrator
Block				
Administer blocks	☐	☐	☐	☑
Comment				
Administer comment types and settings *Warning: Give to trusted roles only; this permission has security implications.*	☐	☐	☐	☑
Administer comments and comment settings	☐	☐	☐	☑
Edit own comments	☐	☐	☑	☑

Figure 9.5 – Drupal's permission management page

As we can see, permissions are mapped to roles. Each permission is grouped by the type of permission. Given the large number and granularity of permissions, leveraging the browser's native page search for lists can be useful.

Permission definition

Permissions are defined by modules. Typically, permissions are statically defined in a module's `[module].permissions.yml` file. Alternatively, a module can leverage Drupal's framework to dynamically generate permissions. This is common for things that change, such as site builders, who develop new content types and then assign permissions per content type to specific roles. Given that a site builder can manage content types, the permissions cannot be statically defined.

Modules own specific functionality. Not only do they define the permissions, but the module contains the logic to enforce the permission. Permissions can be reused in modules since a module can define dependencies; a dependent module may define permission leveraged by another module. The following code block demonstrates enforcement logic for the manage user permission:

```
if (\Drupal::currentUser()->hasPermission('manage users')) {
    // perform some action
} else {
    // prevent user from performing some action
}
```

This code example can be embedded in any of the PHP code found in the module, which allows that module to check permissions within any of the functionality it provides. Note that user 1 is automatically authorized to perform any action.

Permissions define what actions a user can perform that are tied to their assigned roles. They are managed through Drupal's administrative user interface for users who have been granted the correct access. Permissions are defined by the modules that also contain authorization logic within the code to check for permissions before executing certain actions. Setting up users, roles, and permissions in combination helps ensure users are granted capabilities tied to their desired persona.

Summary

Users, roles, and permissions help Drupal manage access for various personas. These features are used by Drupal to provide fine-grained access controls to users of the Drupal system. Drupal can then perform authorization tied to specific system actions. These features exemplify Drupal's extensibility for use cases tied to various personas and the specific actions each persona can be allowed to perform. Drupal's modules help define the actions as permissions and the logic to authorize actions. The next chapter covers a complex but powerful feature in Drupal called **Views** that is used to create dynamic content displays.

10
Drupal Views and Display Modes

Drupal has a feature called Views that helps deliver dynamic content displays. This is one of the more popular features of Drupal, as it allows site builders to take existing structured content and reuse it in additional ways. This helps content authors avoid duplicating the same content that may be delivered in multiple places throughout a Drupal application. This chapter helps define Views, covers its features, and walks through how to use the feature. The chapter also touches on a complementary feature called display modes, integrated with Views. The combination of these two features empowers site builders to address a large number of use cases with little or no code. While complex, the chapter will address the purpose, offer hands-on development with these features, and provide the foundation to build more advanced use cases.

In this chapter, we're going to cover the following main topics:

- Defining Views
- Defining display modes
- Using Views and display modes

Defining Views

Views, as a feature, is one of the most compelling and most complex features for site builders. It is in core, which means it is out of the box with Drupal. At a high level, it is a dynamic display builder. Being able to learn and leverage its features effectively is not easy, but the results can be empowering.

Overview

Defining Views is tricky. It is important to dissect this definition significantly more.

The term *display* in this context has a broad definition. Drupal maintains structured content, which can be used within any display. In a traditional sense, **content management systems (CMSs)** store content that then gets displayed like a page on a website. Even Drupal does this with content types, nodes, and rendering nodes. However, recall earlier chapters where the problem of content duplication could be addressed by CMSs in favor of copying the same content repeatedly and pushing the burden onto content managers to do a lot of manual work. At a high level, a display could be defined by any place content is served, with a desire to create multiple displays of the same content over duplication. So, by definition, a display extends well beyond a typical page.

The term *dynamic* is important as well. There is an implied relationship between the content and its displays. If the content can change, the display should also change. Drupal manages this relationship, and it handles the dynamic nature of a display.

Bringing this together, a dynamic display builder is a tool that allows site builders to create displays for Drupal's content. A site builder configures the display and Drupal handles the rest. Drupal integrates the display with its native request and rendering capabilities. It handles content updates, which automatically update the related displays. Content authors gain the benefit of managing content in one place but reusing it where they expect the same content through their application.

Another useful analogy is a **database management system (DBMS)**. If we consider Drupal to handle the structure and storage of its content, the display of the content is one form of data retrieval. Views is one of those forms and solves similar problems to SQL. While SQL is transactional, some statements support retrieving information. Given DBMS often stores structured data, SQL helps specify fields from tables, relationships, filters, and even functions that transform the returned rows. Views do this for Drupal data and without code.

Views features

Views are intended to address many use cases around dynamic displays. To do so, Views has a large number of capabilities and configurations that can help a site builder create what they need.

At a high level, Views starts with a display and incorporates the following high-level features:

1. Selecting entity types for the display
2. Filtering and sorting by fields or bundles
3. Incorporating different types of displays (pages, blocks, view modes, field-based displays, feeds)
4. Managing the display settings and formatting of fields and/or content
5. Static content through header, footer, no results messaging, and more

6.   Incorporation of linked, relational data across entities

7.   Various APIs to customize Views behaviors through modules

It starts with enabling site builders to manage Views. The Views UI is a separate module and one that needs to be enabled to provide the backend configuration screens for Views. A user will then be able to log in to Drupal's backend and access the interface to manage Views, given the correct permission.

A View is a wrapper around one or more displays. A View has basic metadata, such as the name and description of the View. It is also possible to restrict access through permissions. The same View can have one or more displays, often designed to address similar displays that may have minor variations across use cases.

Creating a new View starts with a default display. The default display has a full definition for the display, which can be subsequently copied and overridden for similar displays within the View. The definition covers all of the configurations of Views features for a specific Views display. Subsequent displays inherit the configuration from the default and only specify changes relevant to the secondary display.

Given the broad definition of a display, a View starts with a display type. This integrates with other Drupal displays by offering a page (similar to rendering a node), a block that can be placed on a page, or even web services such as RSS feeds, XML, and more.

Each display type has options relevant to that display. Given that Views is in core and well integrated with other features of Drupal, it is common for display types to be able to be configured with similar capabilities. For instance, a page display has a path, but a block display leverages Drupal's native block placement, so it does not have a path. Block displays maintain the metadata of the block, such as the title.

Each display integrates with Drupal's structured data by selecting the relevant entity type and fields. Selecting the entity type allows for the specific selection of fields to display. Every field type has its own different ways to configure the display. As an example, you can pick the relevant format for displaying date fields, such as "10/20/2023" or "October 20, 2023". Images can select the specific image style.

Beyond formats, Views also has some transformation capabilities relevant to the field type. A title can be converted into a link to that node. A body can be truncated and summarized to provide visitors with a glimpse into the content on a page. A Boolean field can be transformed into more descriptive information, such as on/off, yes/no, or selected/unselected for the specific use case. While this is not exhaustive, it is reasonable to expect additional, common transformations found for the type of field within the display.

Views also has support for relationships where one field references another entity. By creating a relationship, all fields of the related entity can then be used within Views. Again, one of the most important aspects of normalized data is the avoidance of repeated information. Using relationships in Drupal stores the data in one place, and relationship fields allow an entity to reference another entity. Suppose a display has the first and last name of an author (a user entity) from a listing of blog posts (nodes from a content type). By selecting the content type of `blog post` and adding a relationship to the `user`, Views can subsequently pull the first and last name fields from the user profile.

Filters are another useful feature that allows for a display to refine the entities returned. As an example, suppose a blog has a relationship field to a taxonomy called a `category` that identifies a blog post by subject matter. A display can filter blog posts by the subject matter, such as `sports` or `politics`. Using this feature allows various displays to more explicitly define what content is needed.

Views also have support for context through contextual filters. Context can be a broad and nuanced topic and one that expands well beyond Views. There are several common types of context, such as the date or time of a request, a user that is logged in (or anonymous), parameters that may be passed through a request, or a language passed through a browser in the request header. Natively, Views can filter displays based on the context. Showing blog posts that a user has authored is possible with a contextual filter of blog posts that uses the user authenticated at the time of request.

Exposed filters are another useful feature. A filter does not simply need to be through the definition and configuration of a View display. An exposed filter allows for a display to expose one or more filterable options within the display. This allows those who access the display to see a full list and subsequently pare down by specific field values at their discretion. To extend the blog post example, a View can show all categories but have an exposed filter that allows a user to filter down the results of the View by the category they are interested in.

Several other features exist in Views that expand on the functionality mentioned in this chapter. It is useful to get hands-on with Views and explore it in greater depth, as it is a fairly complex feature.

Customizing Views

Views have several typical means of customization, the most popular of which is through contributed modules. Through the community, one can find extended display types such as calendars, trees, accordions, or integrations with popular JavaScript libraries. More functional capabilities with Views can be added through **Views Bulk Operations** (**VBO**) or data exports. It is useful to explore the Views category of projects to learn more.

> **Important note**
>
> One of the most important aspects of developing a Drupal application is effectively finding and adopting contributed modules before considering custom code. Views, in particular, has a robust set of contributed modules that already address a large number of use cases. Views are well integrated with other contributed modules such as field types, entity types, and more.

While Views is largely aimed at helping site builders avoid code, it can be common to override Views templates within custom themes. Views expose a naming convention and various types of templates, which allows a custom theme to provide its own Twig templates to override Views default markup. It is recommended to explore all site-building options before creating custom code.

Also, Views has a fairly robust framework for backend developers to create custom modules that extend the out-of-the-box capabilities. This can often help for advanced use cases where third-party

·data needs to be interfaced with Views or there is a need to filter the data provided to Views with advanced business logic not possible with site building. Views provide various APIs that allow a custom module to extend it in code.

Views is a complex but useful feature of Drupal core that helps create dynamic displays. It is well connected to the rest of Drupal, with entities, fields, blocks, themes, and more. Views' ability to work with context, provide filters, and transform data helps address important use cases for displays without touching code.

Defining display modes

Drupal's display modes feature takes a different approach to creating displays and is complementary to Views. Conventionally, this feature starts with being able to control display settings for a content-type rendering on a page. However, additional display modes can be configured to display the same content in different ways as needed.

Overview

Display modes look at displays tied to a content type. A content type defines structured content. The same node within a content type can be displayed in different ways. Each display may be able to fine-tune which fields are displayed, labels, formats of field values, ordering of fields, and more. A content type can have as many display modes as needed to address any desired use case. Each content type can select a default display mode, which is most commonly used for rendering nodes.

This may be confusing concerning Views, given Views also allows for the building of displays. Display modes only define displays for content types. To create a display, a display mode must integrate with another Drupal feature. Also, display modes are used more broadly than just Views such as rendering nodes, providing display capabilities for nodes in blocks, and displaying nodes in Layout Builder. Views is a far more robust display system that can work across content types, against several display formats, and more.

> **Important note**
> Given display modes can help create displays, it may not be required to leverage Views to build a display. Display modes are more lightweight, integrated throughout Drupal core display features, and help configure displays specific to a content type. If a display matches these criteria, use display modes.

Views do have native support for display modes. This saves time by allowing for the use of existing display configurations tied to a content type. In favor of selecting specific fields in a content type, a site builder can harness all of Views' features but simply select a full entity and a corresponding display mode. And, in the case of entity references found in fields, Views allows for selecting a display mode in addition to field selection of the referenced entity.

Display modes are also integrated into Drupal's theming system. While the feature helps site builders rapidly configure displays for a content type, a display mode still may need to be customized visually. Thankfully, display modes have corresponding templates that allow a developer to enhance a Drupal theme to modify the markup or CSS.

Popular use cases

Display modes can be leveraged in several common use cases:

- **Node-based default displays**: A display mode allows for flexibility to configure node-based displays across several use cases. A key benefit of Drupal is the ability to reuse the same content as needed across several displays. However, it's not assumed each display is the same. A display mode allows a site builder to create any number of displays for the same content type and node based on any desired use cases and variations. A variation may be as simple as not showing the authoring information of a node in one part of the Drupal application if the default node display shows the author information. It may also involve tweaking an image to show a thumbnail and not a fully rendered image only on the home page or within a specific View listing.

- **Teasers**: One of the most popular use cases for display modes is known as a teaser. Typically, a default display mode is a full representation of the visible fields of a node. A teaser is intended to introduce or summarize the same content, often so that one can click on the teaser to view the full details. The same idea can be extended to a display mode where a node is featured and the content is more prominent than other displays. The Umami demo distribution leverages a teaser display mode for its home page listing.

Display modes help configure displays, similar to Views, but are more directly tied to variations in displaying nodes' content types. Features for display modes can be used in Views but also other Drupal features. Using display modes helps address common use cases such as teasers and features that use the same underlying content as full-page views.

Using Views and display modes

Using Views is one of the more difficult tasks for site builders given its vast configuration options. While this chapter affords hands-on options, it is important to explore the feature in greater depth and to get more practice with time.

All the following examples leverage a blog content type with a primary use case of building different blog-related displays in the Drupal application. For the sake of clarity, the content type has fields for title, body, featured, and a banner image. Also, it's assumed the Views UI module is enabled for the next screenshots and that a user is logged in with the correct permissions.

Creating a teaser display mode for blogs

An effective teaser could be as simple as a title of the blog linked to the full page with some preliminary, summarized body content.

Follow these instructions to create a teaser:

1. A teaser display mode can be created by going to **Administration | Structure | Display modes | View** and pressing **Add new Content view mode**. This prompts a simple form to enter the name of the display mode. This enables the display mode for all content types, which can now be configured for the blog content type.

2. On the content type listing page, found at **Administration | Structure | Types**, the blog content type will have a drop-down list of options. Selecting **Manage Display** allows a site builder to manage its display mode configuration. At the bottom of the page, the following screenshot shows **Custom display settings**, which are used to enable or disable specific display modes for each content type:

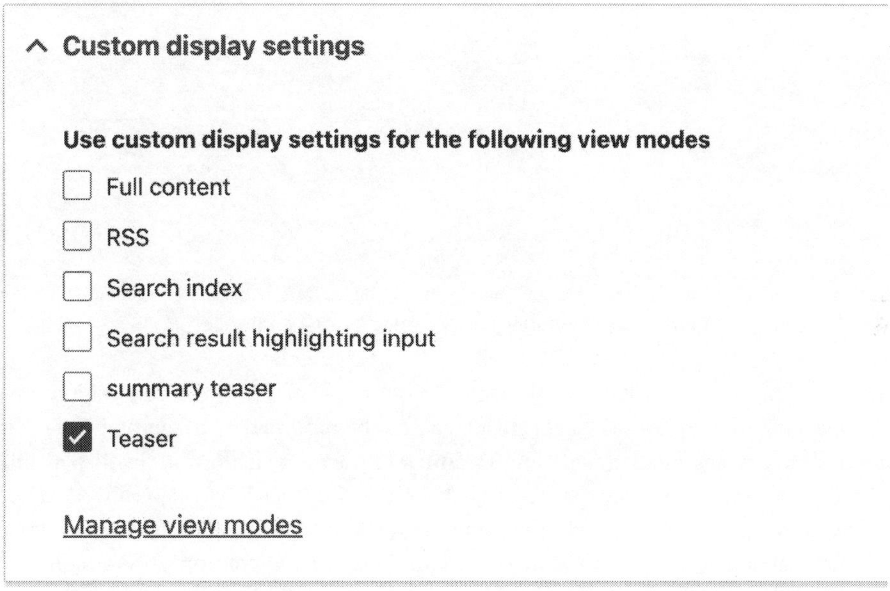

∧ **Custom display settings**

Use custom display settings for the following view modes

☐ Full content

☐ RSS

☐ Search index

☐ Search result highlighting input

☐ summary teaser

☑ Teaser

Manage view modes

Figure 10.1 – Custom display settings for content types

3. After creating the new display mode, the display mode must then be enabled for the content type you wish to leverage. The **Teaser** checkbox is selected in the preceding screenshot, signifying that the blog content type has the teaser display mode enabled.

4. Once the display mode is enabled, a tab will exist at the top of the blog's **Manage display** page for the specific display mode. The following screenshot shows the blog with teaser enabled:

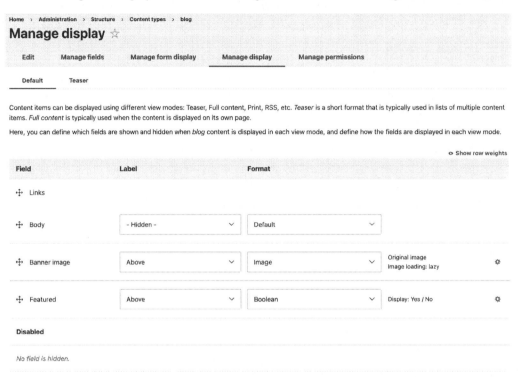

Figure 10.2 – Managing display modes for a content type

5. After clicking on the **Teaser** tab, this page allows for several different configurations for display modes. First, the order of the fields displayed can be modified by dragging the far-left toggle up or down. Dragging the toggle into **Disabled** removes the field from the display mode. For the specific teaser use case, the featured checkbox and links have been moved to **Disabled**. The second column demonstrates the label. This allows a site builder to select whether or not the field label is displayed in the display mode. The **Format** column provides different ways to render the field depending on the field type. Given the body field is to be summarized, the format for that field is set to **Summary or trimmed** for our use case.

This effectively creates our teaser display mode for the blog content type. Additional rendering options exist for each field display by pressing the gear icon on the far right of each row.

Creating a View for a blog listing – option 1 with teaser display mode

Now that the blog content type has a teaser display, a View can be created that harnesses the display mode for a blog listing. Start by going to **Administration | Structure | Views** and pressing the **Add View** button. This prompts an initial configuration form to create the View, as found in the following screenshot:

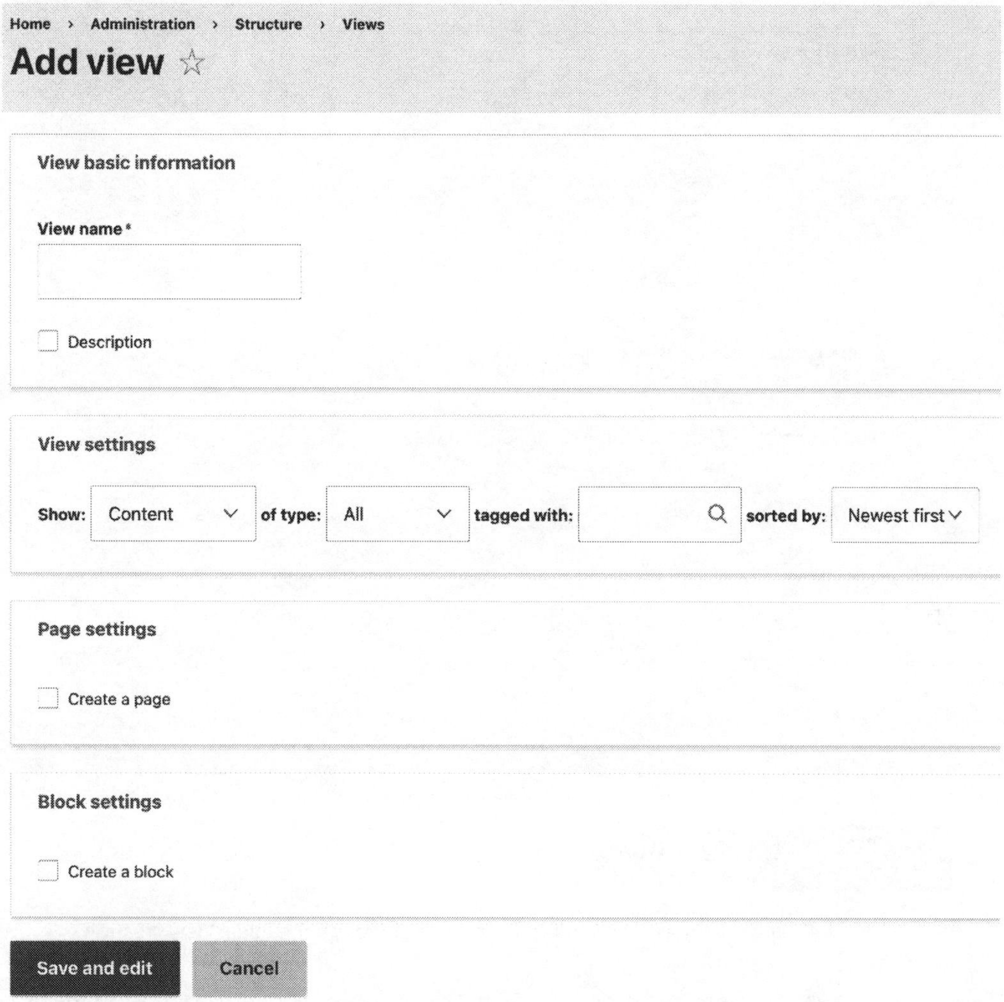

Figure 10.3 – Initial View creation form

This form prompts for the basic metadata of the View and its initial configuration. The name and description help provide the purpose of the View. The **View settings** option helps define the high-level display logic. For the use case of a blog listing, selecting a **Content** option of type **Blog** will get the correct content type, with an option to provide the sorting logic. Finally, the ability to add two initial displays to the View exists by checking boxes for creating a page or creating a block. For the sake of demonstration, a block display was selected to be able to place the same block on multiple pages. The following screenshot immediately prompted more options for the block display:

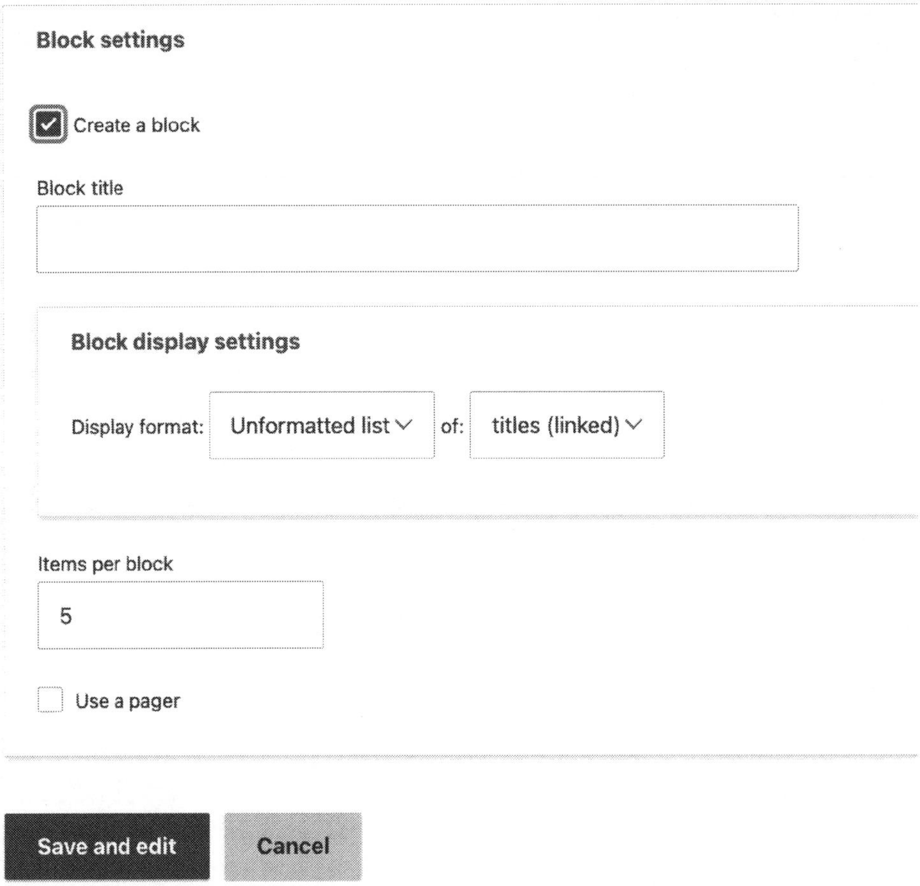

Block settings

☑ Create a block

Block title

Block display settings

Display format: Unformatted list ⌄   of: titles (linked) ⌄

Items per block

5

☐ Use a pager

Save and edit   Cancel

Figure 10.4 – Displaying specific settings for display modes on the initial View creation

This form allows us to configure specific settings of the block display. For the block title, a **Blog teaser listing** helps effectively identify the purpose of the block. The **Display format** selection provides various display options for the block, such as list, grid, and table, all of which have various additional and specific configurations. The second dropdown helps identify what to display and has options for a default linked title, the ability to specify fields or a selection of the display mode for the blog. In this case, **Teaser** is selected for the dropdown. Finally, the block supports a specific number in the list with the ability to paginate. This can be enabled based on the specific use case. By pressing **Save and edit**, the View is effectively created and has the basic configuration of our blog listing with teaser display modes.

Creating a View for a blog listing – option 2 with fields

One of the most common use cases for Views is to use fields within the structured content of an entity. The previous example bypassed Views' field capabilities by harnessing the display mode for the blog content type. This second option produces a similar listing but with fields within Views.

Start a new View, again, by going to **Administration | Structure | Views** and pressing the **Add View** button. The following screenshot demonstrates the form to add this View:

Figure 10.5 – Displaying specific settings for fields on the initial View creation

The preceding screenshot shows most of the same settings by selecting content and picking the blog content type. The notable difference is in the block display settings, where **fields** is selected instead of the display mode in the previous example. After saving, the initial View is created but still requires configuration.

The next screenshot demonstrates the Views configuration interface for each View:

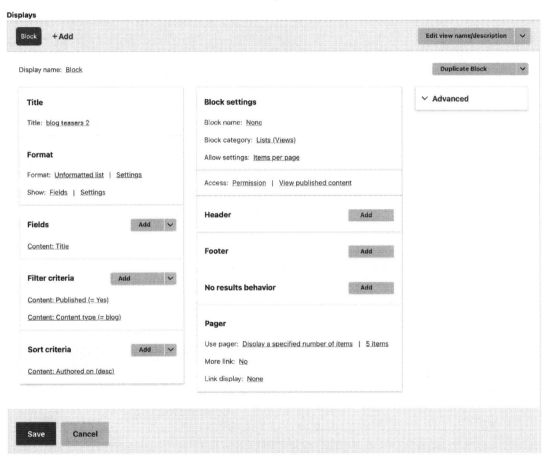

Figure 10.6 – Interface for editing the configuration of a View

To finish the previous example, the View needs to be configured with the specific fields for the teaser. By default, the View has the title field that is linked to the node. To build the teaser, both the banner image field and the summary of the body field need to be added to the View. In the **Fields** section, press **Add**, search for body, check the box, and press **Add and configure fields**, as shown in the following screenshot:

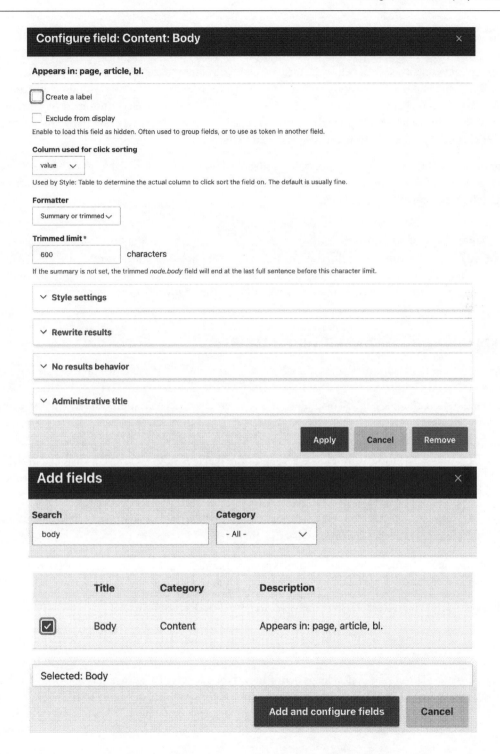

Figure 10.7 – The two steps for adding a new field into a View

The second step, also shown in *Figure 10.7*, prompts a screen to configure the settings for the body field. This includes a label, a formatter, and four different sections of various settings. Each of the four sections contains several helpful features that address common use cases, but the options change per field type, and there is a significant amount of depth in each section that would be difficult to summarize comprehensively in this chapter. For our specific use case, select **Summary or trimmed** for the formatter of the body field with a desired character count to effectively summarize the content. After clicking the **Apply** button, the field is added to the View.

For the sake of brevity, the same process that added the body field can be used to add a banner image to the View. Different configuration options will be prompted for an image field that would be different from the field type of the body field.

> **Important note**
>
> Every time a View is edited through the interface, it is not automatically saved. It stages any changes, and the changes only take effect once the **Save** button is pressed. It is important not to forget to save; otherwise, the View may continue to show the older configuration.

Explaining the Views editing interface

Figure 10.6 demonstrates the Views editing interface, which is full of useful features. While it is not possible to more comprehensively cover these features due to nuances with field types and the breadth of configuration options, it is still helpful to have an overview of each section with relevant use cases.

The top row helps manage the displays for the View and the operations for the View:

- **Displays**: The top row of blocks is each of the displays in the View. The display currently being edited will be highlighted in a different color. The +**Add** button allows for the creation of secondary displays in the same View.

- The dropdown on the right of the top bar allows for editing the metadata of the View, duplicating the View, reordering displays, or deleting the View.

Under the top row is the preliminary display type configuration and a dropdown for the operations of the display. This is useful for changing the display type or for operations such as duplicating the display.

The first column defines the content configuration of the highlighted display:

- **Title**: This is the title of the display, which is typically **Metadata** and can be optionally included in the display.

- **Format**: This configuration helps define how the View gets displayed and the settings for that display format. It also provides the configuration for what gets displayed in the View, which is the selection of fields or a specific display mode. And, depending on what is selected, there are specific settings.

- **Filter criteria**: Just as with querying a database, one or more criteria can be provided to filter the results. In our example of blogs, only published nodes with the blog content type are displayed. **Published** is a specific setting of the node and is one filter. The blog content type is a second filter. Those criteria ensure only the correct subset of all nodes is returned. Additional criteria can be added based on the use case.

- **Sort criteria**: A View can be configured to return results in a specified order. Common use cases are alphabetical by title, by the date published, and more.

The middle column manages the configuration for how the content is displayed:

- **Block settings**: This was the specific display type of the example display, but this section generally shows the configuration tied to the display type. This configuration changes by display type.

- **Permission**: Most display types allow for configuring permission that can perform access control to the display.

- **Header and Footer**: Static content that is delivered before and after the results of the content display, respectively.

- **No results behavior**: Different behaviors can happen if no content exists in the display. Some simple examples would be returning nothing or static text if no content is found.

- **Pager**: Displays that have a large amount of content often need to be able to support pagination. The **Pager** section allows for configuring the amount of content returned and the controls to paginate.

The third column has advanced settings for displays that expand beyond basic capabilities:

- **Relationships**: This provides the ability to use entity relationships within Views. The most common use case is an entity type that has a relationship field to another entity where the View contains information from the other entity.

- **Contextual filters**: The ability to filter content based on context, as described previously. This is useful to provide filters created from other Drupal features, such as the user logged in, information from the request, desired language, and more.

- **Exposed form**: A capability to allow a user to control filters when viewing a display.

- **Other**: There are several ad hoc behaviors or configurations that can be adjusted for the display, such as caching, administrative metadata, or custom CSS classes.

Countless other more detailed use cases can stem from some of the high-level use cases defined previously.

Creating an RSS feed display

Displays in Views do not just apply to content rendered by Drupal through a page or a block. Common web service APIs allow for displays in Views to become a feed for machine-driven content delivery. A common use case is an RSS feed.

Following the aforementioned steps of adding a View without adding a page or a block creates a default display of blog nodes. A feed can be added by pressing the +**Add** button, which prompts a dropdown of different display types, as exemplified in *Figure 10.8*:

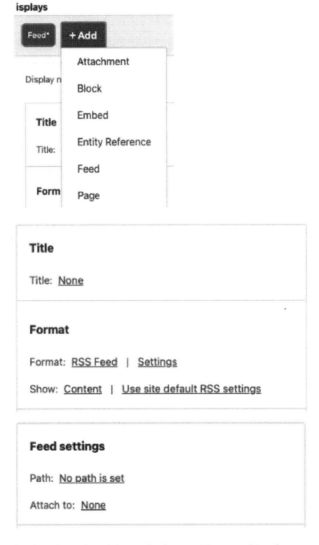

Figure 10.8 – The dropdown for adding a display to a View, resulting format, and settings

By selecting **Feed**, a display is created from the existing configuration set when adding the View. The format, by default, is set to **RSS Feed**, and the display type settings change to **Feed settings** where a path to the feed can be set.

Views can address many nuanced use cases, all rooted in creating dynamic displays that are well-integrated throughout Drupal. Site builders are then given the tools and discretion to configure Views based on the desired use cases of the application.

Summary

Views help provide a robust, feature-rich dynamic display tool for site builders. Its ability to configure features across different types of displays, structured content, and other Drupal features helps Views reuse the same content in different displays and feed-based formats. Display modes help complement Views for displays directly integrated with content types. The combination of both offers two highly flexible tools capable of addressing a large number of use cases.

The next chapter presents media and files that help Drupal manage and deliver static digital assets.

Files, Images, and Media

Drupal's **File** and **Media** systems provide a rich set of features that are commonly used for static assets, such as images, videos, and more. This chapter extends structured content concepts to files and media types and leverages these features as fields linked to other entities. Each feature has various ways to configure both media and files. This chapter covers additional use cases, including Drupal's public and private filesystems for different storage mechanisms. Finally, this chapter concludes with various tutorials that address common asset-based implementations.

In this chapter, we're going to cover the following main topics:

- Assets in Drupal
- Files
- Images
- Media
- Use cases

Assets in Drupal

Assets are a specific type of digital content. Consider reading about a researcher online. When viewing their biography on a University website, an image shows a picture of them, a list of their publications, which are linked to PDF files, and a video of their latest conference talk is featured. These are all assets.

Assets are a vibrant part of the modern web. Social platforms such as Instagram and YouTube are built around images and videos. The emergence of cameras and cell phones has made digital assets ubiquitous. As such, assets are a large part of digital applications. And, assets are a significant part of Drupal.

Use cases

Assets are one part of the longstanding "trifecta" of Drupal: code, database, and files. Files take on two forms: assets and generated files. Configuration, as an example, is generated by the Drupal application, managed by the runtime database, and persistently stored in files for versioning. Drupal's caching also commonly generates files for CSS and JS. Assets are for file-based content.

Drupal has a significant amount of functionality for assets. It can be configured to address use cases similar to that of a **digital asset manager** (**DAM**), while Drupal has many basic, native features of a DAM out of the box. Given Drupal is a digital application with structured content, it should be no surprise that Drupal can manage assets much like other content. Assets have the same problems as other content: managing, storing, rendering, transforming, and authoring. Drupal's asset features cover all of these problems across several use cases.

As an application, everything starts with Drupal managing assets. Drupal can natively manage assets and metadata for assets in tandem with its structured content. It has features that automatically manage metadata, such as the user who uploaded the asset, the file size, the extension, and tracking any derivative files. Drupal can manage the relationship of a file to other content it manages.

Drupal can also handle the storage of assets through both a public and private filesystem. An author uploads a file and Drupal can store it natively. The most common, default storage means is the public filesystem, which creates a public URL to the file managed by Drupal. When authoring happens and the file is uploaded, Drupal handles all of the logic to store the file, which includes name collisions and references to the authored content (when relevant). Drupal can also manage private files, which have gated access based on the context of a request and Drupal's access control mechanisms. For example, if a file is uploaded to a node and that node can only be viewed with certain permissions, the file would be subjected to the same access control. Access to the file would have parity with access to the node and not offer a public-facing URL.

> **Important note**
> Public filesystems allow for direct links to assets. Even if you remove all references to the asset from other content, such as nodes, the file still exists and would be accessible by accessing the URL to the file.

Drupal has various tools that allow it to manage and deliver assets that can address common use cases. Its systems handle the management, storage, and functionality of assets.

Files

The foundational asset management feature in Drupal is called **File**. This feature handles fundamental file management for Drupal's assets.

Subsystem

File has an entire subsystem in Drupal. Like several other systems, it starts with a **File** entity. This entity provides all of the standard CRUD operations for files. This entity maintains all of the file storage and the corresponding metadata for a file. Supporting the entity are all of the functions that help derive file size and file extensions, and also perform file uploads during content authoring. At a high level, the file subsystem performs basic asset storage, retrieval, and management capabilities.

Entities leverage files through the use of a file field. Suppose that the content of a particular content type should have an attached file. A file field can be added to the structured content of the content type, which then allows you to upload a file and associate it with the node. Files uploaded to the public filesystem will have URLs that can be directly linked in content such as WYSIWYG.

The subsystem also has a robust framework that allows other modules to extend this file-related functionality. This can help with triggering specific business processes, adding conditional custom validation of a file, or performing transformations on the file.

Modules and configuration

To enable Drupal's file functionality, simply enable the **File** module under **Field Types** at `admin/modules`. A central, administrative file listing can now be found at `admin/content/files`. The following figure shows the rudimentary file listing:

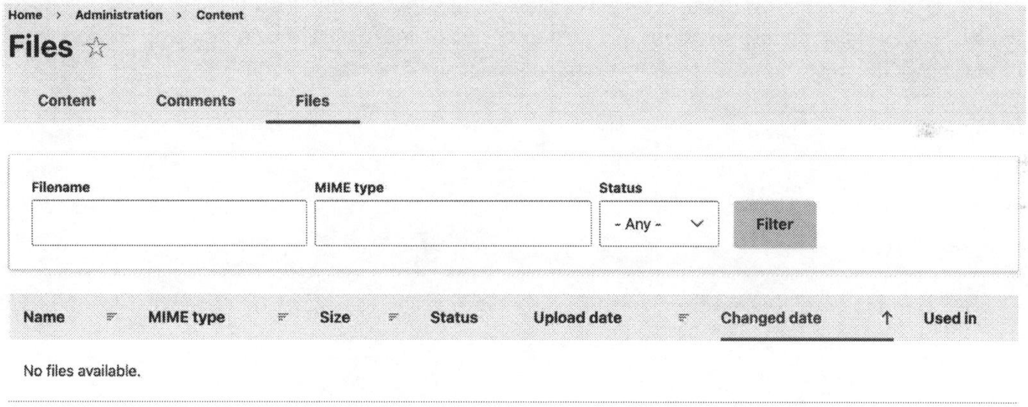

Figure 11.1 – File management screen in Drupal

Content management for files happens with fields of entities. After the module is enabled, any fieldable entity can add a file field that allows each field to be configured for each instance (for example, allowed file sizes and extensions, the use of public or private files, and more). The following figure demonstrates adding an "attachment" file field to a content type:

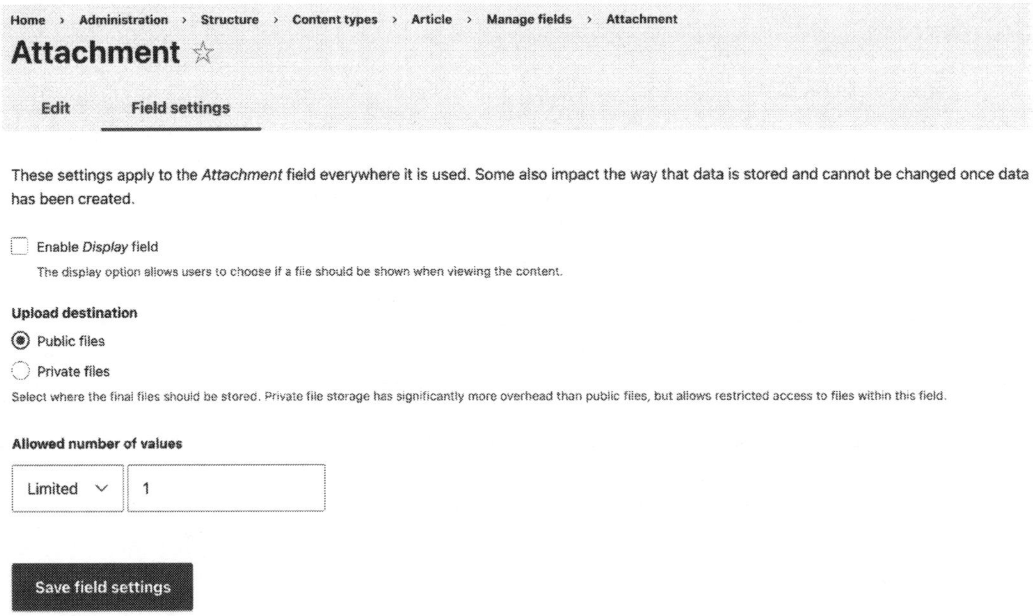

Home › Administration › Structure › Content types › Article › Manage fields › Attachment

Attachment ☆

Edit   **Field settings**

These settings apply to the *Attachment* field everywhere it is used. Some also impact the way that data is stored and cannot be changed once data has been created.

☐ Enable *Display* field
   The display option allows users to choose if a file should be shown when viewing the content.

Upload destination

◉ Public files

◯ Private files

Select where the final files should be stored. Private file storage has significantly more overhead than public files, but allows restricted access to files within this field.

Allowed number of values

| Limited ∨ | 1 |

Save field settings

Figure 11.2 – Step 1 of configuring a file field

This step configures the specific file field settings, including picking public or private file management. It also allows for cardinality selection, which allows one or more files to be uploaded. The following figure shows the next step, which involves managing general field metadata:

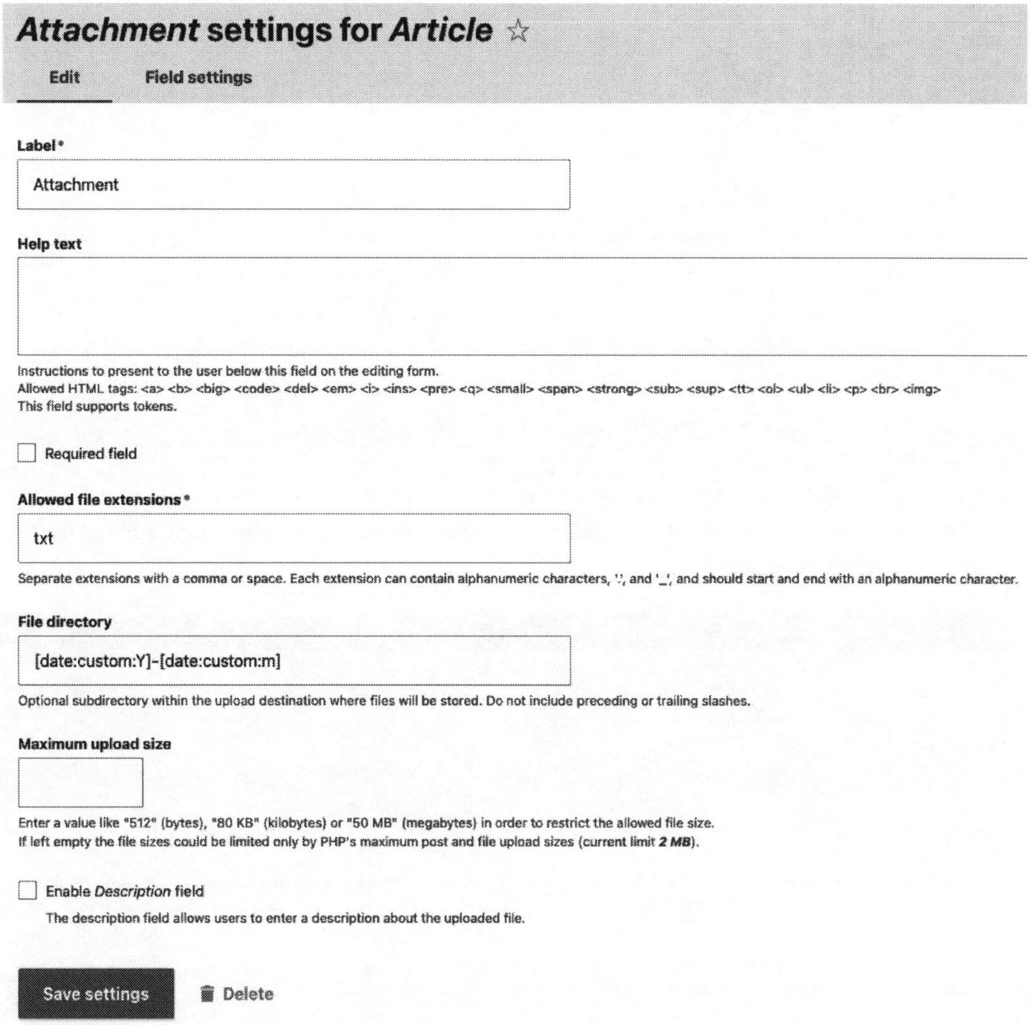

Attachment settings for *Article* ☆

Edit	Field settings

Label *

Attachment

Help text

Instructions to present to the user below this field on the editing form.
Allowed HTML tags: <a> <b> <big> <code> <del> <em> <i> <ins> <pre> <q> <small> <span> <strong> <sub> <sup> <tt> <ol> <ul> <li> <p>
 <img>
This field supports tokens.

☐ Required field

Allowed file extensions *

txt

Separate extensions with a comma or space. Each extension can contain alphanumeric characters, '.', and '_', and should start and end with an alphanumeric character.

File directory

[date:custom:Y]-[date:custom:m]

Optional subdirectory within the upload destination where files will be stored. Do not include preceding or trailing slashes.

Maximum upload size

Enter a value like "512" (bytes), "80 KB" (kilobytes) or "50 MB" (megabytes) in order to restrict the allowed file size.
If left empty the file sizes could be limited only by PHP's maximum post and file upload sizes (current limit *2 MB*).

☐ Enable *Description* field
    The description field allows users to enter a description about the uploaded file.

[Save settings]   🗑 Delete

Figure 11.3 – Step 2 of configuring a file field

Through configuration, each file field has standard field configuration, such as name and cardinality, combined with file-specific functionality, such as extensions, size, filesystem, and more.

When creating a node, a new attachment file field will exist. The following figure shows the field widget:

Figure 11.4 – The authoring experience for a configured file field

You can configure system-wide file behavior at `admin/config/media/file-system`. This is where the public and private filesystems can be configured. The following figure shows the file-related configuration:

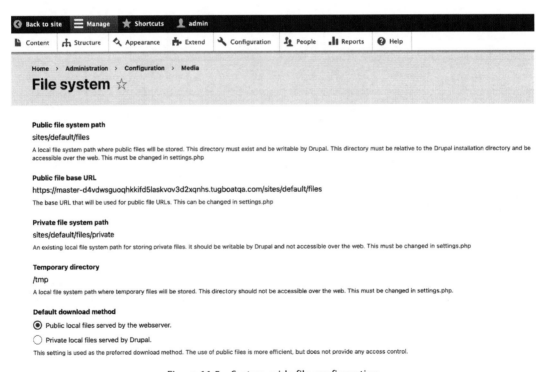

Figure 11.5 – System-wide file configuration

Files provide foundational capabilities for managing assets in Drupal through its existing structured content and configuration capabilities.

Images

Images represent a specific type of file and more specific functionality. Images build those specific features by leveraging files for all of the foundational asset-related functionality, such as CRUD. It also adds image-specific metadata, such as fields for alternate text, which is helpful for accessibility. Drupal may have content that links to a PDF or Word document that was created outside of Drupal. However, web browsers have native support for images of various formats. Given that Drupal serves content for the web, it offers more advanced image-related features beyond simple file linking, which is useful for rendering images and transforming images as part of its content management capabilities.

The responsive web adds more demands on content management systems to ensure images are appropriately delivered to different devices. Some images can be rather large in file size. Imagine the earlier days of cellular networks trying to download a large image on a web page. Content management systems started building features to be more responsive to address this need. Drupal provides image processing functions in the form of image styles that take the same source image and create any number of transformed copies. This is important for harnessing copies of the same image across different devices or types of displays. Each copy can be configured to set a desired size and more. Combined with other features in Drupal, a specific image style can be served to the size of the display.

Like files, images are primarily managed through the structured content of other entities using image fields. Image fields allow for the desired configuration of an image, such as allowed extensions, desired sizes, and association with image styles.

Modules and configuration

The **Image** module, like the **File** module, is grouped under **Field Types** with a dependency of the **File** module to harness its functionality at `admin/modules`. Any images added to Drupal will be listed under the central file listing, as shown in *Figure 11.1*. After enabling the **Image** module, like the **File** module, Drupal now offers a reference-based field type that can be added to any fieldable entity type, similar to what is shown in *Figure 11.2*. The authoring experience for images resembles what's shown in *Figure 11.3* but with some slight variation in how images are displayed after the image is uploaded. Finally, Drupal allows some centralized configuration of image tooling at `admin/config/media/image-toolkit`, which is more commonly used for advanced use cases.

> **Important note**
>
> Image processing tooling is largely dependent on the underlying platform. Most platforms have a PHP library known as GD2, which is required by Drupal. Image manipulation can be a resource-intensive operation and difficult to manage from the underlying platform.

Image style functionality is also available after the **Image** module has been enabled and can be configured from `admin/config/media/image-styles`. This functionality is a generic configuration of sizes for any image and is not specific to one image. The following figure shows the image style configuration listing to help you understand this functionality:

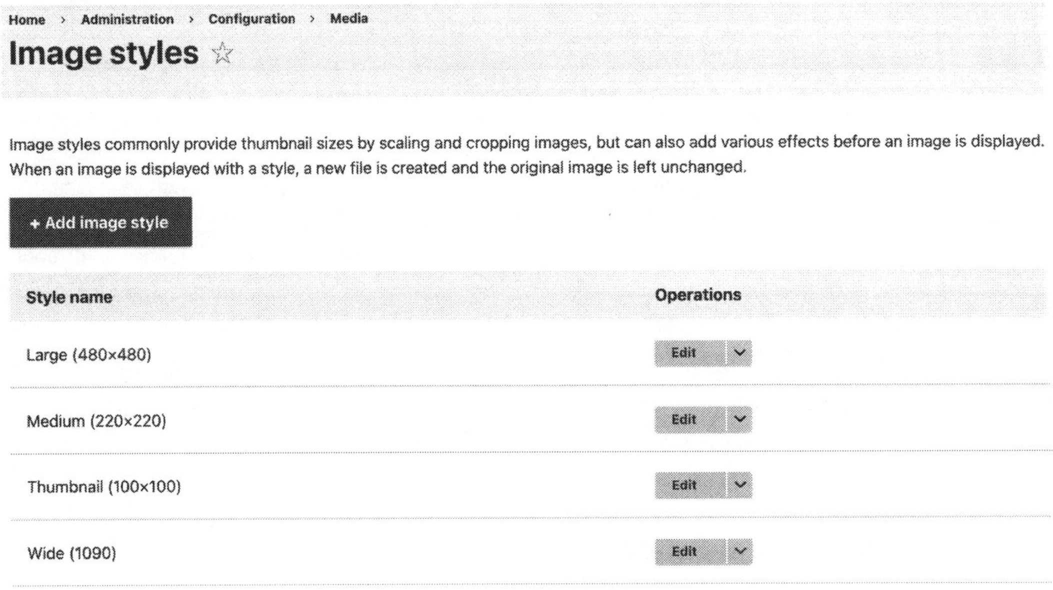

Home › Administration › Configuration › Media

Image styles ☆

Image styles commonly provide thumbnail sizes by scaling and cropping images, but can also add various effects before an image is displayed. When an image is displayed with a style, a new file is created and the original image is left unchanged.

+ Add image style

Style name	Operations
Large (480×480)	Edit ∨
Medium (220×220)	Edit ∨
Thumbnail (100×100)	Edit ∨
Wide (1090)	Edit ∨

Figure 11.6 – Listing of image styles

Figure 11.6 shows the general categorization of sizes for images, as exemplified by **Thumbnail**, **Medium**, and **Large**. These categories demonstrate fixed sizing. **Wide** represents an image that only has a width; the height of the image would remain both relative and variable. All of this can be configured based on the desired functionality in the Drupal application, including the use of the original image.

Images require Drupal to be aware of different displays to be able to effectively harness image styles. Drupal has a dependent module called **Breakpoints** to help Drupal recognize the size of the display. There is no user interface for breakpoints as it is most common to find breakpoints associated with Drupal themes, which need to provide responsive styling through CSS and media queries. A theme can configure the breakpoints from a specified YAML file with the `[theme].breakpoints.yml` naming convention. This is exemplified in the following code sample with a fake theme named `mydesign`:

```yaml
mydesign.mobile:
  label: mobile
  mediaQuery: ''
  weight: 0
  multipliers:
    - 1x
mydesign.narrow:
  label: narrow
  mediaQuery: 'all and (min-width: 560px) and (max-width: 850px)'
  weight: 1
  multipliers:
    - 1x
mydesign.wide:
  label: wide
  mediaQuery: 'all and (min-width: 851px)'
  weight: 2
  multipliers:
    - 1x
```

Note the use of `mediaQuery` in the code sample, bolded in the preceding code, which helps provide the sizing criteria of displays mapped to a breakpoint recognized by Drupal.

Responsive image is a second module that harnesses breakpoints and uses a new feature in CSS3 to adjust to devices. It creates logical groupings that build on media queries and maps image styles. It provides support for standalone responsive image logic or integration with breakpoints defined in themes. The following figure demonstrates the configuration for one responsive image definition:

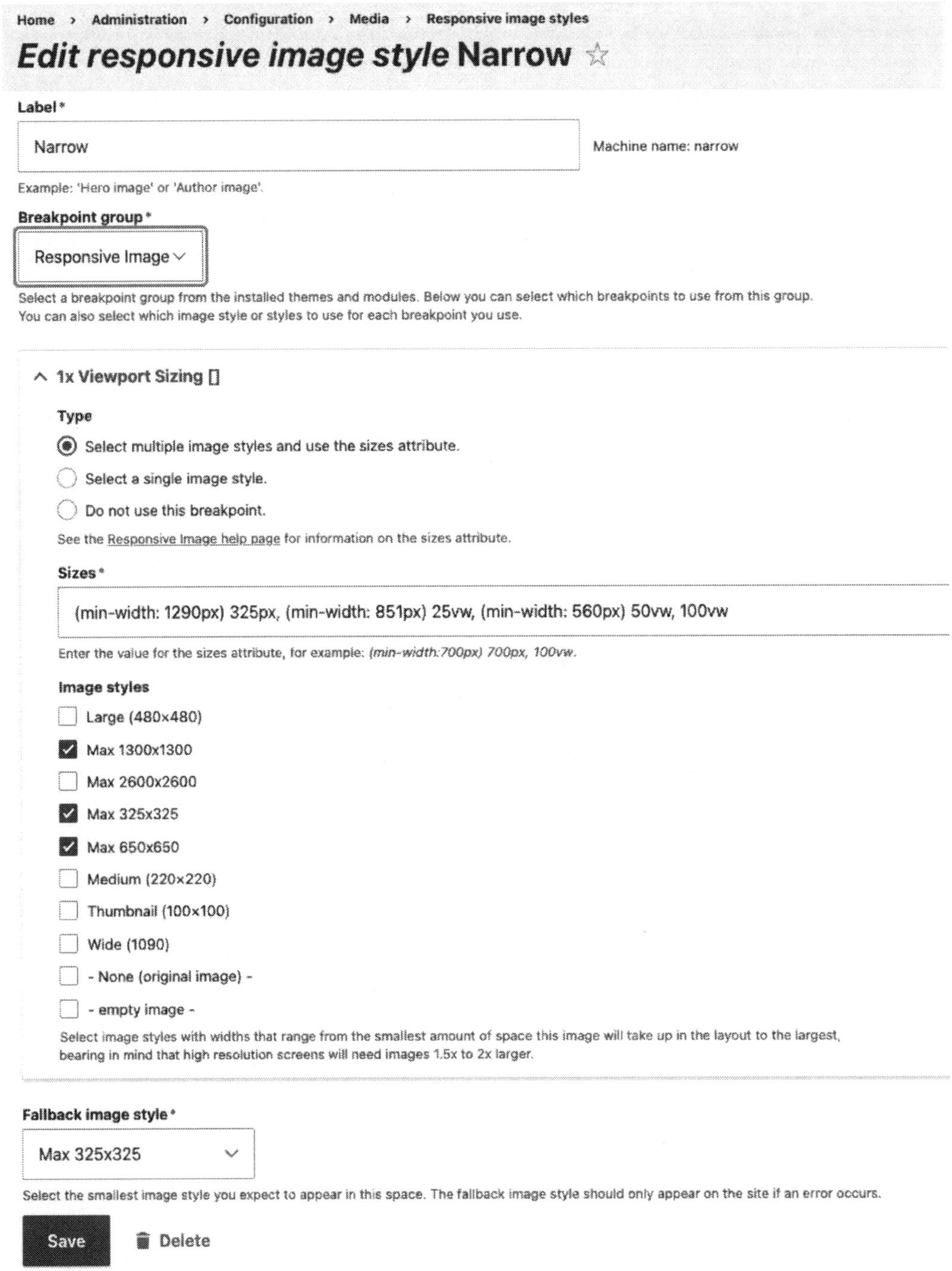

Home > Administration > Configuration > Media > Responsive image styles

Edit responsive image style Narrow ☆

Label *

```
Narrow
```
Machine name: narrow

Example: 'Hero image' or 'Author image'.

Breakpoint group *

```
Responsive Image ∨
```

Select a breakpoint group from the installed themes and modules. Below you can select which breakpoints to use from this group. You can also select which image style or styles to use for each breakpoint you use.

∧ **1x Viewport Sizing []**

Type

◉ Select multiple image styles and use the sizes attribute.

○ Select a single image style.

○ Do not use this breakpoint.

See the Responsive Image help page for information on the sizes attribute.

Sizes *

```
(min-width: 1290px) 325px, (min-width: 851px) 25vw, (min-width: 560px) 50vw, 100vw
```

Enter the value for the sizes attribute, for example: *(min-width:700px) 700px, 100vw.*

Image styles

☐ Large (480×480)

☑ Max 1300x1300

☐ Max 2600x2600

☑ Max 325x325

☑ Max 650x650

☐ Medium (220×220)

☐ Thumbnail (100×100)

☐ Wide (1090)

☐ - None (original image) -

☐ - empty image -

Select image styles with widths that range from the smallest amount of space this image will take up in the layout to the largest, bearing in mind that high resolution screens will need images 1.5x to 2x larger.

Fallback image style *

```
Max 325x325                    ∨
```

Select the smallest image style you expect to appear in this space. The fallback image style should only appear on the site if an error occurs.

[Save]   🗑 Delete

Figure 11.7 – An example responsive image style

Please note that the **Sizes** field resembles media query definitions and the selection of existing image styles. The fallback image style allows a responsive image style to default to an image style if multiple styles match or no styles match.

Images extend basic file functionality by harnessing standard file management combined with image-specific features layered on top. This helps provide more advanced content management for images, such as a more native image display, different image styles, and responsive display integration.

Media

Media extends both files and images to provide more centralized management of digital assets and perform greater integrations across assets managed by Drupal and assets managed outside of Drupal. This centralized management offers a different experience for managing assets and structured content. Out of the box, media works well with files and images but has tools such as oEmbed to work with remote, third-party assets such as YouTube, Instagram, and more.

The media framework provided by Drupal allowed the community to produce a vast ecosystem of media-related modules found on drupal.org. **Media** has been extended for Google Docs, Spotify, social networks, and much more. The framework allows media sources for custom systems, which, in turn, allows Drupal to integrate media throughout an enterprise.

Media types provide a structured, fieldable entity type for digital assets and metadata. A media reference field offers integration with other entities that can associate specific media entities through the media's native management experience.

The most popular media management experience is known as the media library. It is a visual catalog organized by media type and allows you to easily search through media and add new media all in one screen. This works well with media fields, given it provides a more visual experience to select or add media and subsequently associate it with the base entity. A similar experience exists with Drupal's WYSIWYG, where media can be embedded within a WYSIWYG field.

Modules and configuration

Media has two primary modules – the **Media** module for the general features and the **Media Library** module for the enhanced cataloging experience. Enabling the **Media** module provides basic constructs, such as the default media listing found at `admin/content/media`, which resembles the central file listing in *Figure 11.1*. General media settings can be found at `admin/config/media/media-settings`, and they can help address some use cases. However, the area shown in the following figure, which can be found at `admin/structure/media`, shows the media type listing that's used to configure media types:

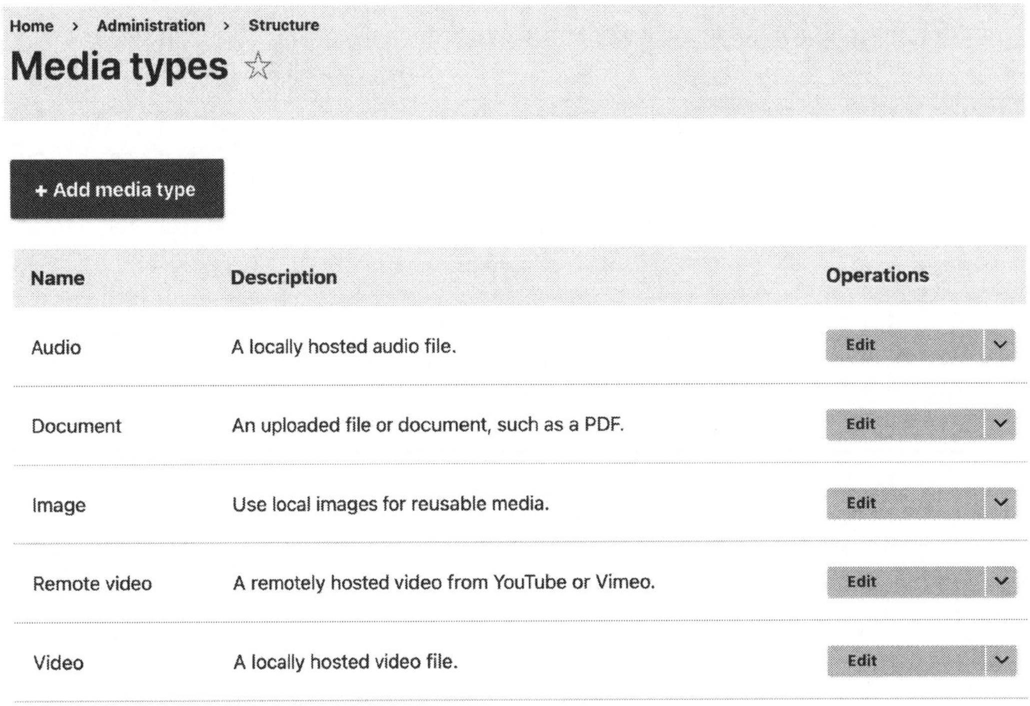

Home › Administration › Structure

Media types ☆

+ Add media type

Name	Description	Operations
Audio	A locally hosted audio file.	Edit ⌄
Document	An uploaded file or document, such as a PDF.	Edit ⌄
Image	Use local images for reusable media.	Edit ⌄
Remote video	A remotely hosted video from YouTube or Vimeo.	Edit ⌄
Video	A locally hosted video file.	Edit ⌄

Figure 11.8 – Management listing of media types

Note that this figure exemplifies both media assets owned by Drupal and a remote, third-party video asset. Configuring any of the media types resembles the same fieldable entity interface, such as managing a content type to configure fields, manage displays, and more, as we covered in previous chapters.

Like images and files, a media field exists for integration with fieldable entity types. The field settings show the selection of media types you can find when creating fields:

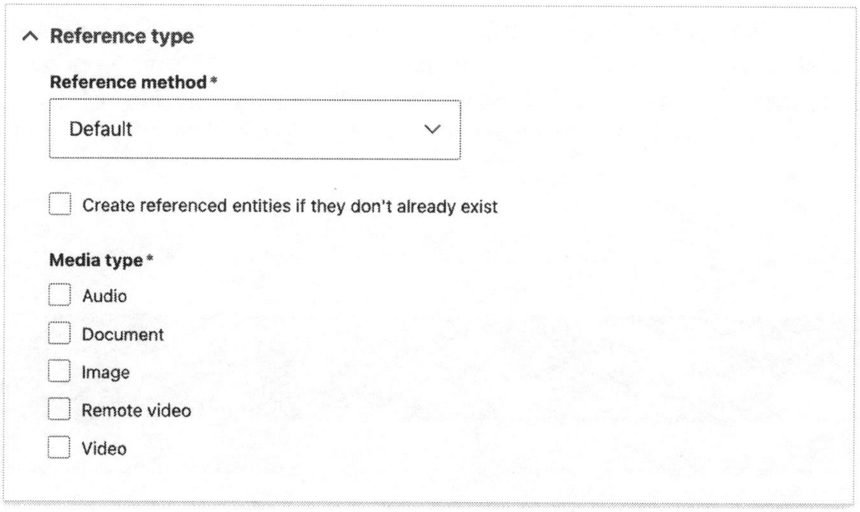

Figure 11.9 – Field settings for media fields

The reference method allows you to select the "default" media type selection or use **Views** to have more fine-grained control of media selection. You can do this by using the **Views** native filtering capabilities.

The authoring experience of the media field depends on whether or not the media library is enabled. The following figure demonstrates the default media authoring experience for the "Related assets" media field:

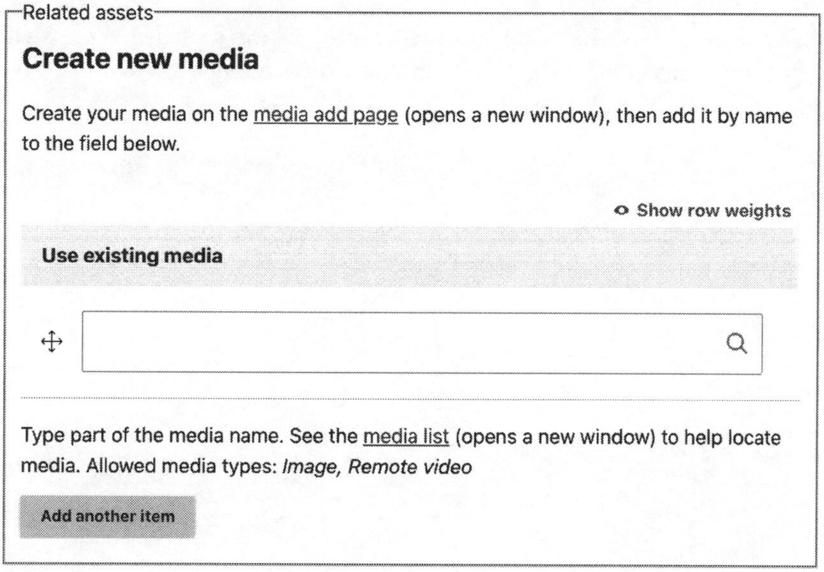

Figure 11.10 – Default media authoring experience

This experience primarily relies on the metadata of images, such as the name of the media. Given a lot of assets are visual, including images and videos, this type of experience is commonly less ideal. This was what motivated the use of Drupal's **Media Library**. After installing the **Media Library** module, field settings can be updated to use the **Media Library** field widget, as shown in the following figure:

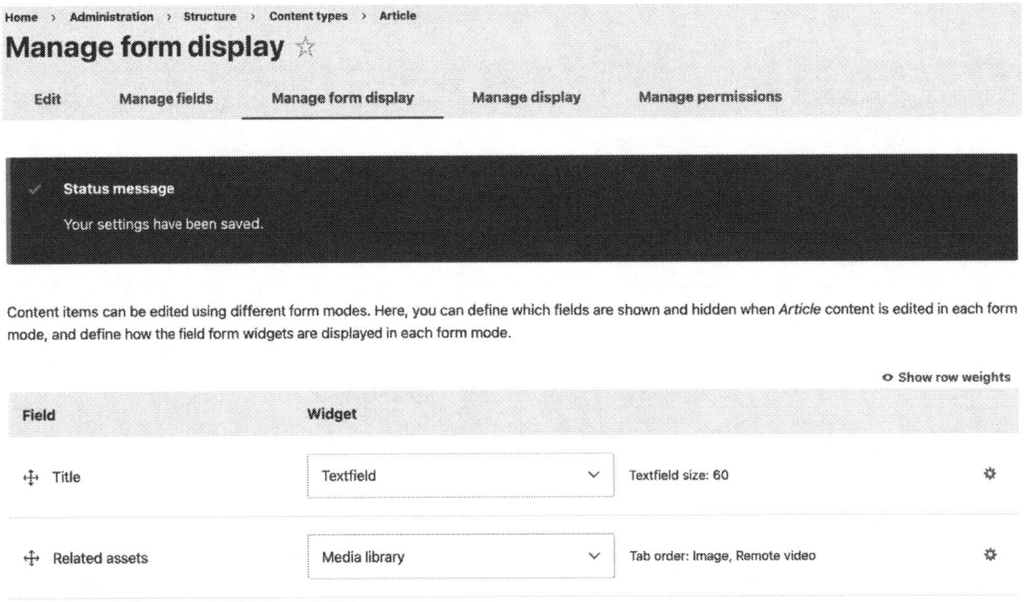

Figure 11.11 – Changing the field widget for Media Library

This figure demonstrates how the example-related assets field was switched to the **Media Library** widget for the article content type. Then, the authoring experience updates to use the media library for this field, as shown by the following figure:

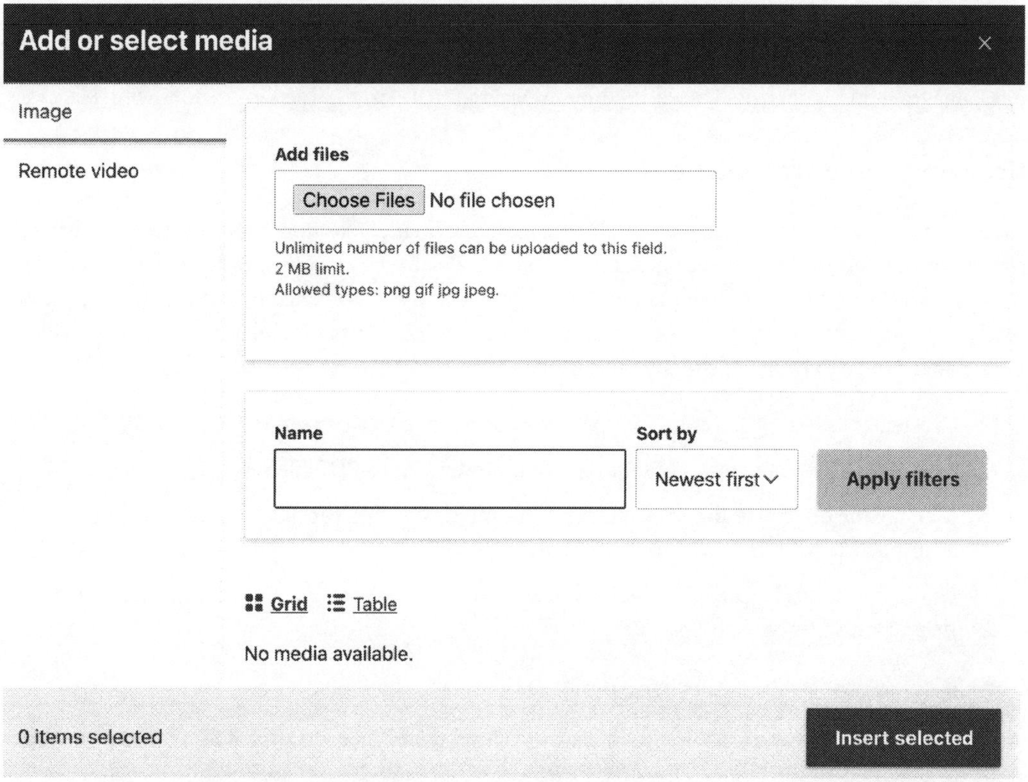

Add or select media   ×

Image

Remote video

Add files

Choose Files   No file chosen

Unlimited number of files can be uploaded to this field.
2 MB limit.
Allowed types: png gif jpg jpeg.

Name   **Sort by**

Newest first ∨   Apply filters

⠿ **Grid**   ☰ Table

No media available.

0 items selected   Insert selected

Figure 11.12 – Authoring experience for fields with Media Library

Media types that were configured for the field are displayed on the left. The ability to add new media is native in **Media Library**, as shown by the **Add fields** section per media type. And, while this figure does not contain any images yet, any available media would be visually displayed where "no media available" is listed for selection. This type of experience is often easier for content authors as they can visualize images or thumbnails of videos so that they can incorporate them into their Drupal-managed content.

Media helps Drupal solve challenges around the experience of digital assets and helps build the breadth of functionality for assets managed by Drupal and those managed by remote, third-party services. While media features naturally extend both file and image functionality, they have the potential to have more robust structured content through media types and a far greater ecosystem of media-related integrations that help media incorporate a broader set of third-party systems or custom enterprise capabilities.

Use cases

Files, images, and media can be used in different ways and are exemplified in the following use cases.

Creating research papers

Suppose that researchers are Drupal users who can highlight their publications in the content management system for their academic institution. A researcher can also be a user role in Drupal, which allows for fine-grained access control of that persona. This use case can be completed by linking file fields to the research papers content type. Most research papers are published as PDF files, not images or videos. Follow these steps to perform the site building that's needed for this use case:

1. Create a research paper content type under `admin/structure/types/add`.

2. Add a file field to the new content type that's restricted to PDF file extensions.

3. Manage the display of the research papers content type to create a teaser display that provides a simple link to the research paper file field.

4. Grant the researcher role permissions to add and edit their publications at `admin/people/permissions`.

This effectively enables the authoring experience of research papers.

An additional use case is displaying publications on the researcher's user profile. You can use Views to do this:

1. Create a new View form called `admin/structure/views/add` that shows the content of research papers with the "create a block" selection checked.

2. Enable the block to show the teaser display mode for the research papers content type.

3. Create a contextual filter for the author of the research paper based on the page being accessed (in this example, the user profile page).

4. Go to the block placement page.

5. Find the research papers block, drag it into the desired theme region, and press **Save**.

6. Edit the research papers block and, under **Visibility**, select the **Pages** tab and enter `user/*` to restrict the block visibility to user pages.

This allows the site builder to create a feature for research papers and display each researcher's papers on their user profile.

Icons for sports

Drupal's taxonomy system is a common entity that's used for categorization. However, many designs that display content show images that represent the categorization. Exploring the use case of sports, each sport may be a category but visually, an icon could be a stick for hockey, a ball for baseball, or a soccer ball for soccer. The following example assumes image fields are enabled and that there is a configured thumbnail image style. This use case can be performed with an image field linked to a taxonomy term:

1. Create a `sports` taxonomy vocabulary at `admin/structure/taxonomy`.
2. Select **manage fields** in the vocabulary and add an image field for the `icon`.
3. Select **manage displays** in the vocabulary and press the gear next to the icon.
4. Select **thumbnail** for the image style.

This effectively configured an icon for a sports taxonomy and configured the display of a sports taxonomy to show a thumbnail of the icon in its displays.

Tutorials found in YouTube videos

Media provides support for remote assets based on oEmbed that address this use case. After enabling the **Media** module, a default media type exists for remote videos that can be harnessed. Follow these steps to enable this:

1. Create a `tutorial` content type.
2. Add and configure a media field for the content type that's limited to the `remote video` media type.
3. Configure the desired display settings in the tutorial to ensure the video is rendered as desired.

Note that the `Media` module offered fields that were specific for the remote video media type, which is key to understanding the differentiated value of the **Media** system. This created structured content for tutorials that harnessed the media reference field for YouTube videos.

Summary

Digital assets have become an integral part of content management, especially as mobile phones have become more ubiquitous. Content management has had to better support photos and videos and integrate with third-party services, such as social media, that readily incorporate digital assets. Drupal affords a customizable experience through its files, images, and media features, all of which address these use cases. Files provide the foundation for Drupal to manage an asset. Images help offer specific capabilities, such as image styles and responsive images, that provide more targeted content management. Finally, media helps offer tools for a more robust structured content mechanism and refined experience that helps you manage digital assets more broadly.

In the next chapter, we'll learn how to implement search within Drupal.

12
Search

Drupal offers a native search feature that is well integrated with structured content. This chapter will explain the search feature, walk through how to enable search on a site and outline configuration options. Drupal also offers more advanced search features and abilities to execute different types of searches. By design, there are common Drupal modules that extend search out of the box to address common use cases.

In this chapter, we're going to cover the following main topics:

- About the feature
- Configuring search
- Extending search
- Use cases

About the feature

Content management systems, especially those with a large amount of content, practically require that content to be searchable. Search engines such as Google have made search features ubiquitous, as users expect to find what they want and need as quickly as possible. Drupal is built to manage content and is capable of managing content at scale. As such, the search function is a widely used and popular feature that is built into the Drupal core and is highly extensible. Next, we explore how search capabilities are built into Drupal.

Implementation

The search function is a specific feature built on top of existing content entities. Other systems introduce their entity types, but the functionality provided by the search function is only designed for the existing content-related entity types. This feature is provided by the `Search` module in Drupal core.

Implementing a search function requires an index for storage. At a high level, this can be considered a mapping between terminology and content. An out-of-the-box search function harnesses Drupal's database schema to create relational data for a search index. Changes to content in Drupal are queued up for processing and are indexed on `cron` (`www.drupal.org/docs/administering-a-drupal-site/cron-automated-tasks/cron-automated-tasks-overview`). Once indexed, the content is searchable.

Drupal offers various user interfaces for search by default. A search page exists that handles both search results and a search form widget. Drupal also offers a block with the search form widget, which can be placed on any page using the block system. The search form widget is an interface to the search page. Searches executed through the widget display on the search page and invoke Drupal's backend search processor. All of this is out of the box in the search subsystem found in Drupal core.

The subsystem also has a robust framework that helps address various use cases that extend search. Indexing in Drupal's native database can cause the database to grow significantly. There are common search indexes, such as Apache SOLR or Elasticsearch, that are built to address search-related needs. As such, the use of the search framework can replace Drupal's built-in index with a third-party system.

Frontend experience

The frontend search experience is offered through the search form and the search results page. Both work in tandem to take search terms as input and display content that matches. All frontend interfaces are customizable from Drupal's theming system and have several experience-related contributed modules that can be used based on the desired use cases.

The following figure shows Drupal's search form from the Umami demo:

Figure 12.1 – Out-of-the-box search form

Figure 12.1 demonstrates the search block that is placed within Drupal's Umami theme. Typing in any search term and pressing the **Search** button reveals the search results:

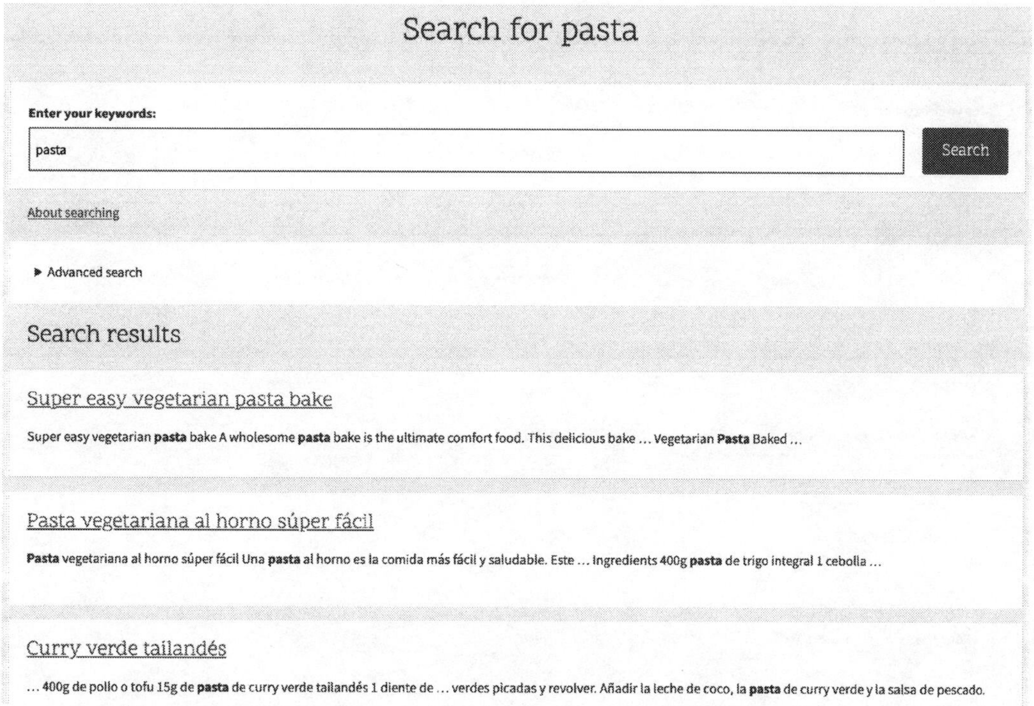

Search for pasta

Enter your keywords:

| pasta | Search |

About searching

▶ Advanced search

Search results

Super easy vegetarian pasta bake

Super easy vegetarian **pasta** bake A wholesome **pasta** bake is the ultimate comfort food. This delicious bake ... Vegetarian **Pasta** Baked ...

Pasta vegetariana al horno súper fácil

Pasta vegetariana al horno súper fácil Una **pasta** al horno es la comida más fácil y saludable. Este ... Ingredients 400g **pasta** de trigo integral 1 cebolla ...

Curry verde tailandés

... 400g de pollo o tofu 15g de **pasta** de curry verde tailandés 1 diente de ... verdes picadas y revolver. Añadir la leche de coco, la **pasta** de curry verde y la salsa de pescado.

Figure 12.2 – Out-of-the-box search results page

Figure 12.2 shows the result after the user makes a search, which goes to search/node. The input parameter is added to the end of the search page as exemplified by search/node?keys=test for the search performed in *Figure 12.2*. A small About searching link provides a help page where users can read more about advanced search querying.

The search form also has an advanced search feature. The following figure shows the various options:

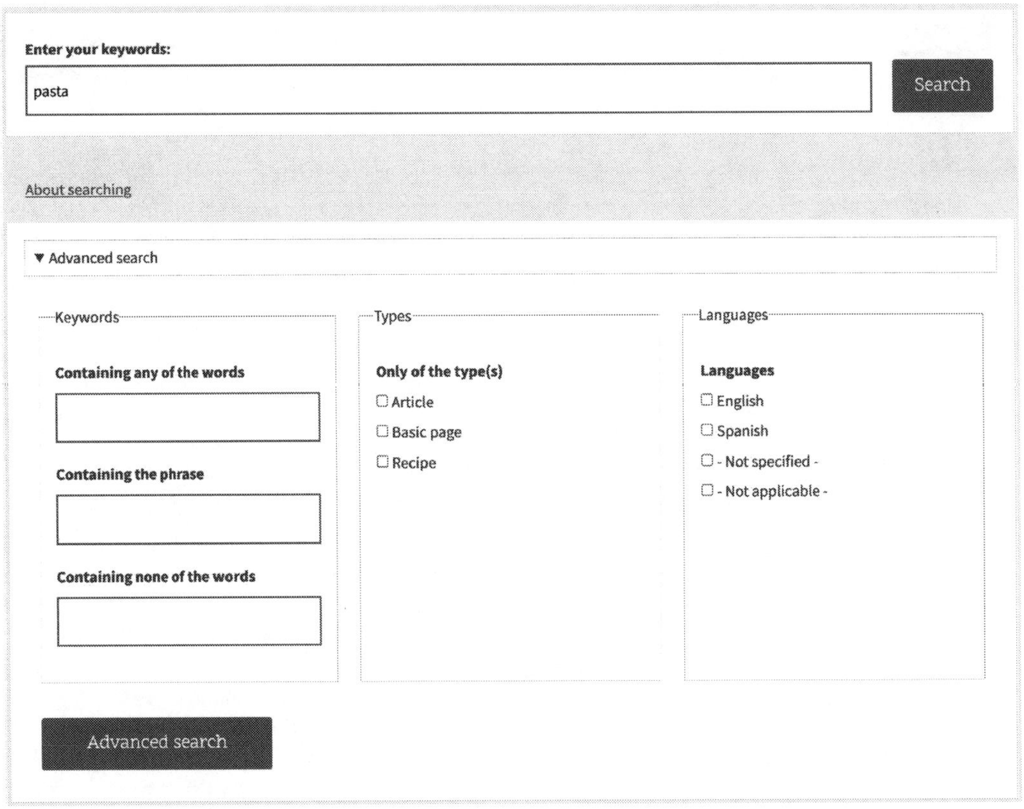

Figure 12.3 – Advanced search on the search page

Advanced search allows the end user to extend the standard search term input with more options to filter by content type or to ensure the results exactly match the search term or contain keywords.

The combined experience of the search form widget, blocks, and search pages helps Drupal offer end users both general and more targeted means of finding the content they want.

Backend

The search form interface triggers the backend search processing. The processor takes the search input and queries the index against the desired configuration logic.

The backend also handles content changes in the Drupal application, as previously mentioned. Such changes are queued up and processed via CRON, which perpetually refreshes the search index.

Important note

Drupal's search index may change by environment, especially for third-party integrations. Drupal may not correctly report the status of the index in all circumstances. Third-party integrations, such as search indexes, must have their setup for Drupal's environments. Each environment should have their own search index to ensure search services and content are separated. This mapping happens through Drupal's configuration and must account for environment-specific changes.

Consider a development workflow that refreshes a Dev environment from content found in a production environment. Search-related configuration Dev environment may not be accurate until configuration has been synchronized, and even then, it may show inaccurate status until the Drupal application has effectively synchronized with the service. The most common way to do this is through re-indexing, given that there can be a large number of content changes found in production between the last environment synchronization. An index for Dev may be woefully behind the production index given that CRON processes production changes periodically. It is important to be aware of the configuration and the state of the indexes when dealing with multiple environments.

Drupal's search feature is split into the frontend, which offers experiences, and the backend, which handles indexing, processing, updates, and configuration. All of this makes up Drupal's search subsystem, which is both configurable and extensible.

Configuring search

The search settings can be found at `admin/config/search/pages` and are shown in the following figure:

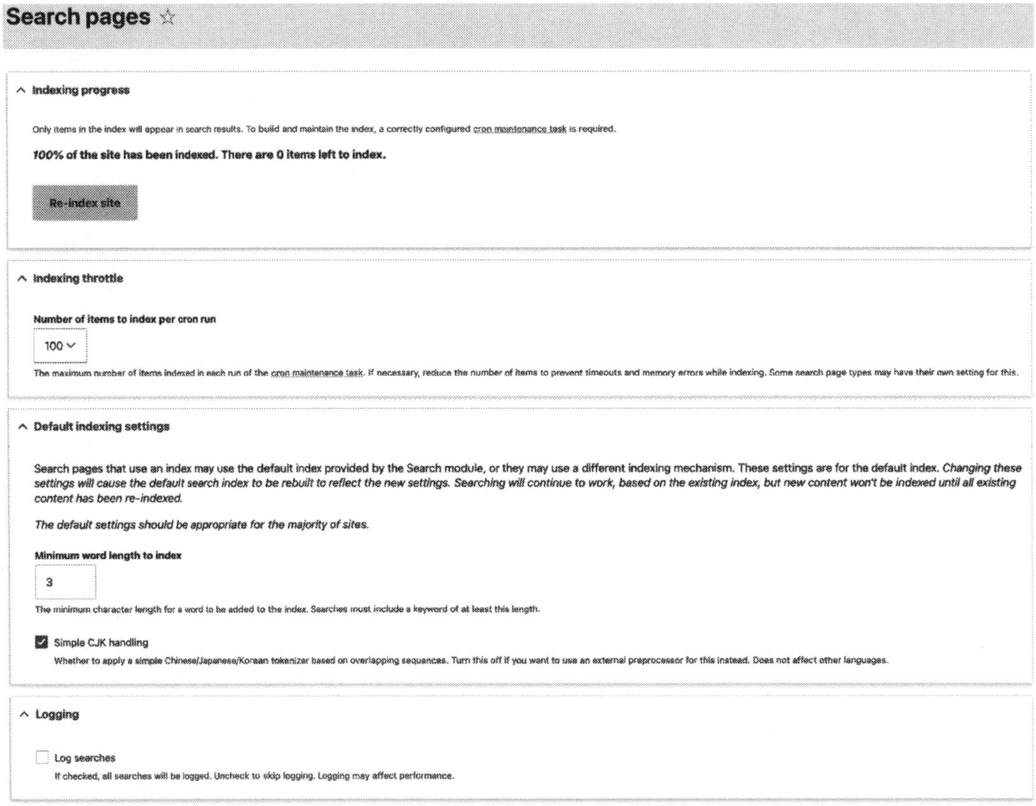

Figure 12.4 – Out-of-the-box search configuration

The first section of *Figure 12.4* highlights both the status of the index and the ability to re-index the entire Drupal application. Recall that Drupal leverages a queue to collect content changes and synchronize the index. This section demonstrates the state of the queue, which can help you understand if the index has all of the changes in Drupal or if CRON needs to process changes for the index to match Drupal's content.

> **Important note**
>
> The indexing process can be very helpful in triaging issues with search. CRON runs periodically, and changes to content should not remain in the queue indefinitely. Having a large number of items to index can often be a sign of an issue. A safe starting point is checking Drupal's logs for errors related to searches.

Figure 12.4 also shows different settings that may need adjustment. Index throttling will control how many content changes will be sent to the index per CRON run. This may need to be tuned based on the performance of the hosting platform. Default indexing settings help provide a word-length check to filter out common words such as "so," "it," or "to" from indexing. Finally, you can also enable Drupal to log searches.

Being able to access the search function is tied to Drupal's permissions. It is common for anonymous users to be granted the "use search" permission to be able to search content on the site. There is also permission for "use advanced search" and "administer search." All of these settings can be adjusted according to the desired use case of the application.

Search pages

Search pages can also be configured in `admin/config/search/pages`, as shown by the following figure:

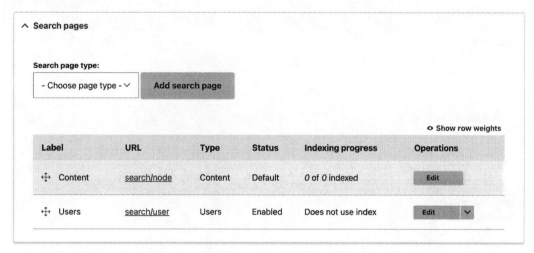

Figure 12.5 – Search pages listing on the search configuration page

This demonstrates the various search pages on the site. By default, Drupal has two search pages: one for the Node entity and one for the User entity. The Node entity is the most popular for content-related search and is the default. The user search page can be removed if an application does not have a lot of engagement found in community-like applications. Search pages can be added that can address specific desired search logic through a customized page. The following figure shows the configuration of a search page accessed by pressing **Edit** on a specific search page:

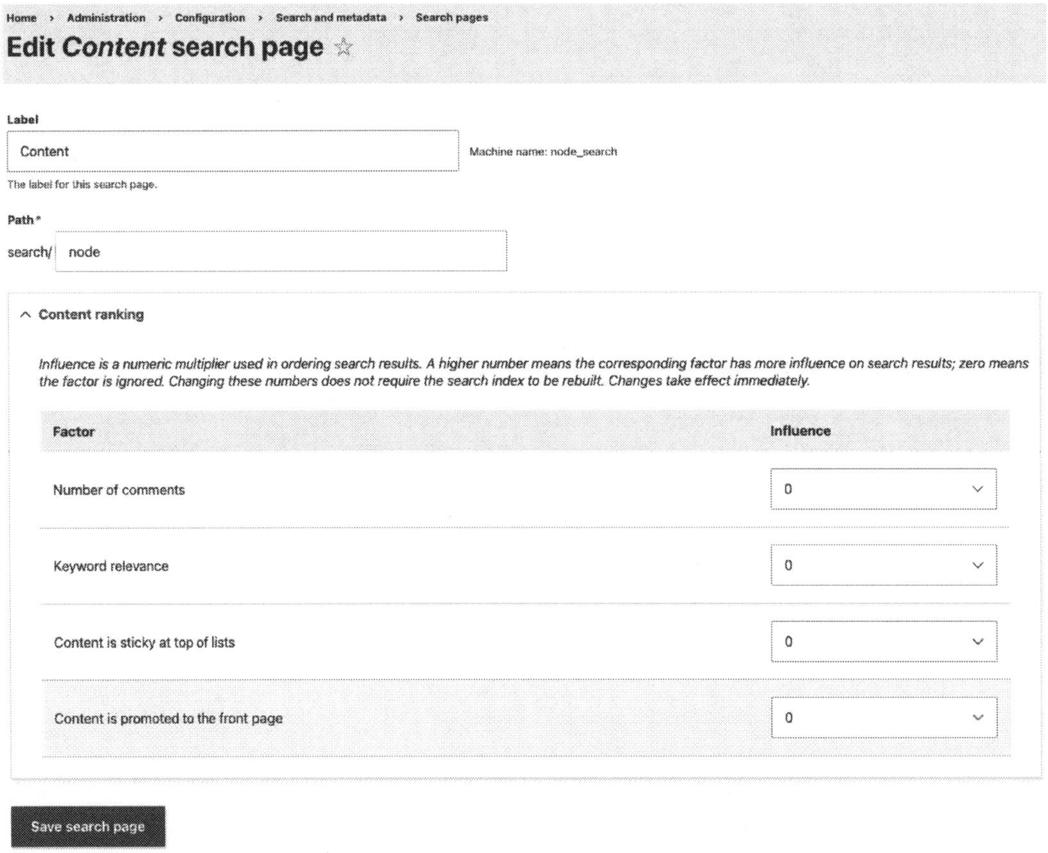

Edit *Content* search page ☆

Label

> Content

Machine name: node_search

The label for this search page.

Path*

search/ | node

⌄ Content ranking

Influence is a numeric multiplier used in ordering search results. A higher number means the corresponding factor has more influence on search results; zero means the factor is ignored. Changing these numbers does not require the search index to be rebuilt. Changes take effect immediately.

Factor	Influence
Number of comments	0 ⌄
Keyword relevance	0 ⌄
Content is sticky at top of lists	0 ⌄
Content is promoted to the front page	0 ⌄

Save search page

Figure 12.6 – Search pages listing on the search configuration page

Figure 12.6 demonstrates the page-specific configuration that influences the results of the search processor. One such concept is weighting, which helps provide relevance to specific search keywords. Drupal provides weights through the configuration of a search page tied to content ranking. Content ranking provides ordered relevance and influence weights based on rendered content or the metadata of the content. For instance, if the content has the **Promoted on front page** box selected, it can be weighted higher than other content. HTML is naturally structured into headings, such as H1, H2, and H3, that organize content into a hierarchy. This is provided by the keyword relevance content ranking in Drupal. Given Drupal renders its structured content as HTML, the search can also associate the tag of a word that is mapped to the page. Weighting can be provided by tag, commonly giving priority weighting to heading tags such as H1, H2, and H3 and less weight to DIV and P tags.

Through basic settings, permissions, and search pages, Drupal can configure the search function in a wide variety of ways and can address a large number of use cases for the application.

Extending Search

Like most out-of-the-box Drupal features, search is designed to be extended. Several popular use cases can be addressed by contributed modules.

Facets

Facets (`drupal.org/project/facets`) is a project intended to offer site builders the ability to create additional search filters for end users who use search. Facets work well with Drupal's structured content models. Consider a taxonomy field that categorizes nodes. Being able to filter by a term could be very useful beyond the out-of-the-box advanced search.

Facets go well beyond a term-based selection. Facets can natively change based on the type of field. This can be different form widgets or even different logic for searching fields. Ultimately, site builders can leverage this module to provide commonly used search interfaces tied to the underlying structured content.

Third-party indexes

Drupal offers out-of-the-box search capabilities, but other technologies might be better at allowing an application to provide search indexes. This is especially true as the amount of content in Drupal scales. Separating Drupal's native database that replicates an index from Drupal's content can yield performance gains while adding complexity.

Drupal has a contributed project named Search API (`drupal.org/project/search_api`), which extends Drupal's native framework. This module serves as a dependency for an ecosystem of other contributed modules that help provide integrations with third-party indexes.

Two very common projects exist, primarily due to the popularity of third-party and/or native platform offerings. Apache SOLR is an open-source search index that is likely the most common third-party search index tool leveraged by Drupal applications. It has a corresponding Drupal project (`drupal.org/project/search_api_solr`). First, it is open source. Second, it is commonly offered by Drupal hosting providers. Finally, its popularity has led to a lot of adoption and subsequent polish against a large number of use cases. The second type of search index is Elasticsearch. It offers similar benefits to Apache SOLR. It is less popular, but it offers some more modern features. Elasticsearch has its own Drupal project (`drupal.org/project/elasticsearch_connector`) as well.

Autocomplete

When you use Google, recommendations show up as you start typing. Drupal is also able to offer this kind of search experience. In Drupal terms, this is known as the autocomplete behavior. The Search API Autocomplete project (`drupal.org/project/search_api_autocomplete`) exists to provide this functionality. As an end-user starts using the native search form, suggestions will come up based on, for example, the title of the node.

One of the key benefits of the search function is its extensibility. While there are a lot of projects on `drupal.org` to extend it, popular search cases include facets, third-party indexes with Apache SOLR or Elasticsearch, and autocomplete functionality.

Use cases

Search in Drupal helps both users and site builders create capabilities in applications to find content.

Querying for two different movie titles simultaneously

Drupal's native search form, which invokes Drupal's search processor, supports various search parameters. In the search form, the following can be entered:

```
"Wizard of Oz" OR "Gone with the wind"
```

And, don't forget, Drupal does offer some advanced search options that can abstract Drupal's native search form.

Filter by sport

This use case is perfect for the `Facets` module. After enabling facets, which also enables Search API, facets can be created through Search API's configuration (admin/config/search/search-api). Specific field-type widgets can be implemented through search API processors, specifically a preprocess query processor. Then, leveraging the advanced settings of the search page configuration, the processor can be added and the facets can be configured.

Restricting a specific content type from search

Content types are controlled by Drupal's native search pages. *Figure 12.5* highlights how to configure search pages within Drupal. Edit the search page desired, uncheck any unwanted content types, and save. This may prompt re-indexing if unwanted nodes are already indexed.

Drupal's search offers users the ability to find content and for administrators to configure search behaviors toward common use cases.

Summary

This chapter highlighted both out-of-the-box and extended search features. Configuring search pages and the search form block allows site builders to build search functions into their applications without writing code. Concepts such as indexing were covered both within Drupal and by leveraging popular third-party indexes, such as Apache SOLR. Configuring advanced features, such as facets and autocomplete, can provide additional experiences that can be useful on a case-by-case basis.

The next chapter discusses contact forms in Drupal, which is a feature for user engagement. Contact forms provide a means for users to fill out a form on the Drupal application and reach administrators.

13
Contact Forms

Modern websites have the ability to engage users. One of the ways Drupal engages site users is through contact forms, a feature that allows for users to engage through a website generally or personally through user profiles. This chapter covers the basic concepts of creating and configuring contact forms in a Drupal application, including access control and form submissions. Finally, the chapter covers a few popular ways to extend out-of-the-box contact forms.

In this chapter, we're going to cover the following main topics:

- Contact forms in Drupal
- Configuring contact forms
- Extending contact forms

Contact forms in Drupal

Have you ever gone to a website that has a "Contact us" page where a visitor can fill out a form? That is contact forms in Drupal. They give visitors to a site a means of communicating with those who run it. This could be someone who wants to inquire about hosting a party at a restaurant or leveraging services to remodel a house. It is very common for a website to offer more than just a phone number, especially given the ability to communicate digitally.

Basic information

The contact forms feature comes out of the box with Drupal in the **Contact** module. Forms are commonly exposed to end users that allow for engagement through the Drupal application.

The **Contact** module represents one of the more lightweight systems in Drupal. It is composed of an entity type, and contact forms, with bundles for each form. Form submissions represent instances of the entity. Given that it leverages entities, contact forms are fieldable, much like other structured content in Drupal. Contact forms can leverage the underlying entity **create, read, update, and delete (CRUD)** operations as part of its framework. This has allowed for several projects that extend the default functionality for the entity type.

The module offers two types of forms out of the box:

- **Site-wide forms**: These provide more general-purpose forms meant for general engagement
- **Personal forms**: These are associated with user profiles in Drupal and are intended for engaging with a specific person

Both offer similar functionality in terms of the underlying functionality but are intended to address two different engagement use cases.

Form management

Site builders are also able to build their forms. This interface is provided through Drupal's administrative backend at `admin/structure/contact`:

Figure 13.1 – The primary contact form management screen

Figure 13.1 demonstrates the various operations for a contact form.

The **Edit** operation controls the metadata of the form and has the following useful features:

- **Recipients**: This controls which email addresses receive an email after a user submits the forms.
- **Message**: After submitting the form, you might choose to give the user a message, such as `Thank you for contacting us`.
- **Redirect path**: This controls where to send a user after a form has been submitted, which can be useful if you have created a node with content that provides another means of reaching the site administrator.
- **Auto-reply**: A default auto-reply email can be sent to the user who submitted the form. It is common to acknowledge the recipient of the message or tell them when they can expect a reply.

The **Manage fields** operation manages what fields are on the form, which provides a fieldable functionality that is similar to editing fields for a content type. The entity ships with default fields that cannot be altered. Those fields include the sender's name, the sender's email, the subject, the message, the option to preview, and the ability to send a copy. This is seen in *Figure 13.2*.

The **Manage form display** page configures how the form is shown to users:

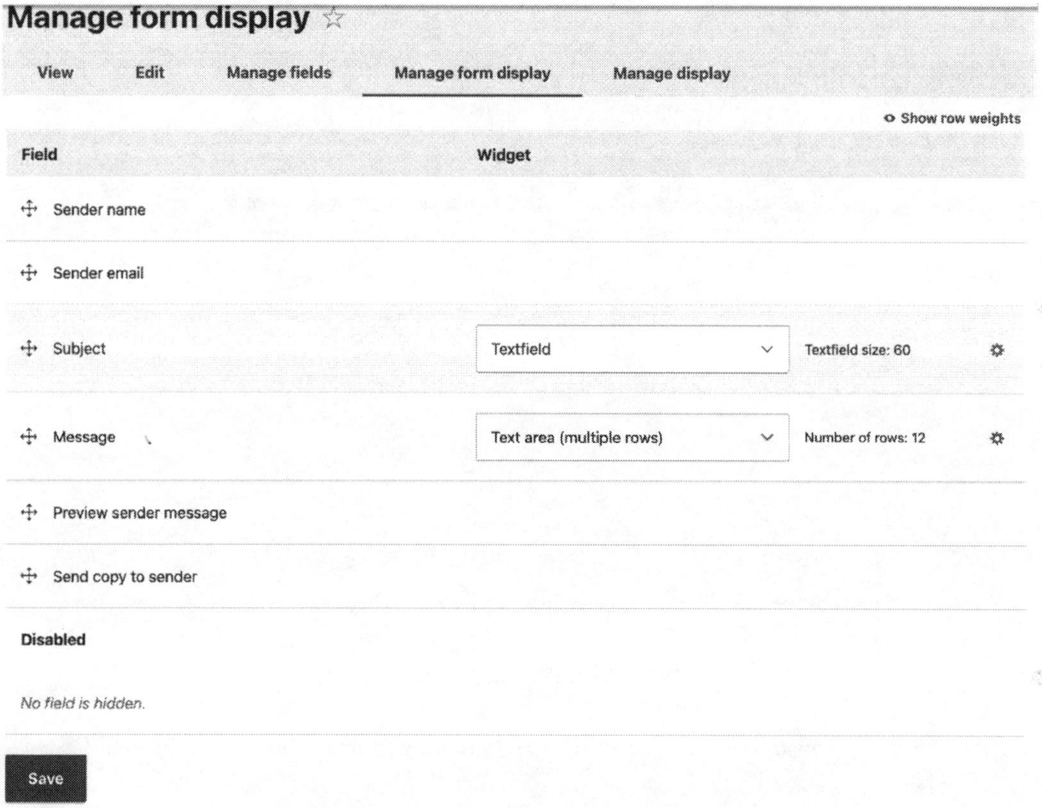

Manage form display ☆

| View | Edit | Manage fields | **Manage form display** | Manage display |

⊙ Show row weights

Field	Widget		
✛ Sender name			
✛ Sender email			
✛ Subject	Textfield ⌄	Textfield size: 60	⚙
✛ Message	Text area (multiple rows) ⌄	Number of rows: 12	⚙
✛ Preview sender message			
✛ Send copy to sender			

Disabled

No field is hidden.

Save

Figure 13.2 – Controlling the display of the form

Figure 13.2 shows how to enable or disable specific fields in the form. It also controls the order of the display, the various widgets to render form fields, and the specific settings for each field.

The final operation, **Manage display**, controls the form submission display. This renders the **Message** field from the form editing interface after a user submits the form.

Form submissions

Form submissions primarily send emails through the **Desired recipients** field defined when editing the form. Out of the box, contact forms do not persistently store the submissions to the form like most entities.

Logging is provided by Drupal's watchdog, which captures form submissions at `admin/reports/dblog`:

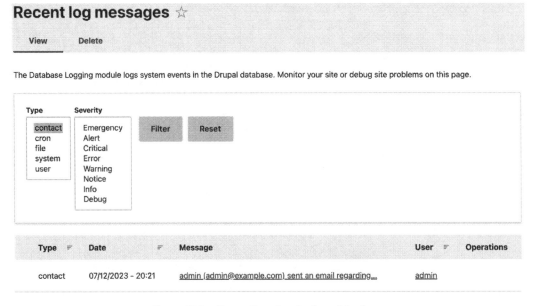

Figure 13.3 – Controlling the display of the form

Figure 13.3 shows how filtering for the `contact` type shows form submissions through Drupal's logging system.

Contact forms provide site builders a means for visitors to engage with the Drupal site and with Drupal users. Forms are fieldable to collect as much information as needed for the specific requirements. Submissions are emailed to recipients and logged in Drupal.

Configuring contact forms

Most of the configuration for contact forms happens through the aforementioned form configuration operations due to their association with structured content in Drupal. There are a few more configurations possible.

User profile configuration

It should not be assumed that a Drupal application wants to have engagement with users. While this feature is provided out of the box, it can be turned off by default globally through Drupal's account settings configuration at `admin/config/people/accounts`. Each logged-in user can enable or disable a form at their discretion by editing their user profile and changing the **Personal Contact Form** setting.

Permissions

Before launching the Drupal application, double-check the contact form permissions:

Permission	Anonymous user	Authenticated user	Content editor	Administrator
Contact				
Administer contact forms and contact form settings	☐	☐	☐	☑
Use the site-wide contact form	☑	☑	☑	☑
Use users' personal contact forms	☐	☐	☐	☑

Figure 13.4 – Permissions for contact forms

Figure 13.4 shows how to map roles to control both who can use or access the forms themselves and who has permission to administer forms.

While most configuration happens through the form editing interfaces, additional configuration exists for both user profiles and permissions.

Extending contact forms

Like most features in Drupal, contact forms can be extended to address a few common use cases not found out of the box.

Viewing and managing form submissions

Unlike other entity types in Drupal, there is no management interface for form submissions out of the box. The Contact Storage project (`drupal.org/project/contact_storage`) provides persistent storage and an administrative interface that allows you to view and manage form submissions. This is a useful feature that helps expose form submissions in Drupal rather than relying on email notifications.

Beyond just a page

By default, the experience of using a contact form is like building a page. However, the Contact Block project allows for contact forms to be exposed as blocks. Managing blocks is covered in greater detail in *Chapter 15*. This allows for a contact form to leverage block visibility settings to be displayed through various contextual options across pages and in specific regions of the Drupal theme.

More robust email notifications

The email notifications that are sent from the Drupal application are basically plain text, and they do not allow for customization. The Contact Emails project (`drupal.org/project/contact_emails`) provides a more robust WYSIWYG interface that can format email notifications. It also can send more than one email notification and message per form for various audiences.

Spam prevention

It is common for forms to be open for any visitor to use. Unfortunately, this can lead to spam form submissions if not managed. Spam management can happen in Drupal through the CAPTCHA project (`drupal.org/project/captcha`) or the Honeypot project (`drupal.org/project/honeypot`). Both have various configuration options available and can work to prevent spam on contact forms.

Several popular modules extend contact forms for common use cases such as form submission management, spam prevention, greater customization of form submission messages, and placing forms with blocks.

More advanced forms

The Webform module (`https://www.drupal.org/project/webform`) is a robust and extensible form-building capability offered through Drupal's contributed projects. This project, along with many of the supporting contributed projects, provides site builders with a tool that creates forms, manages form submissions, and has corresponding capabilities such as email notifications and spam prevention. Multi-step form wizards, modals, and pre-populated values are also included features. Forms are built much like configuring fields with structured content. The community has widely adopted this module and has built an ecosystem of projects that extend it. Such examples include Webform Validation (`https://www.drupal.org/project/webform_validation`) for advanced form validation logic, Webform Views (`https://www.drupal.org/project/webform_views`) for form submission integration with Views, and Webform REST (`https://www.drupal.org/project/webform_rest`), which exposes REST APIs on top of Webform features.

Summary

This chapter covered Drupal's contact forms feature, which is useful for both site-specific and user-specific engagement. Contact forms have various out-of-the-box features, such as response messaging, auto-replies, and more. They are also fieldable to allow you to collect responses with specific information. Extending forms to prevent spam, have persistent form submissions, or have greater control over response messages are all possible through contributed projects.

The next chapter pivots into the experience of managing content and media within Drupal. All site builders must understand Drupal through the experience of content authors, and the next chapter introduces the basics built from Drupal's native structured content.

Part 4:
Using - Content
Management

In this part, readers will understand how the Drupal application can be configured in different ways for content authors and those reviewing content. Various settings for forms and displays will be covered that can adjust the content authoring experience. Tools for configuring and managing the layout help provide some visual content management capabilities. And, editorial workflows build upon users, roles, and permissions to allow different users to author and review content.

This part has the following chapters:

- *Chapter 14, Basic Content Authoring Experience*
- *Chapter 15, Visual Content Management*
- *Chapter 16, Content Workflows*

14

Basic Content Authoring Experience

So far, this book has covered foundational aspects of Drupal and knowledge of how to build Drupal applications. *Chapters 14, 15*, and *16* present the experience offered to content authors. This chapter emphasizes the basic content author experience offered for content types, nodes, and content rendering. Because Drupal can be readily configured, a site builder must have this experience. This chapter highlights how to perform the configuration, what subsequent experience is offered for authoring, and the subsequent rendering of the content.

In this chapter, we're going to cover the following main topics:

- Authoring content
- Authoring digital assets

Authoring content

Never forget the content author who is tasked with using the Drupal application you have built. Drupal has a lot of features, and structured content is not always intuitive. Many content authors who use Drupal for content management think the experience of authoring structured content is technical. It is important to demonstrate, train, and document this experience because content authors may change over time.

> **Important note**
>
> Do not forget about roles and permissions when looking at the experiences of content authors. It can be immensely helpful to have deliberate roles for authors or even different roles for authors who may be responsible for different content in the Drupal application.
>
> The experience of authoring in Drupal can rapidly become better just by removing permissions for activities they do not need to do. This can remove specific administrative actions, such as managing Drupal projects, managing Drupal configuration, and viewing system logs. Roles and permissions can radically simplify what a content author can see, and this is a positive thing. Generally, this follows best practice, given that users are granted only the permissions they need to avoid unintended consequences.

The content authoring experience will be covered for Drupal's basic content management for nodes, menus, and taxonomies.

Nodes

The content authoring experience starts with the node system. Recall that a content type defines the structured content and nodes are specific instances of content types. The activity of content authoring is ultimately creating the raw structured data and metadata for every node. Nodes are then rendered by Drupal to display webpages. At a high level, rendering is the process of taking Drupal's raw structured data and converting it into a delivered webpage based on the context provided (typically a path that is stored as metadata on the node). As such, the basic content authoring experience of editing nodes is a bit disjointed from the visual presentation. A more visual content authoring experience is provided by Layout Builder, which is covered in the next chapter.

This experience starts with the central content listing page, found at `admin/content`. This listing, for which the access is configured by role, is often made available for content authors to have one place to see all of the content they can manage. This also facilitates bulk editing, which can be useful for changing the publishing or even deleting multiple nodes at once.

The centralized listing has a button to add new content and offers the ability to edit each content item listed. The underlying method of adding and editing a node is the same. This can be exemplified by looking at an example node editing form for a page content type. The form itself is configurable by content type by going to the **Manage form display** page found at `admin/structure/types/manage/page/form-display` for the **page** content type. This is shown in the following figure:

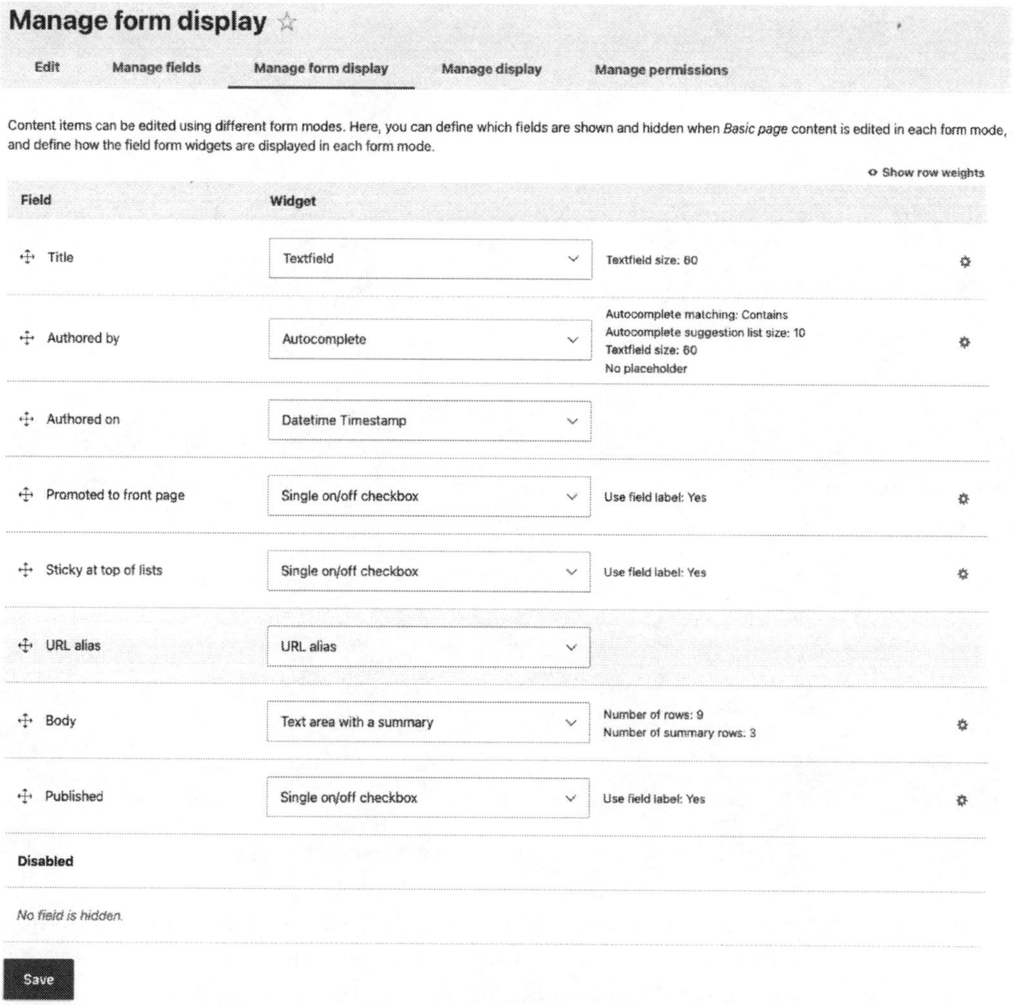

Manage form display ☆

Edit   **Manage fields**   **Manage form display**   **Manage display**   **Manage permissions**

Content items can be edited using different form modes. Here, you can define which fields are shown and hidden when *Basic page* content is edited in each form mode, and define how the field form widgets are displayed in each form mode.

◇ Show row weights

Field	Widget		
✛ Title	Textfield ⌄	Textfield size: 60	✿
✛ Authored by	Autocomplete ⌄	Autocomplete matching: Contains Autocomplete suggestion list size: 10 Textfield size: 60 No placeholder	✿
✛ Authored on	Datetime Timestamp ⌄		
✛ Promoted to front page	Single on/off checkbox ⌄	Use field label: Yes	✿
✛ Sticky at top of lists	Single on/off checkbox ⌄	Use field label: Yes	✿
✛ URL alias	URL alias ⌄		
✛ Body	Text area with a summary ⌄	Number of rows: 9 Number of summary rows: 3	✿
✛ Published	Single on/off checkbox ⌄	Use field label: Yes	✿

Disabled

No field is hidden.

Save

Figure 14.1 – Form display configuration for the page content type

Making adjustments to the form shown in *Figure 14.1* can help you adjust the authoring experience by adding help text or adjusting the form fields to use different widgets. *Figure 14.1* may be difficult to read, but it exemplifies all of the various configuration options available to a site builder to control the display of a content type. Each part of the form, which spans both structured content and metadata, has its available widgets and settings, which are tied to the type of field or type of data. For instance, **Authored on** is a date and time widget that captures the necessary information when a node is created.

To access the form and create a node after logging in, go to node/add, and select the Page content type. This prompts the node editing form, as exemplified by the following figure:

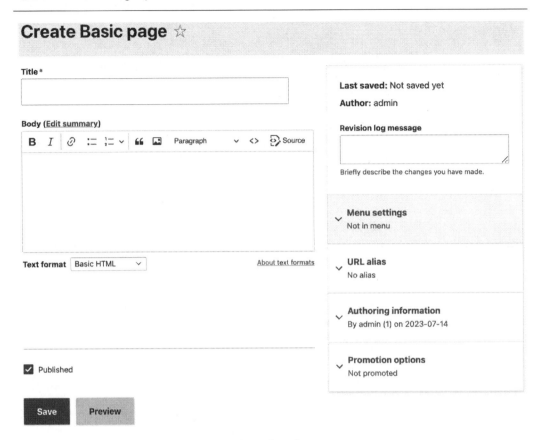

Figure 14.2 – Node editing form for a page content type

The structured content for a Page content type, out of the box, has two fields: **Title** and **Body**. As *Figure 14.2* shows, these fields are two different field types. As such, the experience of editing these fields is different.

The metadata for the node is on the right side. The first box captures the most current revision information and offers the ability to describe the changes made. This description is very useful when reviewing revisions. **Menu settings** allow the node to be placed in a selected menu, provide a title for the menu link, and place the link within the menu hierarchy. **URL alias** allows the author to specify a path to access the rendered node. The authoring information provides the primary metadata for the publishing date and author for the node, which can also be optionally displayed. Finally, **Promoted to front page** and **Sticky at the top of lists** are settings that associate the node with two specific niche features in Drupal.

It should be noted that the **Published** checkbox is also metadata and is used to control the display of a node. This is useful for content that is not yet complete or old content that may no longer need to be displayed but can be kept for archival needs or to enable in the future.

After saving the node with content, the following figure shows how a node is subsequently rendered:

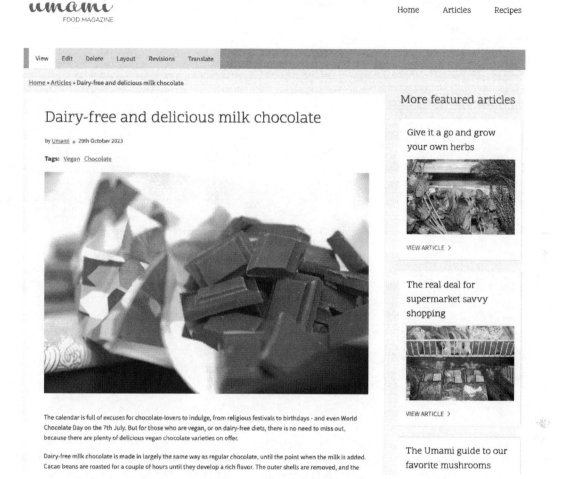

Figure 14.3 – A rendered article node from the Umami demo

A rendered node, as shown in *Figure 14.3*, provides administrative links at the top of the rendered node for those who are logged in and have access. This provides a direct link for you to edit a node, see revisions, or delete a node.

Each field has a different presentation. The visual presentation is handled by both the Drupal theme and configuration. The logic to render content types is provided by the **Manage display** configuration for the content type, found at `admin/structure/types/manage/article/display` for the **article** content type. The following is an example of configuring the article content type:

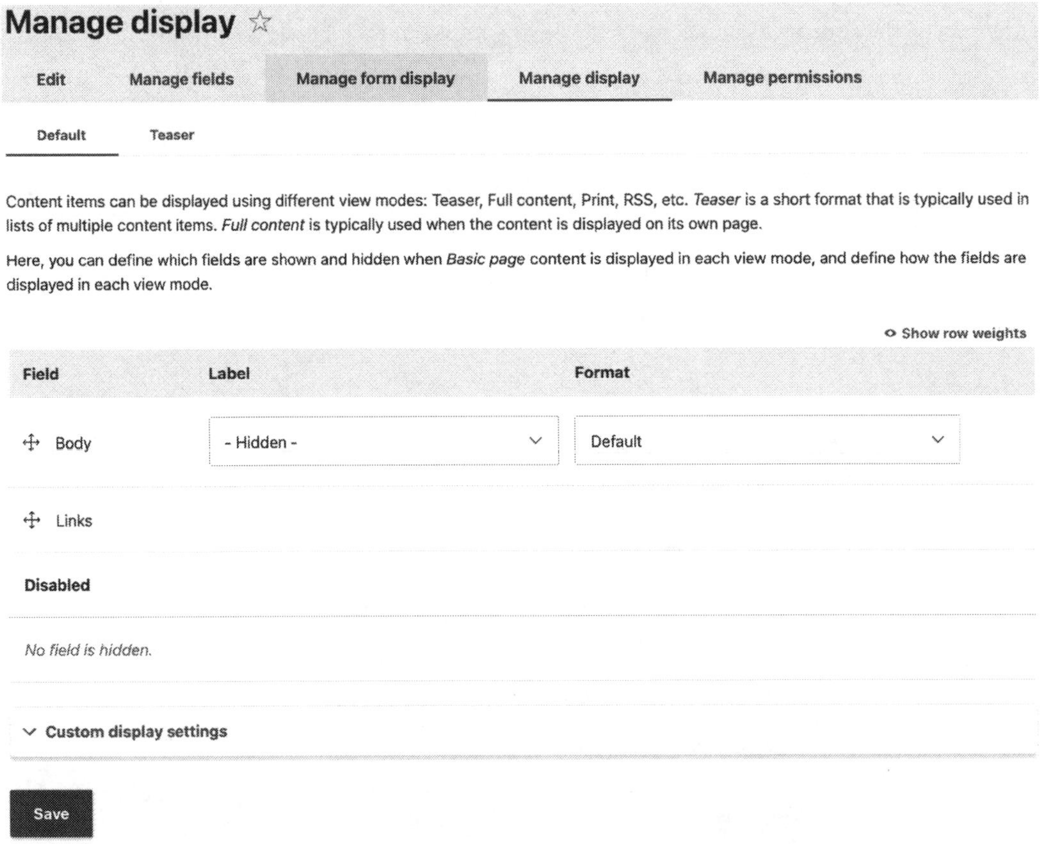

Manage display ☆

Edit	Manage fields	Manage form display	Manage display	Manage permissions

__Default__   Teaser

Content items can be displayed using different view modes: Teaser, Full content, Print, RSS, etc. *Teaser* is a short format that is typically used in lists of multiple content items. *Full content* is typically used when the content is displayed on its own page.

Here, you can define which fields are shown and hidden when *Basic page* content is displayed in each view mode, and define how the fields are displayed in each view mode.

○ Show row weights

Field	Label		Format	
✛ Body	- Hidden -	⌄	Default	⌄
✛ Links				

Disabled

No field is hidden.

⌄ **Custom display settings**

Save

Figure 14.4 – Manage display settings tied to a content type

Changing some of the settings on the **Manage display** page causes the rendering of a node to update accordingly. To show this, the featured image has been hidden and a label has been added to the body field. The resulting rendered node is then updated:

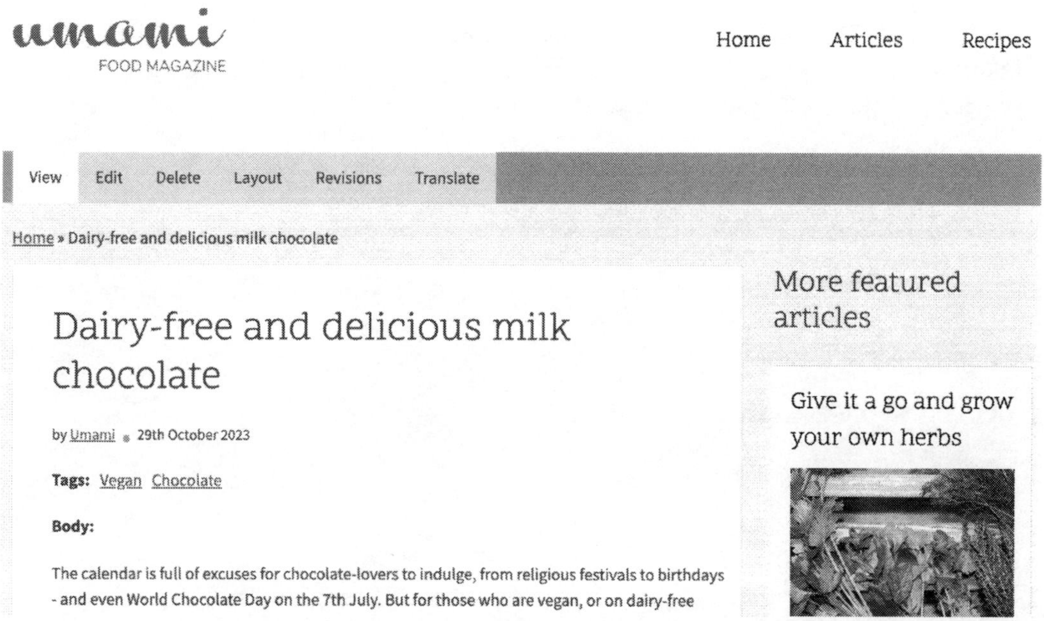

FOOD MAGAZINE

Home   Articles   Recipes

| View | Edit | Delete | Layout | Revisions | Translate |

Home » Dairy-free and delicious milk chocolate

Dairy-free and delicious milk chocolate

by Umami   • 29th October 2023

Tags: Vegan Chocolate

Body:

The calendar is full of excuses for chocolate-lovers to indulge, from religious festivals to birthdays - and even World Chocolate Day on the 7th July. But for those who are vegan, or on dairy-free

More featured articles

Give it a go and grow your own herbs

Figure 14.5 – An updated node rendering

Figure 14.5 shows how updated settings on the **Manage display** page are automatically applied when a node is rendered. The **Manage display** page provides a large number of options for how the node will render. This was covered in greater depth in *Chapter 10*, which also covered additional display modes.

Complexity comes with large content structures. Again, the separation between the visual representation of the field and an editing form can make it confusing to know exactly how a node will be rendered. This is further emphasized when there are a lot of fields, making authors question how all of the fields show up together on a rendered page. It can be helpful to encourage content authors to leverage the preview feature on the node editing page to see changes.

> **Important note**
> Having a lot of fields within a content type or entity is typically a good thing, even if it complicates the authoring experience. Observing atomic principles often requires data to be broken down into its smallest form. Having atomic data gives Drupal control over how each field is rendered in both site building and within themes. It also helps with web service APIs that often return data in highly structured formats.

The editing experience for various field types also goes beyond the **Title** and **Body** fields shown. Out of the box, Drupal supports the following field types, which can be enabled or disabled from the application's project listing (`admin/modules`):

- Dates, date and times, and date ranges
- Boolean (yes or no, on or off, etc.)
- Email
- Numbers
- Selection and lists
- Files and images
- Links
- Options
- Telephone
- Text (short- and long-form text)
- Reference (selecting another entity)

Beyond the editorial experience, each field type offers native validation of field values to promote data integrity. Other core modules offer various field widgets that complement the field types:

- Files, images, and media
- WYSIWYG

> **Important note**
>
> Content authors often ask for WYSIWYG over structured content. The experience offered by WYSIWYG is like that offered by tools such as Microsoft Word. However, WYSIWYG stores content as a blob that is not structured. Overusing WYSIWYG would mean not properly using Drupal features, and it could give content authors too much control over the visual style. This could potentially have adverse effects on how content is rendered visually.
>
> One compromise is configuring Drupal's text formats and editors found at `admin/config/content/formats`. This configuration allows for site builders to change what functionality is available for WYSIWYG. It can be desirable to not let users change fonts, colors, and other things, which is effectively WYSIWYG that keeps the content free of unwanted visual changes.

The following figure shows page node configuration extended with various out-of-the-box field types and widgets which is the same for various other field types and widgets:

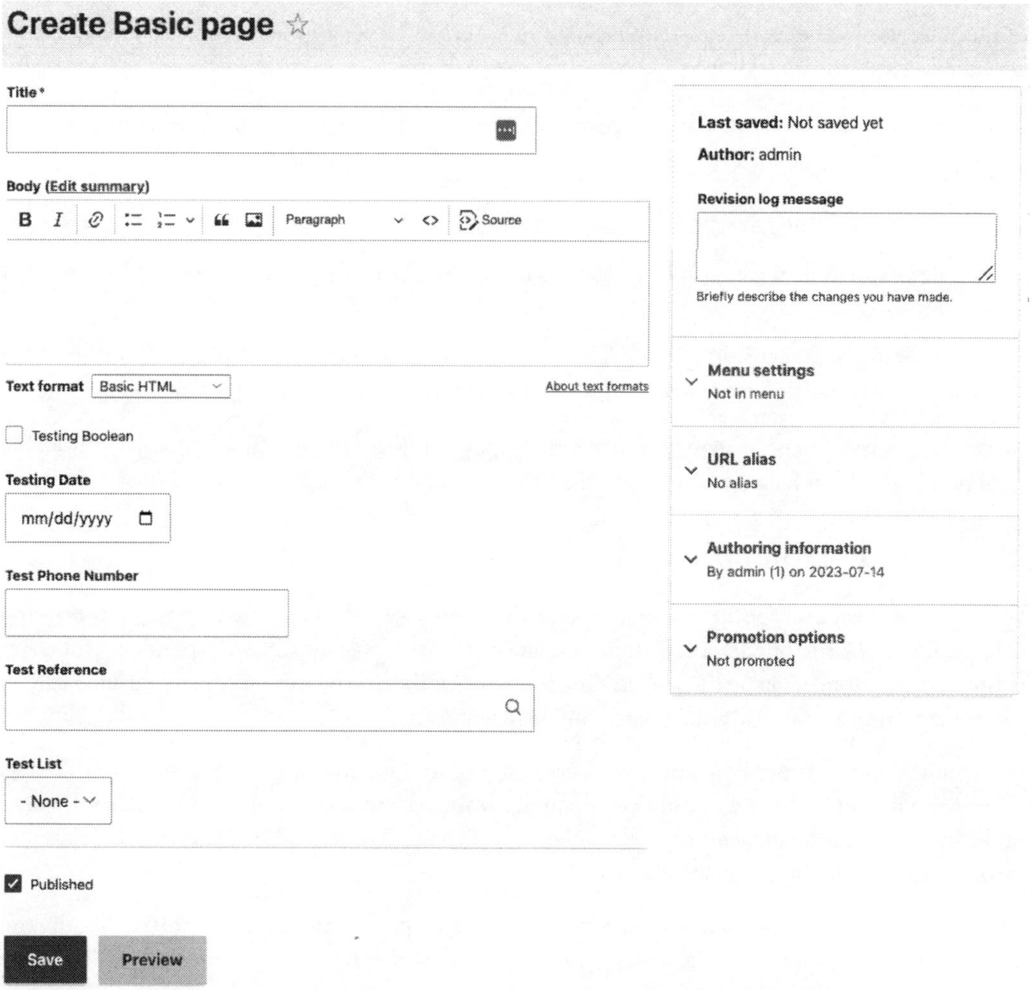

Create Basic page ☆

Title *

[⬚]

Body (Edit summary)

| **B** | *I* | 𝒪 | ≔ | ≔ ⌄ | 66 | 🖼 | Paragraph | ⌄ | <> | ⬚ Source |

Text format [Basic HTML ⌄]   About text formats

☐ Testing Boolean

Testing Date

[mm/dd/yyyy 📅]

Test Phone Number

[   ]

Test Reference

[🔍]

Test List

[- None - ⌄]

☑ Published

[Save]   [Preview]

Last saved: Not saved yet

Author: admin

Revision log message

[   ]

Briefly describe the changes you have made.

⌄ **Menu settings**
Not in menu

⌄ **URL alias**
No alias

⌄ **Authoring information**
By admin (1) on 2023-07-14

⌄ **Promotion options**
Not promoted

Figure 14.6 – A reference node editing form with various field types

Figure 14.6 shows the standard text (**Title**) and WYSIWYG (**Body**) but extended with the following fields:

- **Testing Boolean** (checkbox widget)
- **Testing Date** (date selector popup widget)
- **Testing Phone Number** (text widget)
- **Test Reference** (search and selection widget)
- **Test List** (selection widget)

Contributed projects offer a significant number of other field types and field widgets. Some popular examples include the following:

- The **Color** field (`drupal.org/project/color_field`) allows for a selection of a color
- Field groups (`drupal.org/project/field_groups`) help organize fields into groups
- The **Address** field (`drupal.org/project/address`) provides a field type for addresses
- The **Geofield** field (`drupal.org/project/geofield`) provides various ways to select a location
- The **Select or Other** field (`drupal.org/project/select_or_other`) allows for either a selection of data or the ability to provide a freeform option in the same field

Nodes cover the primary content authoring in Drupal. While it can be complex, giving authors the right permissions can help effectively harness the benefits of both Drupal and structured content.

Menus and taxonomies

While a node best exemplifies the end-to-end experience of structuring, editing, and rendering content across the site builder and author personas, Drupal harnesses similar experiences for other entities with customizable fields, such as the same form authoring process and a similar mechanism for configuration across fields, field types, and field widgets.

Content authors commonly interact with both menus and taxonomies as they author nodes. As we learned from *Figure 14.6*, authors can manage both taxonomies and menus associated with a node directly from the node editing page. There are alternative interfaces for managing menus and taxonomies that are not node-specific.

Drupal has centralized menu management accessible by going to `admin/structure/menu` and subsequently editing a menu. The following figure demonstrates how to edit a menu:

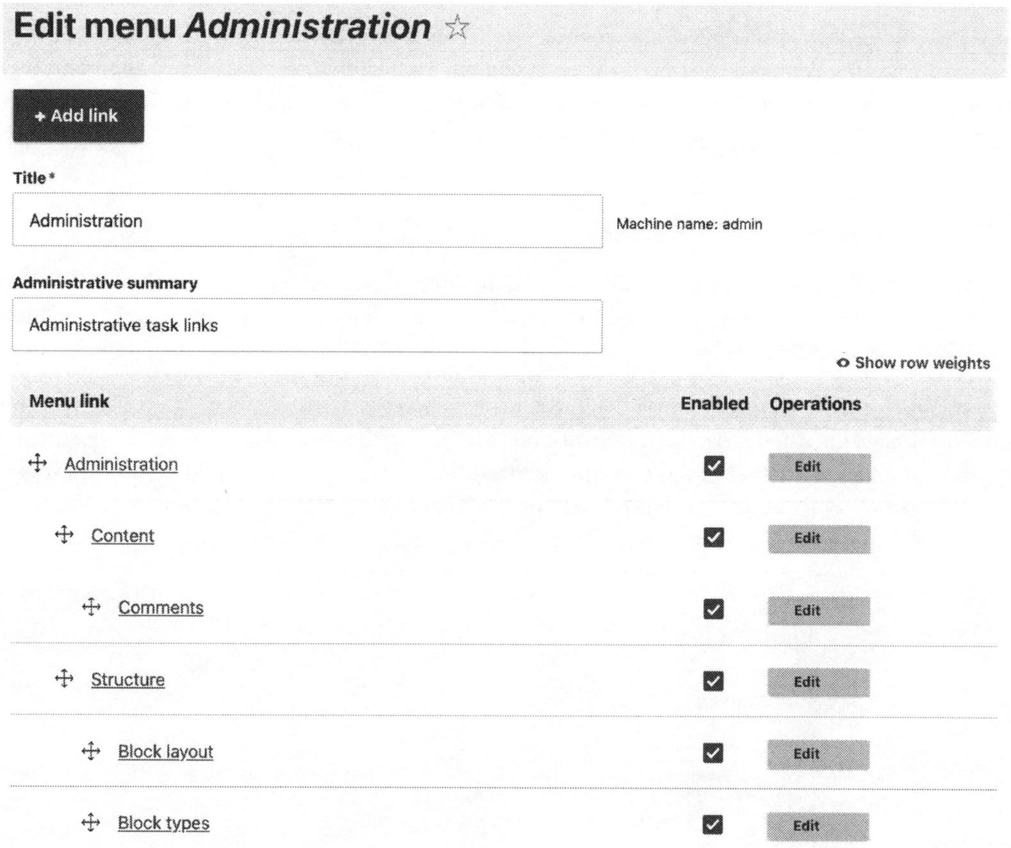

Figure 14.7 – Centralized menu editing for the administrative menu

Figure 14.7 demonstrates centralized menu management with the out-of-the-box administrative menu. It offers the ability to add and edit menu links. A link can also be enabled or disabled within a menu. From the node editing form, it can be difficult to use the **Weighting** and **Parent** fields to see where a link gets placed in a menu. The centralized view helps visualize the full hierarchy of the menu and move items as needed through a drag-and-drop mechanism. Menu links can more readily be ordered and placed under specific pages.

Similarly to menus, taxonomies can be managed centrally and hierarchically through `admin/structure/taxonomy`. Authors often associate taxonomies with a categorization system. While taxonomy management resembles that of *Figure 14.7* for menus, taxonomies have customizable fields. Configuration links, like those shown in *Figure 14.1* for nodes, are available for managing fields, forms, and display settings for taxonomies. Each taxonomy term would subsequently have an authoring experience closer to the fields shown in *Figure 14.6* but without the node-centric features in the right-hand menu.

Anyone building a Drupal application needs to understand the correlation between the configuration for nodes, taxonomies, and menus and the subsequent authoring experience. A content author is a critical person who needs to readily understand how to use the Drupal system. Creating a good experience for them and helping enable them is important for the success of any Drupal application.

Authoring digital assets

Chapter 11 highlights Drupal's capabilities for managing digital assets. In that chapter, the three primary constructs were presented: files, images, and media. All three features offer slightly different experiences for content authors.

Given that entities have customizable fields, digital assets can be associated with an entity. Consider a banner image on a node. Alone, it may not be clear where that image is rendered in the Drupal application. At a high level, the motivation behind the file, image, and media field types was to incorporate digital assets into structured content. The general structure content editing experience is effectively demonstrated in *Figure 14.6*, but there is more nuance for each type of digital asset.

The following figure shows the experience of an editing form that has each of the three digital asset field types:

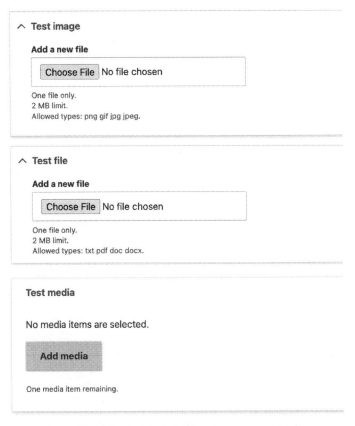

Figure 14.8 – Field widgets for files, images, and media

Figure 14.8 shows that both files and images, which are uploaded to Drupal, allow the content author to select a file from their local system. The experience provides the author with desired parameters, such as file extensions, file size limitations, and more. **Files** will just upload the file and render the file as defined by the display settings for the attached entity. However, images can harness the more advanced image features beyond just upload, such as **Image Styles**, to create transformations of the uploaded image. This functionality is detailed in *Chapter 11* and is largely automated for a content author who simply needs to upload an image.

Figure 14.8 also shows the **Test media** field. Each media field can have two primary authoring experiences, as described in *Chapter 11*. A standard media field provides a rudimentary experience that allows for a content author to select media from a listing categorized by media type. A more robust media library experience is possible from the entity's form display settings if the module is enabled, as shown in the following figure:

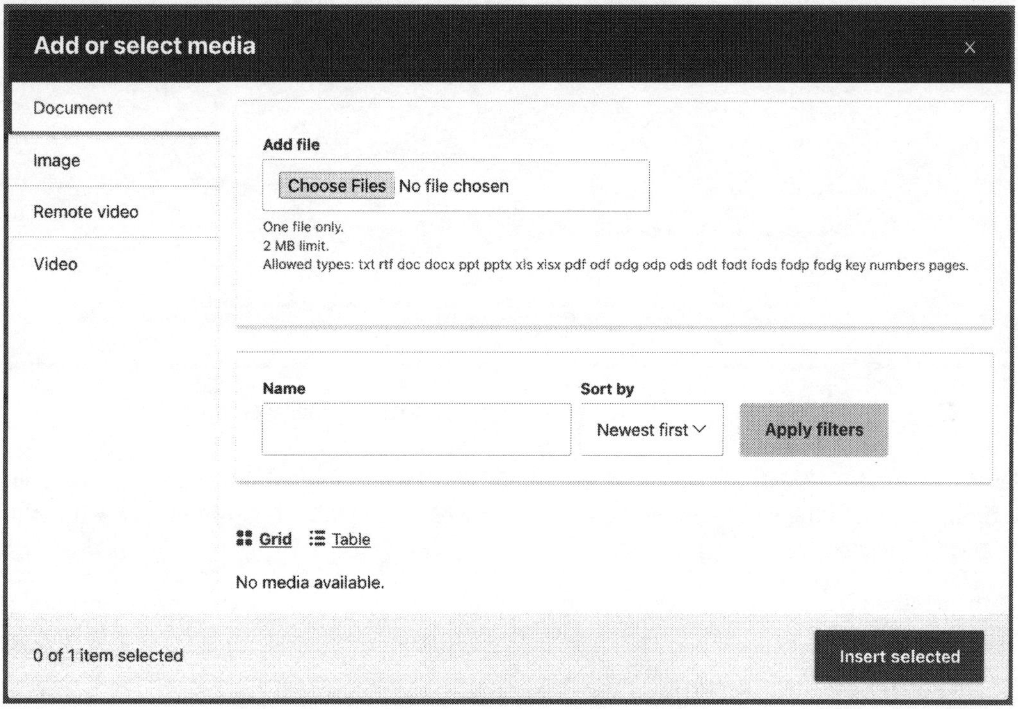

Figure 14.9 – The Media Library field widget

The Media Library in Drupal aims to provide a better, more intuitive media authoring experience. *Figure 14.9* shows the native integration for a specific media field, which can be configured by media type and optionally allows for the addition of media.

Media also is supported for WYSIWYG by embedding media into the unstructured content. After enabling the **Media** and **Media Library** modules, go to `admin/config/content/formats` and edit the desired text formats. Media can be added by moving the media button from the available buttons to the active toolbar and enabling the **Enable Media** setting within the desired text formats. The following figure shows this with an example text format:

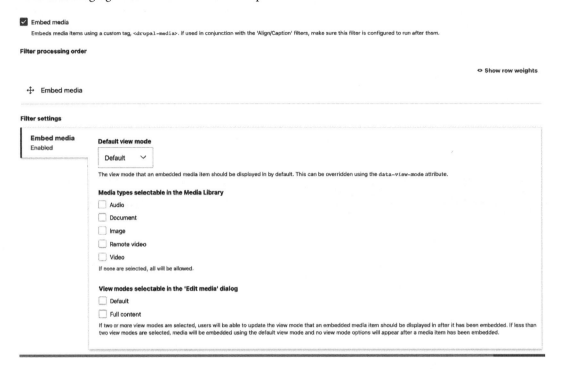

Figure 14.10 – Configuring media for WYSIWYG with the text format

For users who have access to the text format, their WYSIWYG should now have a **Media Library** button that opens the widget in *Figure 14.9*. After selecting media, it will be embedded within WYSIWYG content.

Both menus and media offer experiences that directly impact content authors beyond just nodes. Providing access and properly enabling content authors to use both menus and media can help centrally manage two other important Drupal features.

Summary

Those building a Drupal application must not forget about content authors. The authoring experience is widely configurable and impacts nodes, menus, and digital assets. It is important to properly train, enable, and refine the experience for content authors to ensure the experience of using a Drupal application is intuitive, despite gaps in the experience between structured content and rendering. This gap can potentially be addressed by using Layout Builder, which is the focus of the next chapter.

15

Visual Content Management

Content authors can struggle to map administrative forms with fields for structured content against the resulting rendered visual presentation of that content. While content managers do have tools such as preview, bouncing back and forth between a preview and editing adds effort for authors. This motivated a secondary authoring experience called Layout Builder, which offers visual content management. The feature helps provide content authors with rendered content as changes are made. Furthermore, it extends beyond just nodes by affording the same experience for rendered blocks.

In this chapter, we're going to cover the following main topics:

- Blocks and custom block types
- Layout Builder
- Contributed projects

Blocks and custom block types

Beyond content types, Drupal offers a second fieldable content entity known as blocks. Where a content type renders as its page, a block can be rendered on one or more pages tied to a theme region.

Managing blocks

Out of the box, Drupal comes with many different blocks. Blocks help render menus, content in the header, content in the footer, and much more.

Block management can be found at `admin/structure/block`. The following figure shows the centralized management screen in Drupal:

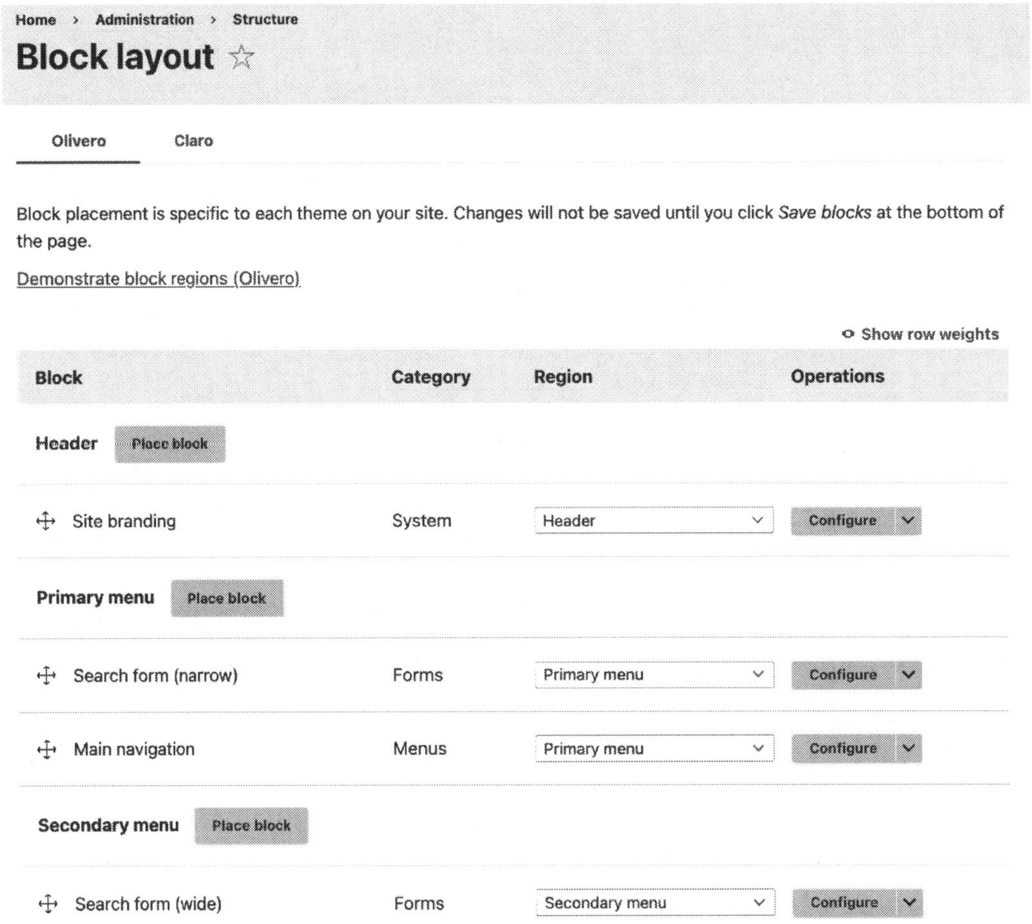

Home › Administration › Structure

Block layout ☆

Olivero   Claro

Block placement is specific to each theme on your site. Changes will not be saved until you click *Save blocks* at the bottom of the page.

Demonstrate block regions (Olivero)

↻ Show row weights

Block	Category	Region	Operations
Header Place block			
✛ Site branding	System	Header ⌄	Configure ⌄
Primary menu Place block			
✛ Search form (narrow)	Forms	Primary menu ⌄	Configure ⌄
✛ Main navigation	Menus	Primary menu ⌄	Configure ⌄
Secondary menu Place block			
✛ Search form (wide)	Forms	Secondary menu ⌄	Configure ⌄

Figure 15.1 – Central block management administrative screen

Figure 15.1 demonstrates block placement. There are tabs at the top for each enabled theme. A block can be placed by pressing the **Place block** button for the region of the theme. This button prompts a modal window that contains the entire block catalog. The modal also provides the option to create a custom block, if needed. Placed blocks can also be moved between regions using the drag-and-drop handle or the region selection option. Various operations exist to disable, remove, or configure the placed block.

The **Configure** operation manages the settings for the block and the block's visibility. The settings of the block may be fields of the content or specific configurations of the block. The following figure shows the block visibility form:

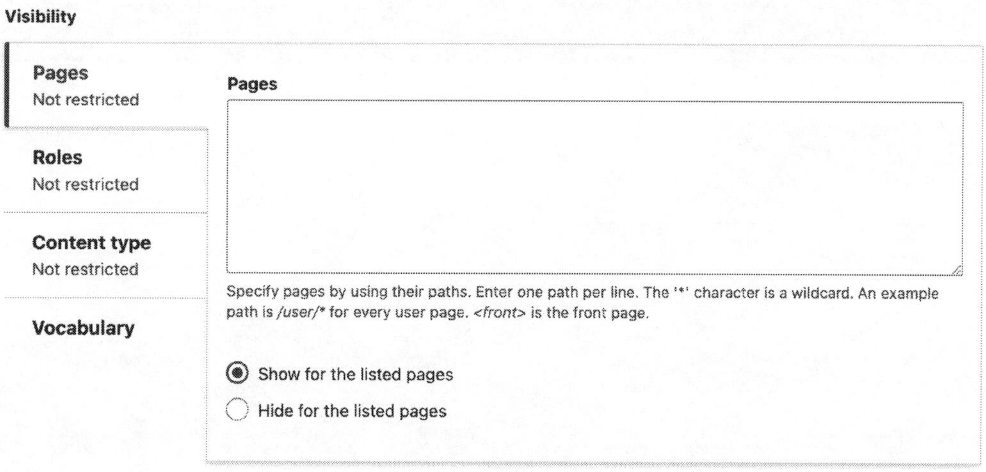

Figure 15.2 – Block visibility configuration for a placed block

Figure 15.2 shows how a block can be placed through various settings. There are various types of context where a block can be rendered; these areas are shown as tabs. The **Pages** tab allows for the * character, which means it gets rendered on any page or one or more paths can be provided to render on specific pages. The **Roles**, **Content type**, and **Vocabulary** tabs allow block visibility to be restricted to those entities.

Custom block types

Beyond Drupal's out-of-the-box blocks, blocks with custom content can be created through custom block types. A custom block type is a fieldable content entity where each type is a bundle. This observes a similar set of features to managing content types. Drupal offers a central block type listing at `admin/structure/block-content` with a button to add a new block type. When adding, the basic block type metadata is entered and saved. There's also a **manage fields** operation to alter the content structure of the block. Furthermore, a **manage display** operation exists to control how blocks of that type get rendered.

Custom blocks can be created after pressing the **Place block** button under a theme region of the central block management screen. The following modal will appear:

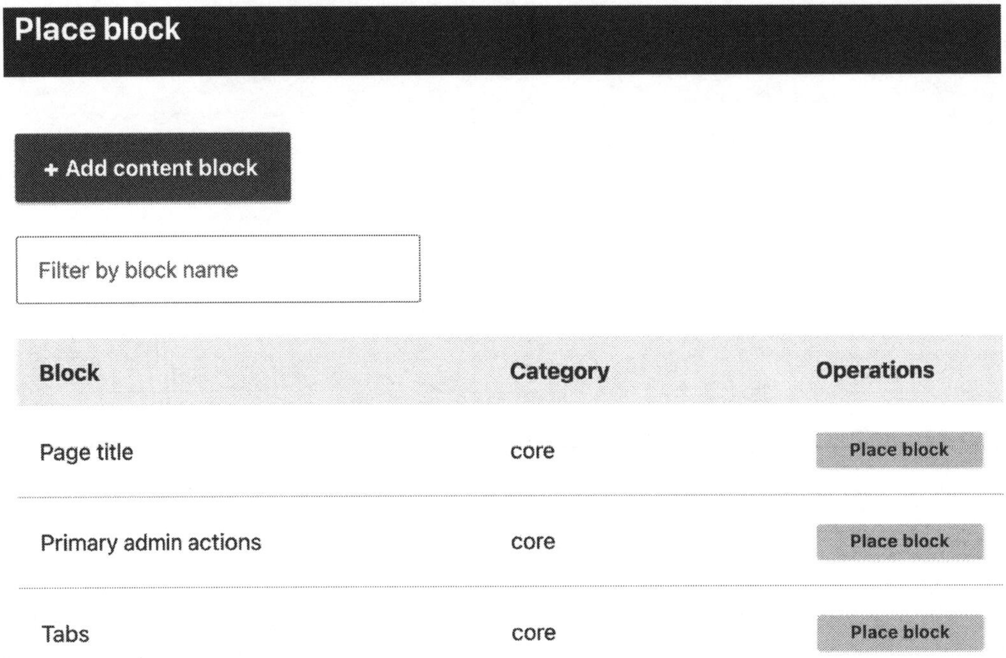

Place block

+ Add content block

Filter by block name

Block	Category	Operations
Page title	core	Place block
Primary admin actions	core	Place block
Tabs	core	Place block

Figure 15.3 – The Place block modal window

Figure 15.3 shows how to either place a block from the library or create a new content block through the **Add content block** button. The **Add content block** button prompts you to select the desired block type, which subsequently prompts a form with all of the fields in the block type. After adding the custom content block, it can be configured with the same visibility settings shown previously.

Blocks allow you to manage the same content across multiple pages within a theme region. It can be managed centrally through block visibility, which configures the logic of when the block is rendered. Custom block types afford structured content for blocks similar to content types with fields, display settings, and more.

Layout Builder

Structured content can be confusing for content authors. Ensuring that Drupal promotes usability and ease of use for content authors helps ensure a Drupal application can be adopted. Authors often struggle to understand how specific fields map to different, rendered visual presentations. Layout Builder attempts to provide a visual experience for content authors to see content change. This combined experience helps the author more directly and easily see how a change is displayed when the change is made.

Layout Builder stays with a layout. Think of this as a series of places on a page where the content can be rendered. From the perspective of structured content, each field in a node can be placed within the layout. Blocks rendered on a page can also be placed within a layout. This allows Layout Builder to author content beyond just the structured content on a page and from the experience of what is rendered, not just the underlying fields.

Placement has context as well. Recall a recurring theme from earlier chapters around the importance of context. Context serves as a series of conditions Drupal uses for dynamic processing. Layout Builder supports context through various types of placement. Consider a block that is placed on all nodes of a content type. A content author would have to place the block node by node without context. Layout Builder supports context for placement that allows a block to be placed on one or more nodes with configuration of the context.

Layout Builder manages content within a layout only. It does not manage content in all regions of a theme, nor does it replace the global block system and the context it manages. Consider a theme with regions for the header, footer, left menu, and main content. Layout Builder may manage a layout in the main content region only.

Configuring a default layout

The experience of using Layout Builder must be configured within each content type. The configuration starts at the bottom of the **Manage Display** form on a content type; this can be found at `admin/structure/types/manage/article/display` for an `article` content type. A checkbox to **use layout builder** exists. Once checked, an additional option exists called **Allow each content item to have its layout customized**. To use the same layout for each content type, leave the second box unchecked.

Saving the **use layout builder** change for the content type removes the field-specific display options and replaces them with a button to manage the layout. Pressing this button prompts the following figure:

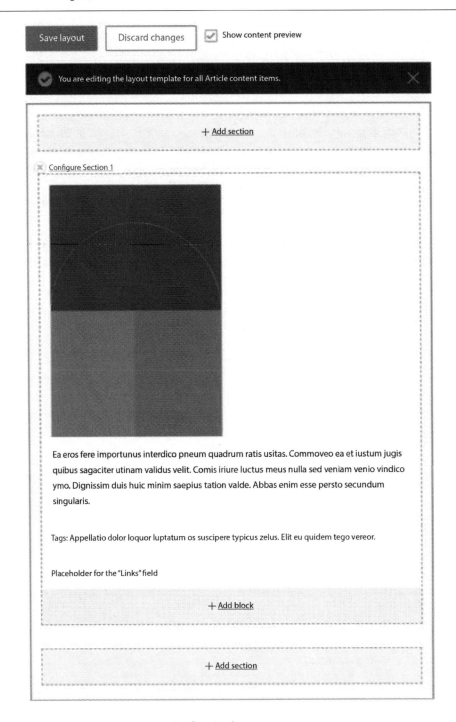

Figure 15.4 – Configuring layouts on a content type

Figure 15.4 shows the structured content in the layout. The article content type has two fields, an image and a body. Both are converted into field-specific blocks. The figure demonstrates a section in a layout where the image field is placed above the body field. The layout configuration is interactive. Each field can be dragged above another field. And, hovering over a field shows a pencil icon that contains the form for settings of that block. The settings include the option to render labels or control the display mode of that block.

Figure 15.4 shows the ability to add sections or blocks to a section. This provides you with an interface to place additional blocks within the layout. This is shown in the following figure:

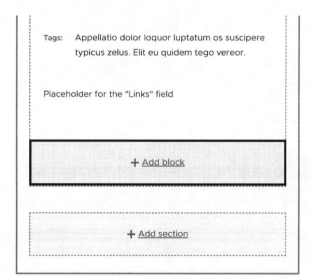

Figure 15.5 – Block placement for layouts

Figure 15.5 shows the ability to place additional blocks from the block system or content fields as blocks into a section. Again, this configuration applies throughout the content type. Do not forget to scroll up and click **Save Layout** to apply the changes.

Layout Builder allows content authors to manage a default layout for content types and blocks placed within the layout. This helps site builders manage structured content as field-specific blocks to promote a consistent rendering of content within a region of a theme.

Node-specific layouts

Each node can have its layout and this affects the experience for content authors. Recall the second checkbox, **Allow each content item to have its layout customized**, which is configured within the content type. This setting, and its corresponding permission per role, offers content authors control over the layout. Content authors are then afforded a new tab to manage the layout per node with the ability to override the default layout.

When viewing a node, authors will see a **Layout** tab, as shown in the following figure:

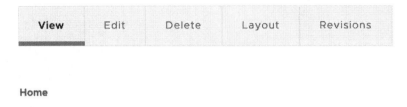

Figure 15.6 – The Layout tab for nodes

Pressing the **Layout** button prompts the same layout manager found in *Figure 15.1* and *Figure 15.2*. However, node-specific layouts have some additional functionality, as exemplified in the following figure:

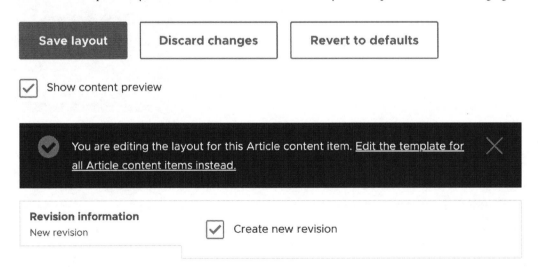

Figure 15.7 – Node-specific operations for managing layouts

While the standard operations for saving and discarding layout changes exist, a **revert to defaults** operation can be used to restore a node to its default layout configured with the content type. Authors are shown a message saying they are managing the specific content item, with a link to edit the default layout found in the content type. Also, note the **Show content preview** option, which provides a visual interface for content authors to see the node-specific content as authors are managing the layout. Finally, layouts per node can be revised, which means they can be reverted, and you can view a log of change.

Setting up Layout Builder

To enable this feature, you must enable the Layout Builder module by going to `admin/modules`. Doing so enables both Layout Builder and a dependent module known as Layout Discovery, which manages the underlying API framework. This module turns on the functionality that can subsequently be configured.

To ensure the feature can be used, configure permissions for each role by going to `admin/people/permissions/module/layout_builder`. It is important to enable the use of Layout Builder for roles that are expected to perform content management.

> **Important note**
>
> Drupal community members often discuss testing as different users through a utility known as "Masquerade." Starting with Drupal 7, the community developed the Masquerade module, which helps a site builder switch to another user in the Drupal system. This can be incredibly helpful in testing the different experiences across roles. When making changes to permissions, masquerading as a user with a different role can provide a quick way for a site builder to see the results for a different user. In the context of this chapter, it can be helpful to enable Layout Builder for some roles and allow a site builder to see the change in experience without explicitly logging out and logging in as another user. Different browsers with different user sessions also can be used in favor of logging in and out of the same browser.

Layout Builder allows layouts to be managed not just within a content type but also in nodes. Doing so affords content authors with a visual experience for controlling the placement of structured content and other system-wide blocks.

Contributed projects

Several contributed modules exist on drupal.org that are complementary to the concepts in this chapter. Please note that the following projects are not necessarily recommended given that, in some circumstances, core maintains similar functionality.

Paragraphs

Paragraphs (`https://www.drupal.org/project/paragraphs`) is a vast ecosystem of modules based on a content structure similar to blocks. Its purpose was to offer an alternative content authoring experience to Drupal's default block management. The Paragraph entity has a bundle called Paragraph Types. The community has developed several out-of-the-box contributed modules for paragraph types:

- `https://www.drupal.org/project/ept_accordion` – accordion
- `https://www.drupal.org/project/ept_basic_button` – a button
- `https://www.drupal.org/project/ept_carousel` – a carousel
- `https://www.drupal.org/project/ept_image_gallery` – an image gallery
- `https://www.drupal.org/project/ept_quote` – a quote
- `https://www.drupal.org/project/ept_micromodal,` – a modal

Gutenberg

In 2018, WordPress 5.0 released Gutenberg, a block editing system (`https://wordpress.org/documentation/wordpress-version/version-5-0/`). The key difference between this and other block editors was its ability to perform visual editing. Gutenberg was introduced to Drupal as a contributed module (`https://www.drupal.org/project/gutenberg`) that provides support for visually editing Drupal blocks. Gutenberg efforts were selected from the DrupalCon Pitchburgh competition, demonstrating community interest. However, it is not in core and likely does not meet the core standards around accessibility.

While Layout Builder focuses on where blocks are placed, Gutenberg allows a block to be directly edited on the page. Authors then get the ability to see the content changes visually. This type of experience is often more intuitive for authors who can see the visual changes immediately instead of using administrative backend forms, clicking on the preview to render a node with changes, and subsequently saving it.

Setup starts by downloading the contributed module. Gutenberg is configured per content type through its administrative settings. The following figure shows the content type settings tab once Gutenberg is enabled:

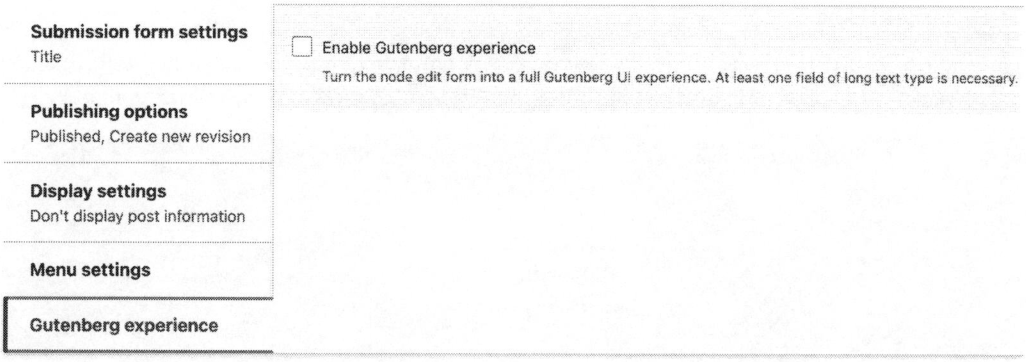

Submission form settings
Title

Publishing options
Published, Create new revision

Display settings
Don't display post information

Menu settings

Gutenberg experience

☐ Enable Gutenberg experience

Turn the node edit form into a full Gutenberg Ui experience. At least one field of long text type is necessary.

Figure 15.8 – Enabling the Gutenberg editor for a content type

After checking the checkbox, more advanced options are available. Given that Drupal heavily leverages blocks, there are blocks for everything. Gutenberg allows for block selection to allow site builders to control which blocks editors can access. This is shown in the following figure:

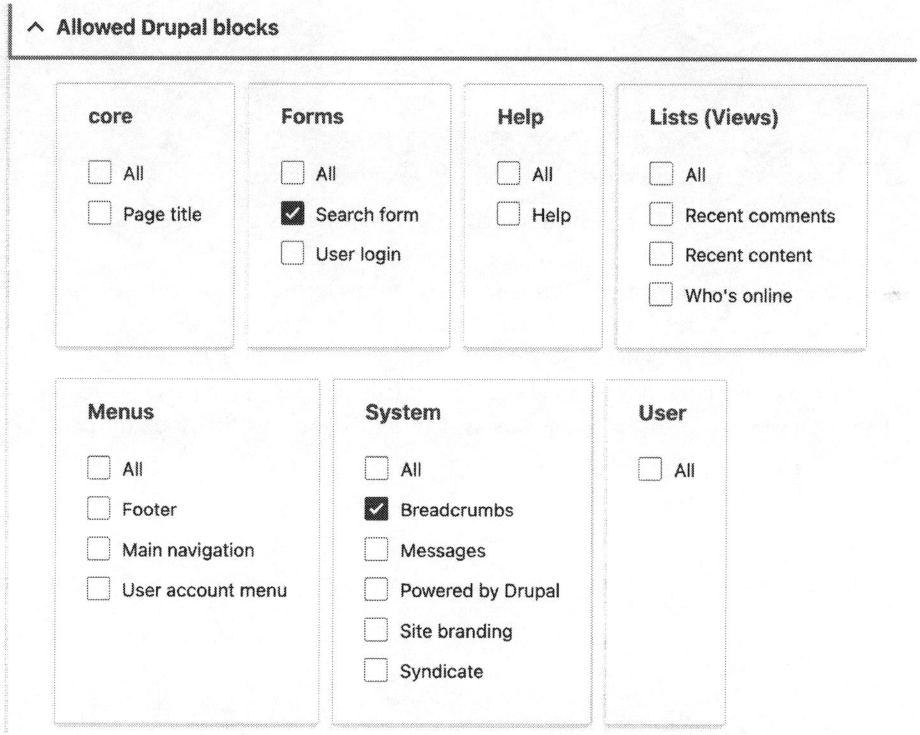

∧ Allowed Drupal blocks

core
☐ All
☐ Page title

Forms
☐ All
☑ Search form
☐ User login

Help
☐ All
☐ Help

Lists (Views)
☐ All
☐ Recent comments
☐ Recent content
☐ Who's online

Menus
☐ All
☐ Footer
☐ Main navigation
☐ User account menu

System
☐ All
☑ Breadcrumbs
☐ Messages
☐ Powered by Drupal
☐ Site branding
☐ Syndicate

User
☐ All

Figure 15.9 – Block selection in Gutenberg for a content type

Once configured, Gutenberg replaces the default, administrative form for adding new nodes. After going to node/add and selecting a content type with Gutenberg enabled, an author will see a new splash page and a completely different authoring experience, as shown in the following figure:

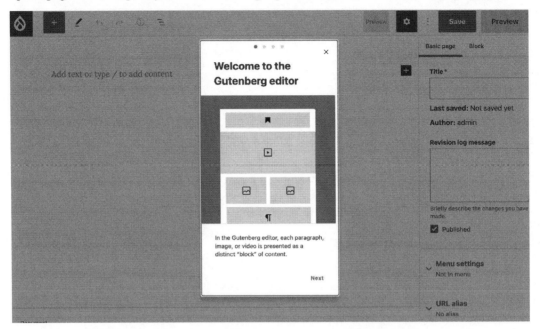

Figure 15.10 – The initial content editing experience in Gutenberg

The splash modal window provides a brief overview of how to use the Gutenberg editor for users who first access it. The node's administrative fields/metadata area still exists as a tab on the right sidebar, but the content is managed in the middle of the page. Free-form text can be added as a paragraph simply by typing in text. Blocks can be added by pressing the plus (+) sign icon, which prompts a modal window for the available blocks. This is all done visually within the page, as shown in the following figure:

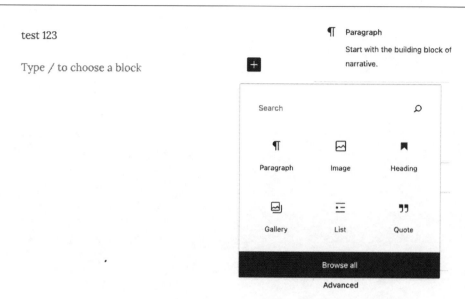

Figure 15.11 – Initial content editing experience with Gutenberg

The same experience highlighted in *Figure 15.11* covers editing beyond just initial node authoring.

For Drupal, the Gutenberg project is still nascent. However, it was a project that was selected as part of the 2023 DrupalCon Pittsburgh's new Pitchburgh concept where some funding was set aside to promote ideas that the community voted on. The Gutenberg project should continue to evolve and help offer content authors a fairly intuitive and modern content editing experience.

Summary

Drupal has a core feature for visual content management called Layout Builder. Layout Builder leverages Drupal's blocks feature, which offers structured content entities. Layout Builder provides a different content authoring experience beyond the default block management by adding a new concept of a layout that has a default layout managed per content type and the ability to manage layouts per node. This feature helps manage the presentation of rendered content within a specific region of a theme. This works for both system-wide blocks and custom block types. Node-specific layouts afford context where a block can be placed only on a node and not on a default layout, which would apply to all nodes using the default. Layout Builder offers site builders and content authors more control over where and how a specific field can be rendered but also adds block-specific content authoring within node-specific layouts. Drupal has other contributed solutions similar to Blocks and Layout Builder, which include Paragraphs and Gutenberg.

The next chapter will explore content workflows in Drupal, which are helpful for editorial processes and content governance.

16

Content Workflows

Content often has to be reviewed and approved before publishing. Much like with print, editors perform reviews, request changes, or authorize content for publishing. Drupal offers a feature that allows content to go through a workflow before publishing. Leveraging roles and permissions, Drupal can customize workflows for various users during an editorial process.

In this chapter we're going to cover the following main topics:

- Configuring workflows
- Using workflows

Configuring workflows

Content workflows in Drupal have two different modules relevant to configuration:

- Content moderation, which offers additional publication states for content
- Workflows, which manage state, transitions, and corresponding workflows

This section explores how those modules are configured to deliver workflows tied to Drupal content. It is broken down into subsections on the configuration needed to manage states, transitions, and workflows and with the user permissions required to grant specific roles.

Managing states

Workflows help define different states of content. Consider the different states of an article. A writer drafts content. An editor reviews the draft, may perform some editorial corrections, and approves or rejects it for publishing. The authored content may come in different states. This could be a draft state or an approved/published state, or it might get sent back to draft if it's rejected.

Managing transitions

Transitions capture the action of moving between states. This helps define a workflow by understanding how content moves between states. For instance, a draft can be published for those who are allowed to perform that action. A draft would not be able to move to an archived state, given that it never got published. Configuring a transition defines the business logic of the state changes that happen for content.

Managing workflows

Both states and transitions are managed per workflow. All workflows are managed from `admin/config/workflow/workflows`, with a default **Editorial** workflow added upon installation.

The management form has multiple sections. The following figure demonstrates the states:

Label *

| Editorial | Machine name: editorial |

∧ **States**

⟳ **Show row weights**

State	Operations
✛ Draft	Edit
✛ Published	Edit
✛ Archived	Edit ⌄

Add a new state

Figure 16.1 – Managing states in a workflow

States can be ordered and edited, and new states can even be added. Out of the box, an archived state exists, which can be removed. Draft and published states are also out of the box but not editable.

The following figure shows transitions in the workflow:

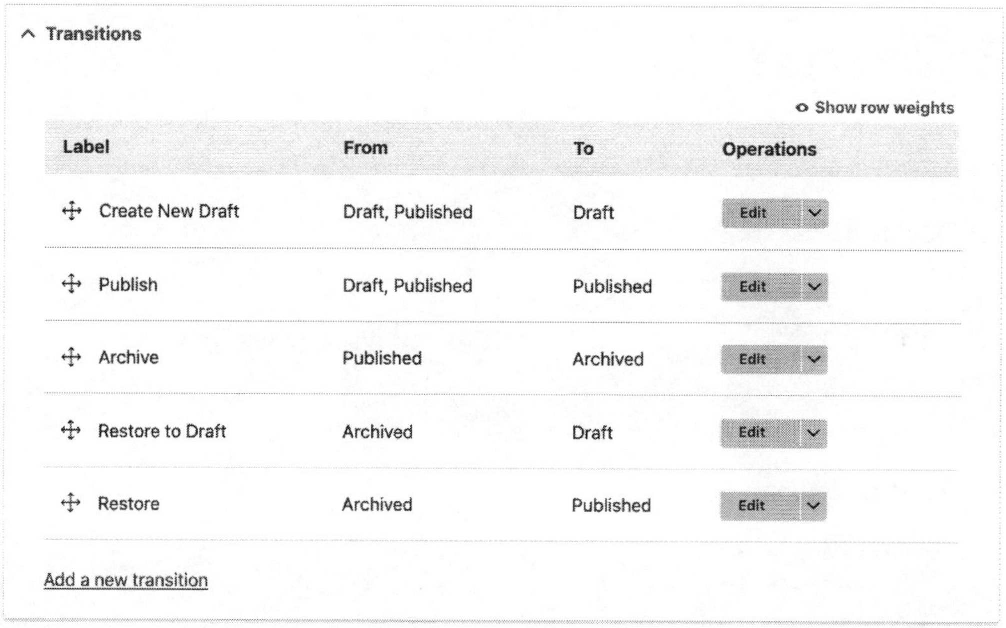

Figure 16.2 – Managing transitions in a workflow

Figure 16.2 shows that transitions have labels (which refer to the action) and **From** and **To** states. This helps define the workflow by mapping states to their corresponding actions. Transitions are the business logic of the workflow. In this example, a draft can be published or sent back for another draft. Published content can have new drafts or be archived. Transitions can be customized as needed based on the desired use case. All changes are logged through Drupal's revisions.

The following figure shows where the workflow is applied:

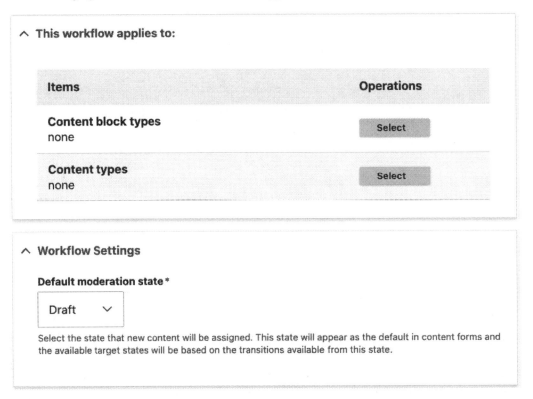

Figure 16.3 – Applying the workflow

Figure 16.3 shows content entities that can apply the workflow. This allows for different configurations for each content entity and bundle. For instance, if only the article content type required workflows, all other content types could have standard Drupal content authoring and publishing.

Managing permissions

Role-based access control, as Drupal provides by assigning users to roles, treats transitions as permissions. Given that a transition is an action, such as "an editor can publish," a role can exist for an editor and they can be granted permissions for publishing transitions.

The following figure exemplifies the out-of-the-box workflow permissions:

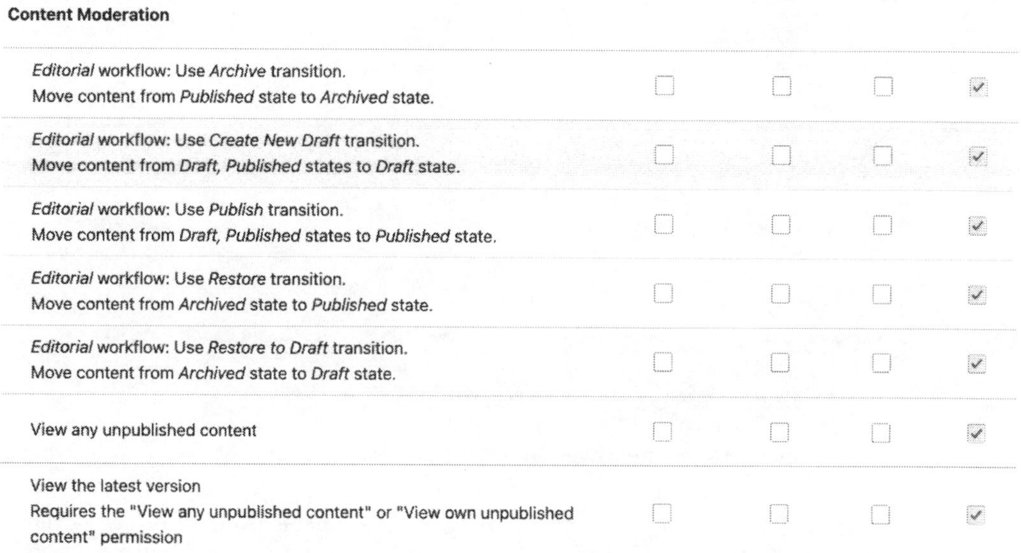

Content Moderation

Editorial workflow: Use *Archive* transition. Move content from *Published* state to *Archived* state.	☐	☐	☐	☑
Editorial workflow: Use *Create New Draft* transition. Move content from *Draft, Published* states to *Draft* state.	☐	☐	☐	☑
Editorial workflow: Use *Publish* transition. Move content from *Draft, Published* states to *Published* state.	☐	☐	☐	☑
Editorial workflow: Use *Restore* transition. Move content from *Archived* state to *Published* state.	☐	☐	☐	☑
Editorial workflow: Use *Restore to Draft* transition. Move content from *Archived* state to *Draft* state.	☐	☐	☐	☑
View any unpublished content	☐	☐	☐	☑
View the latest version Requires the "View any unpublished content" or "View own unpublished content" permission	☐	☐	☐	☑

Figure 16.4 – Example of transition-based permissions

Each role can be configured to their allowable transitions. It is expected that there are different roles that can be assigned to users based on the different actions that can be performed in workflows. This experience is exemplified in the next section.

Using workflows

Workflow features are incorporated into Drupal's standard content management capabilities. The community has contributed additional capabilities that can be added on. Some examples include the **Scheduler** module (https://www.drupal.org/project/scheduler), which integrates time-related events with the **Content Moderation** module, a bulk publishing module for use within **Content Moderation** (https://www.drupal.org/project/moderated_content_bulk_publish), and a notifications module also tied to **Content Moderation** (https://www.drupal.org/project/content_moderation_notifications). The following section highlights the usage of out-of-the-box content workflow features in Drupal only.

The main content listing has a new **Moderated content** tab for viewing workflow states within the content. It is found at admin/content/moderated and is shown in the following figure:

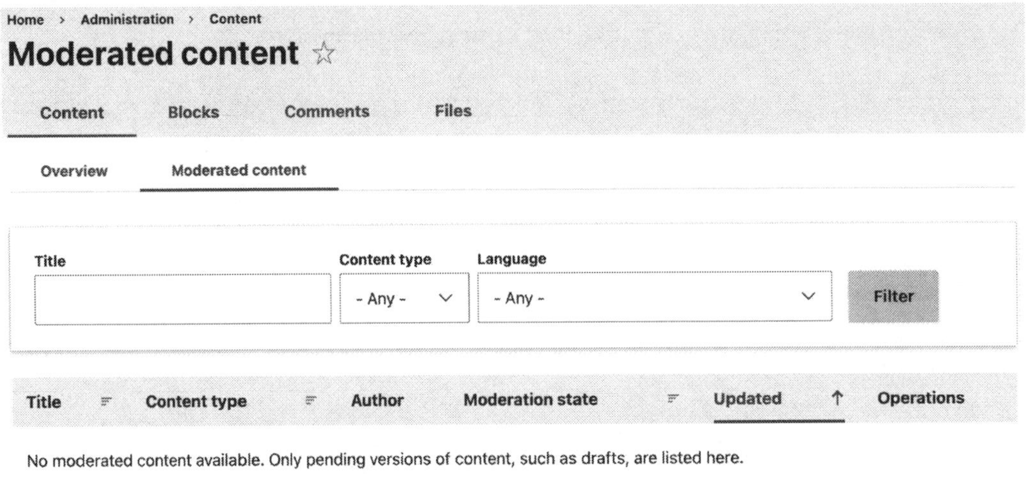

Figure 16.5 – Content overview for the Moderated content tab

This listing is different from the standard content listing because it has a **Moderation state** column and can be filtered by state.

The content management form is updated to provide controls for content authors of various roles to manage workflows for the specific content. For this example, an *article* content type was configured for Drupal's default editorial workflow. The content form now has a workflow field, as shown in the following figure:

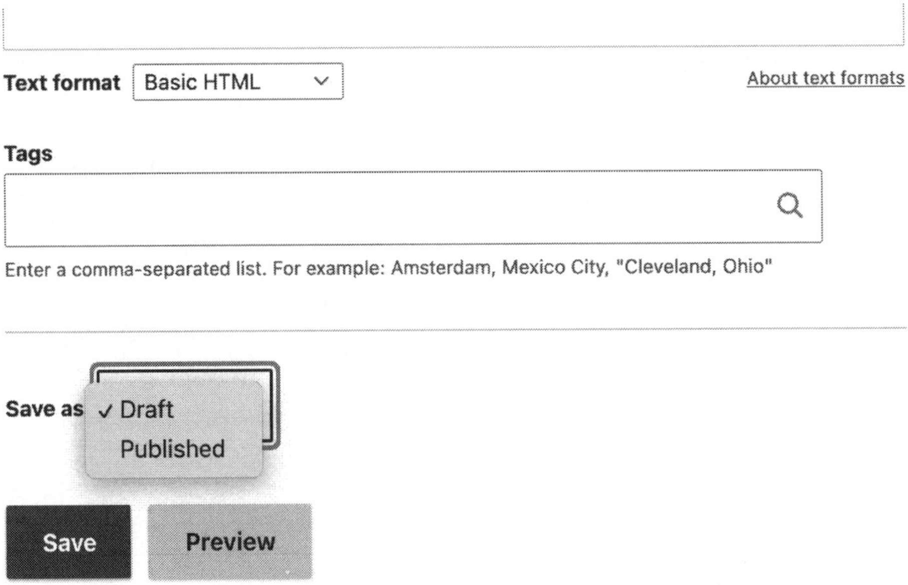

Figure 16.6 – Workflow state field on the article

The workflow state field values change based on context. The values of the dropdown change based on the current state. For instance, if it is new content, it will apply the draft state because the content is not yet published. The only allowable values will be in the **To** state for the current **From** state of the content. If a user does not have permission for the transition, field values will be restricted to the states to which they have access. For instance, an author may see only the draft state while an editor may see draft and publish states.

Use case

Suppose a public company has regulatory compliance, requires all earning reports to go through a review, and has a specific publishing date. This example assumes the **Content Moderation**, **Workflows**, and **Scheduler** modules are enabled. The following steps can be done to configure this use case:

1. Create an earnings report content type with any file fields configured to use the private filesystem from `admin/structure/types/add`

2. Configure the earnings report content type to use the scheduler by enabling the checkbox Enable scheduled publishing for content items under the Scheduling tab when configuring the content type.

3. Add a new regulatory workflow of type "`content moderation`" at `admin/config/workflow/workflows` with at least draft and published states and at least one transition from draft to publish.

4. Select the earnings report content type when configuring the regulatory workflow.

5. Create a role for the regulatory governing users.

6. Assign relevant permissions for the regulatory role, including the following two permissions:

   - Set the publish transition of the regulatory workflow to **Use Publish transition**
   - Set the scheduler permission to **Schedule publishing and unpublishing of content**

7. Remove the scheduler permission from other roles so that only regulatory users can schedule.

This creates a new workflow that handles this regulatory use case.

Summary

Workflows allow for content to go through editorial processes. By harnessing Drupal's native users, roles, and permissions, site builders can configure states and transitions and control actions for each user, which can be applied to content entities and bundles. Like editorial processes for print, Drupal offers various checks done by different users before the content is published.

The next chapter explores advanced topics in Git, Drush, Composer, and DevOps that developers and operators should understand.

Part 5: Advanced Topics

This part explores more advanced topics. Several of the earlier parts emphasize a site builder persona configuring Drupal. This section dives deeper into tools for managing code and command line tools necessary for development. Both module and theme development are introduced to provide readers a brief overview. More advanced features, like web services, content migrations, and multi-site are covered for more niche use cases Drupal solves natively.

This part has the following chapters:

- *Chapter 17, Git, Drush, Composer, and DevOps*

- *Chapter 18, Module Development*

- *Chapter 19, Theme Development*

- *Chapter 20, Delivering Drupal Content through APIs*

- *Chapter 21, Migrating Content into Drupal*

- *Chapter 22, Multisite Management*

17

Git, Drush, Composer, and DevOps

Much of the book so far has covered installing and configuring Drupal to meet a variety of use cases. However, even if you are not a developer, it can be difficult to maintain a Drupal application or contribute to the community without some basic technical skills. While this is an advanced topic, a brief primer in technologies such as Git, Drush, and Composer that enable developers can serve as a foundational launchpad into future development practices. These technologies bridge development and operations through practices known as DevOps. Getting started with this technology helps work toward the 80/20 rule, as discussed in previous chapters.

In this chapter, we're going to cover the following main topics:

- Git basics
- Drush basics
- Composer basics
- DevOps practices

Technical requirements

This chapter moves beyond installing, using, and configuring Drupal. Many of the items in this chapter run on the command line through a terminal and are well-suited for Mac and Linux machines. Support for Windows exists, but Mac and Linux have well-vetted paths adopted by many in the Drupal community.

Technical requirements change by tool. For instance, Git may have certain system dependencies that are different from a PHP-based tool such as Composer. Much of the requirements are abstracted by installers that run on the local operating system and set up the tools.

Some commands may require **Secure Shell** (**SSH**), either to access a machine remotely or for use by the tool on the local system to connect to remote systems. This is often important for connecting to environments that run Drupal applications or working with code repositories. Configuring SSH often needs to be set up locally and on remote systems. Some SaaS vendors offer user interfaces that allow for public SSH keys to be uploaded to a user account, instead of directly configuring a system.

Git basics

Git is a distributed code versioning system. A repository is what stores the code, which is revised by changes known as commits. Each repository can configure remotes, which help synchronize code between repositories by fetching code from one repository to another. Remotes communicate via HTTPS with basic authentication credentials or the SSH protocol, which can leverage SSH keys. There is significant documentation on the internet on generating SSH keys and configuring SSH in Git that changes, based on operating systems and hosted Git platforms. Repositories maintain branches that help maintain a series of commits that relate to a change. Code in a branch is often merged into a main branch, which serves as a baseline for code to be accepted into a repository.

SaaS vendors have helped make Git more ubiquitous. Vendors such as GitHub and GitLab run managed Git repositories with a UI and various complementary features. It is common for a Drupal application to manage code on one of those platforms and harness continuous integration features that automate some of the mundane building and deploying of code. Developers can clone these managed Git repositories to their local systems as an upstream remote. This provides a central code repository that all developers can contribute to and pull from.

The term GitOps refers to events around a Git repository. These events, such as creating a new branch, committing to a branch, and merging a branch into a main branch, all signify events that can be automated. Certain technologies, such as ArgoCD and even GitHub and GitLab, leverage GitOps to perform tasks when the events occur. The most common feature is known as a `pull or merge` request, which is an event in which a developer submits candidate code from a branch to be merged into the main branch. GitHub and GitLab offer user interfaces to review code by peers and perform automated checks, before accepting code into a main branch. This helps to instrument developer workflows with scripts that can help perform code deployments that update environments, run automated tests to verify changes, and so on.

Setup

Git is a command-line tool built from open source software that has several installation methods that change by operating system. Some operating systems even offer it by default. More instructions can be found in Git's online documentation (`https://git-scm.com/book/en/v2/Getting-Started-Installing-Git`).

Git can also be installed as a **graphical user interface** (**GUI**). The GUI can be useful to abstract some of the complexities of running Git commands on the terminal. However, Git is a complex system, and troubleshooting concepts such as remotes and rebasing can be difficult through a GUI. It is valuable to learn the CLI to properly understand what is happening instead of seeing an abstraction through a GUI. GUIs can change per platform (e.g., GitHub Desktop) and have different support per operating system. However, the command-line tool is the most consistent.

Common commands

After installation, the `git` command should be available from the command line. The following commands are helpful when managing code through Git repositories. Note the use of placeholders in brackets where specific parameters are required:

```
$ git init
```

This command initializes a repository in a directory where none exists:

```
$ git clone [link to remote repository]
```

This command copies a remote repository by creating a new directory and pulling the code from the remote:

```
$ git remote -v
```

This command lists the remotes configured with the Git repository, including the name and URL:

```
$ git remote add [name] [link to remote repository]
```

This command adds a new remote, which can be used to add remotes for **Software as a Service (SaaS)** vendors or Drupal hosting providers:

```
$ git commit -a -m "[enter a message describing the change]"
```

This command creates a new commit for a code change, with a message describing the change:

```
$ git checkout -b [branch-name]
```

This command makes a new branch to organize a series of commits common with trunk-based development:

```
$ git branch -v
```

This command lists out branches and shows the active branch:

```
$ git branch -a
```

This command lists out branches found with remotes:

```
$ git fetch --all
```

This command refreshes metadata from remotes on branches and their corresponding commit references:

```
$ git reset --hard [remote]/[branch]
```

This command destroys changes on the current branch and replaces it with the commit found in a remote branch. This requires a fetch to get updated information before running this command:

```
$ git log --stat
```

This command shows abbreviated information on the commit history of the branch.

Learning Git is critical for managing code on Drupal applications. Becoming familiar with even a basic few commands can help perform Drupal updates, manage code from a local system through deployments, and so on.

Drush basics

Drush is a command-line tool that runs operations on a Drupal site. Because Drupal has a backend administrative area, users with the appropriate permissions can log in and operate a Drupal application. However, there are times when an application is unavailable, such as when it has pending database updates or requires a cache clear. Also, developers want to be able to run commands remotely and in scripts during events such as code deployments, without having to subsequently log in through the web application.

Operations is an overloaded term in technology, but with Drush, operations are focused on actions that run on the Drupal application – things such as logging in as a user, clearing the cache, or updating configuration from code to the application. Drush does not manage code in Drupal.

Like Git, Drush can leverage SSH to manage remotes. This feature is known as site aliases in Drush. Site aliases are helpful for developers who work on multiple Drupal applications and manage different environments found in a Drupal application.

Setup

Installing Drush is dependent on the major version of the Drupal application. Installation instructions for Drush 12, which is compatible with Drupal, can be found through Drush's online documentation (https://www.drush.org/12.x/install/). There is a compatibility matrix for Drupal and Drush versions, also available online (https://www.drush.org/12.x/install/#drupal-compatibility). Modern versions of Drush require the use of Composer for installation, given that is how Drupal manages its code, and it affords parity between the major version of Drupal and Drush itself. Also, note that Drush has specific PHP version requirements.

Common commands

Drush has a lot of commands, and each command has different parameters that can be used as needed. The following commands, while not exhaustive, help serve as a few common examples to understand Drush basics. While all examples do not have an alias, which assumes Drush is run directly against a Drupal application, an alias can be provided by adding @[alias] directly after drush in the following commands. Also, note that Drush also has shorthand commands known as aliases that can be found in the online documentation:

```
$ drush user:login --name=[user name]
```

The preceding provides a link to the Drupal application to log in as a specific user:

```
$ drush user:password [user name] '[updated password]'
```

The preceding resets a user password in the Drupal application:

```
$ drush site:alias
```

The preceding shows configured site aliases in Drush that can be used within any Drush command to run the command against a remote application:

```
$ drush updatedb
```

The preceding performs any updates made available after deploying new code to an application:

```
$ drush config:import
```

The preceding updates the active Drupal application configuration from code:

```
$ drush cache:rebuild
```

The preceding clears the cache in a Drupal application:

```
$ drush pm:list
```

The preceding shows projects in code and the installation status on the Drupal application:

```
$ drush pm:enable [project name]
```

The preceding enables a specific project on a Drupal application:

```
$ drush watchdog:show
```

The preceding displays logs on a Drupal application.

Drush is a helpful way to execute commands against a Drupal application. Whether it's deploying new code or helping a user reset their password, it is immensely helpful for developers on both local and remote applications.

Composer basics

Composer is a command-line tool for managing code in PHP-based applications such as Drupal. PHP has a vast ecosystem of components, libraries, and so on, including the catalog of Drupal projects and various Symfony components used by Drupal. Like a package manager, Composer helps assemble and update the PHP-based parts of an application.

Composer starts with a project. Not to be confused with a Drupal project, a Composer project is the high-level scaffolding for an application. Drupal applications are initialized as a Composer project. Composer projects have installed packages, and each package has its own dependencies – all of which can be managed by Composer through Composer projects.

Once a Composer project is initialized, Composer has a few key constructs. A `composer.json` file manages a developer-friendly list of projects, versions, and constraints for the Drupal application. A constraint in Composer is a set of directives defined per project to help manage versions of projects. For instance, the tilde constraint, such as `~1.0.0`, allows for all releases of a project before 2.x to be loaded upon update. A `composer.lock` file manages the state of code loaded in a project by commit. This is akin to code deployment and helps Composer differentiate between building code in an application and updating code in an application, based on the constraints. `Composer.json` manages what projects exist and what updates are acceptable, while `composer.lock` manages what versions of projects should be built.

Code that can be built does not need to be persistently stored in a code repository. It is common to persistently version the `composer.lock` and `composer.json` files, as these files define what gets installed. However, any open source code pulled from the broader PHP ecosystem can be ignored, as it can be readily loaded from Composer. For Drupal, core and contributed projects can be ignored. Custom code cannot. Ignored code can be managed through a `.gitignore` file managed persistently in the Git repository. There can be multiple `.gitignore` files within different directories found in the repository. All of the scaffolding for core, contributed, and custom conventions are loaded by default with the Composer project for Drupal applications.

Setup

Composer is a PHP-based command-line project that can be set up on any system. Installation instructions are based on the operating system and can be found through their online documentation (`https://getcomposer.org/doc/00-intro.md`).

Like Drush, Composer will be tightly coupled with the version of PHP running on the system. However, Composer is not tightly coupled with the Drupal application. Composer is capable of loading the correct updates based on the version of PHP on the system, and for notifying known incompatibilities of projects that have strict PHP version dependencies.

Common commands

Following is a list of Composer commands:

```
$ composer create-project --no-install drupal/recommended-project [site]
```

The preceding starts a new Drupal application as a Composer project:

```
$ composer install
```

The preceding builds code from a predefined Composer install file:

```
$ composer outdated -D
```

The preceding views the available updates from the composer.lock file within the Drupal application:

```
$ composer update
```

The preceding performs code updates on a Drupal application:

```
$ composer require drupal/[project name]
```

The preceding adds a new Drupal project to the Drupal application.

Composer is the command-line tool to manage code in Drupal applications. It performs the management of Drupal application code definitions, loads projects from both the broader PHP ecosystem and Drupal community, and scaffolds new Drupal applications.

DevOps practices

Historically, software engineers would delegate management, coordination, and execution of releases to operators. The practice of DevOps brought those practices together, primarily through continuous learning and the use of automation. Summarizing DevOps can be challenging, given it spans a set of practices and technologies that enable that practice. At a high level, it manages operations in code through configuration and scripts. Both development and operations teams can perpetually learn from issues that arise and update code based on that knowledge. This philosophy promotes consistency, given the same code is used repeatedly to perform the same actions on repeat.

Drupal best practices have evolved as DevOps has become more emergent. DevOps for Drupal applications closely align with events found in GitOps, practices tied to continuous integration, and the desire to have repeatable and frequent code deployments. Developer workflows often create new branches, review code pushed to those branches, merge code back into a main branch, and have desired deployments to environments based on release tags of the code repository. The desire to automate specific events helps promote consistency across developers and provides engineers the ability to update scripts when, or if, they learn of better ways to do things.

Drupal has specific scripts that can exist for each of these events. Automation can harness Git, Composer, and Drush as part of the scripts.

Consider the following GitOps events and corresponding concepts.

A developer pushes a new commit to a development branch

To do this, the following steps can be performed:

1. Create a new remote testing environment.

2. Deploy code from the branch to the environment.

3. Build the code.

4. Bring database and file content down from production and sanitize a production database and files.

5. Perform standard Drupal deployment steps.

This can be performed with the following example `bash` script, from a `dev-001` branch in the `origin` remote after an environment is created (which is functionality-specific to hosting providers, if offered):

```
git restore .
git fetch --all
git checkout -b dev-001 origin/dev-001
composer install --no-dev
drush sql:sync @prod @self
drush rsync @prod:%files @self:%files
drush deploy
```

Note that the script runs on the provisioned environment that was created to test the change. It should also be noted that a continuous integration tool can trigger the script to run on the environment, during the appropriate GitOps configuration.

Developer reviews and merges code into the main branch

Given trunk-based development, merging code into a main branch suggests code was accepted. This often corresponds to automatically updating environments, such as a development server, where the main branch is deployed. Thankfully, a slightly modified script can be used for this:

```
    git restore .
git fetch --all
```

```
git checkout -b main origin/main
composer install --no-dev
drush sql:sync @prod @self
drush rsync @prod:%files @self:%files
drush deploy
```

Tag-based deployments for release candidates

Release candidates often harness Git tags over branches. This is common for staging and production environments, given that development environments often maintain parity with accepted code found in main branches.

The script can be augmented to do this, with the introduction of two variables to conditionally check the target environment and supply the tag:

```
    git restore .
git fetch --all
if [[ $TARGET_ENV = staging ]] or [[ $TARGET_ENV = production ]]
then
    git checkout tags/$GIT_TAG -b main
else
    git checkout -b main origin/main
fi
composer install --no-dev
drush sql:sync @prod @self
drush rsync @prod:%files @self:%files
drush deploy
```

Addressing production deployments

The same script can be reused with different parameters to perform deployments across all environments. Parameters can be passed for the environments, the code tag, and the desired branch to deploy beyond just the main branch.

> **Important note**
>
> Production environments should be non-destructive, given they are the source of ground truth. This impacts the synchronization of the database and files, in particular. You cannot run the same common deployment script for production and non-production environments.

Consider the following script that adds environment logic and parameters for a tag or branch:

```
TARGET_ENV=$1
GIT_BRANCH=$2
```

```
GIT_TAG=$3
git restore .
git fetch --all
if [[ $TARGET_ENV = staging ]] or [[ $TARGET_ENV = production ]]
then
    git checkout tags/$GIT_TAG -b $GIT_BRANCH
else
    git checkout -b $GIT_BRANCH origin/$GIT_BRANCH
fi
composer install --no-dev
if [[ $TARGET_ENV != production ]]
then
  drush sql:sync @prod @self
  drush rsync @prod:%files @self:%files
fi
drush deploy
```

This script, saved as an example `script.sh` file, can then be invoked with parameters. The parameters can be filled in through GitOps systems tied to events. The following example shows how to run a script to deploy to a staging environment, with a main branch and `v.1.1.0` tag:

```
$ bash script.sh staging main "v.1.1.0"
```

When performing DevOps in practice, automation can be built to maintain consistency in deployments and address all of the nuances of development workflows across environments. This harnesses several aspects of Git, Drush, and Composer.

Summary

Git, Drush, and Composer all are tools that Drupal developers are required to learn. Each of the tools handles different aspects of development. Git manages distributed code versioning from local systems through deployments. Drush manages operations that run on Drupal applications. Composer manages Drupal's projects, dependencies, and code. All of these can be combined to do automation, which is common for consistency in code deployments.

The next chapter explores creating custom modules with Drupal's development framework.

18

Module Development

The 80/20 rule in Drupal relies heavily on having a robust development framework to address functional gaps found in the 20%. While some of the 20% effort applies to visual theming, enterprise Drupal applications often require customization. Drupal modules offer this capability. Modules can integrate with third-party services, add custom business logic, define unique data structures, or develop workflows when something happens within the Drupal application. Modules help developers create custom modules for Drupal applications or contribute to modules found in drupal.org for core and contributed use cases. Learning how to code can be complex, but this chapter offers an overview to help with the basics of developing a Drupal module. A comprehensive guide on developing Drupal modules is a far greater subject and one that is covered in depth by other books.

In this chapter, we're going to cover the following main topics:

- Concepts
- Design patterns
- Module definitions

Concepts

Drupal offers a robust development framework in core that allows for the creation of modules. All types of modules leverage the same framework. A module can be found in core, be contributed to drupal.org, or be a custom module that exists only for a specific use case found in a Drupal application. Use of the framework promotes consistency and helps readily learn across modules.

Modules are set up as projects. Drupal core offers the ability to manage projects per application. This handles the installation, enabling, and disabling of projects. Some projects are intended for specific use cases only, such as debugging on a local system or performing testing on a non-production environment. This allows the same module to exist in a code base but to be managed within a specific application or environment of that application.

As a reminder from earlier chapters, module development should observe the 80/20 rule. Developing Drupal applications starts with site building. Normally, this covers a high percentage of use cases (80%). The remainder, also known as the 20%, should be completed by leveraging custom modules and/or themes. It is only after the site building has occurred and known gaps exist should module development happen.

Early Drupal concepts

Drupal modules are all about conventions. Each module has its own directory in a specific part of the application's code base (`/modules`). The code inside of the module has specific files and naming conventions to be considered a module. Even the code itself has specific standards for comments, style, and more.

Much like PHP, Drupal has gone through a transformation. During its inception, PHP was used as a scripting language. The development practices were known as **procedural**, given that the code was executed sequentially from when the script was loaded. Libraries could be created and included in PHP scripts, organized by functions and with global variables. Drupal 7 was the last major version of Drupal that primarily leveraged procedural PHP.

To this day, there are still module concepts in Drupal that are procedural. The most obvious example for modules is known as the **hook system**. At a high level, a hook is a naming convention for a function that can be considered a specific event that either core or another module defines and invokes. Some event examples include overriding a form definition, CRUD for entities, a user logging in, and more. A module defines the hook by providing a unique name for the hook and its parameters. It is common for the defining module to have a `*.api.php` file (example: `https://api.drupal.org/api/drupal/core%21lib%21Drupal%21Core%21Form%21form.api.php/10`) that provides examples for hooks and their usage. A calling module leverages the specific naming convention within its own `.module` or included PHP file to invoke the hook. This will be demonstrated in code later.

Modern Drupal concepts

Modern PHP has shifted to **object-oriented** development practices (`https://www.php.net/manual/en/language.oop5.php`). Starting with Drupal 8, Drupal also started adopting object-oriented PHP. Following several other PHP communities, Drupal was able to replace some of its foundational code with Symfony components, commonly adopted by the broader PHP ecosystem. The Symfony components introduced their own best practices and coding paradigms beyond the existing module conventions in Drupal. This includes the use of Composer, which is a standard for managing code in PHP applications.

Object-oriented development replaced several earlier aspects of module development. Hooks and procedural code have been gradually deprecated (flagged for removal and subsequently removed in later releases) by object-oriented alternatives such as **EventSubscribers**, **Controllers**, and **Services**. Drupal 8 introduced this new architecture and was a significant refactoring of Drupal core. Each major version of Drupal continues to deprecate more procedural code in favor of object orientation. This is the kind of maintenance one can expect when keeping a module up to date.

Drupal 10 module development covers both procedural and object-oriented development practices, largely through the introduction of Symfony components in Drupal 8. Module developers can expect Drupal-specific conventions and common development paradigms brought in from Symfony and the broader PHP ecosystem.

Common patterns

As mentioned, all Drupal modules follow specific conventions and patterns that bring uniformity across core, contributed, and custom modules. While not exhaustive, there are some common patterns used within modules.

PHP patterns

Object-oriented PHP makes use of PSR standards (`https://www.php-fig.org/psr/`). PSR-4, which deprecated PSR-0, is a method of autoloading files. This is how Drupal modules, Symfony, and other PHP applications can make use of specific filenames and paths to load files. Files loaded in specific paths help register the code of specific patterns. For instance, a new service class can be placed in a `src/Service` directory to register a service.

Namespaces are PHP conventions used to organize classes, which are leveraged by Drupal modules. Every auto-loaded file makes use of this pattern, as demonstrated by a namespace for a `MyService` class:

```
namespace Drupal\my_module\Service;
```

Every class in a module uses the same base namespace to keep code organized, as shown in bold here. Other classes can then readily reference the object, as demonstrated by the following examples:

Here's an example leveraging a `use` statement with namespaces:

```
use Drupal\user\Entity\User;
$user = User::load(\Drupal::currentUser()->id());
```

Here's an example leveraging a full namespace:

```
$user = \Drupal\user\Entity\User::load(\Drupal::currentUser()->id());
```

Both examples show how the `User` entity class is loaded from the namespace furnished by the user module.

Composer helps Drupal assemble code from the PHP ecosystem. Every Drupal application has a `composer.json` file that defines what version of core and contributed modules exist. It also defines dependencies of core, which brings in the various Symfony components. Drupal modules also make use of `Composer.json`. This pattern allows for modules to have their own dependencies for other modules or even other PHP projects. A module's `Composer.json` file is exemplified by the Password Strength module (`https://git.drupalcode.org/project/password_strength/-/blob/8.x-2.x/composer.json?ref_type=heads`), which harnesses a third-party library for scoring passwords:

```json
{
  "name": "drupal/password_strength",
  "description": "Integrates the Password Strength into Drupal's
Password Policy module.",
  "type": "drupal-module",
  "require": {
    "bjeavons/zxcvbn-php": "^1.3",
    "drupal/password_policy": "^3.1|^4.0"
  }
}
```

The example demonstrates the basic metadata of the module with a name, description, and type.

Symfony capabilities

New development patterns were introduced by underlying Symfony capabilities. While not exhaustive, several of them are commonly used in Drupal modules:

- **Events**: Modules often leverage interfaces for **EventSubscriber** and **EventDispatcher** to register and listen to events. While modules still define and implement hooks for a similar purpose, many of the newer Drupal subsystems, such as configuration management, harness events over hooks. More information can be found on drupal.org (`https://www.drupal.org/docs/develop/creating-modules/subscribe-to-and-dispatch-events`), which explains these differences in greater detail.

- **Routes**: Drupal has implemented the routing concept from Symfony. Modules can define a `.routing.yml` file to statically define paths for the Drupal application. Those paths are triggered by a browser through the URL of the request. Routes can invoke both Drupal and Symfony capabilities from controllers, direct calls to services, rendering forms, viewing an entity, and more. It also has configuration for various access controls. More information can be found on drupal.org (`https://www.drupal.org/docs/drupal-apis/routing-system/structure-of-routes`).

- **Controllers**: Symfony harnesses a controller as a means of configuring a request, defining how that request is processed, and returning a response. Controllers are classes that can process routes, invoke services, perform redirects, and return various forms of response classes based on the use case. Various conventions can be used, such as specific types of code comments, that can help define how the class should function.

- **Services**: A lot of procedural processing logic that would commonly be found in a `.module` file, which is a conventional PHP file found in a module, has been moved into services. A service is a specific type of class that is registered in a `services.yml` file within the configuration of a module. This helps any module invoke the same code in a service over duplicating code within modules.

- **Container**: A service container is a Symfony construct that exists to register all services for the application. This registration model helps centralize how services are managed and can control how they are implemented. This is often the underlying tool that enables modules to invoke services within Drupal.

- **Dependency injection**: Controllers and plugin classes often define their dependent services and parameters that can avoid calling the services container. This pattern harnesses configuration to define the relevant services and their parameters. Registering dependent services is more performant and recommended as best practice.

Drupal patterns

As an application, Drupal may harness Symfony components, but it does maintain its own specific patterns based on Drupal-specific features.

Drupal modules have their own standards beyond just the Symfony capabilities. First, a module is encapsulated in its own directory. This directory has all of the configuration and code for the module. The configuration and code often follow specific naming conventions, as previously mentioned. Each module often has its own `composer.json` file. Modules apply the PSR-4 standard from the module's `src` directory given the need for autoloading and leveraging Symfony conventions from within a module. These specific Drupal conventions for a module still work very similarly to other PHP communities but support the modularity Drupal promotes.

Drupal has a novel object-oriented Plugin API that harnesses PSR standards to extend Drupal features. A plugin type defines the expected code and conventions to extend a feature and then a plugin is an instance of the plugin type with its own class, specific functions relevant to the plugin type, and associated metadata. A plugin harnesses annotations in coding comments to provide the metadata of the plugin. Plugin Managers perform the central management of plugins and types and are also extensible. Many core features harness the plugin pattern to allow modules to extend specific features, such as specific Views features, field formatters, blocks, conditions, and more. The use of plugins is very common in Drupal modules and is well documented on drupal.org (`https://www.drupal.org/docs/drupal-apis/plugin-api`).

The submodules pattern is another pattern specific to Drupal. A submodule is often an optional feature that comes packaged with a module. This is common for UI modules that can be turned on or off if a UI is needed. Submodules are often just directories within a module and follow all other module conventions. An example can be seen with the source code of the Password Policy module (`https://git.drupalcode.org/project/password_policy`) given each submodule is a specific rule that can be enabled as needed to enforce specific password validation.

As mentioned, even with the move to object-oriented code, Drupal still leverages hooks within modules. A module can define its own hooks to extend Drupal's framework. Drupal modules can also extend hooks by following specific naming conventions of functions commonly found in the `modules .module` file. Hooks provide a procedural pattern for registering an event and having listeners from any Drupal module.

Automated tests are also recommended in modules to ensure code is tested when it changes or is maintained. This is an in-depth topic with several different patterns and operational differences from standard Drupal application functionality. Drupal harnesses the PHPUnit framework as a significant part of its automated testing. Module developers have various interfaces to use based on the type of testing desired. This includes unit tests, kernel tests, functional tests, browser tests, and more. Drupal also has testing standards for JavaScript. These tools provide fundamental features, such as mocking, that work with Drupal and Symfony features (services, controllers, etc.). Drupal.org covers a significant amount of information on automated testing within their documentation for modules (`https://www.drupal.org/docs/develop/automated-testing`).

Drupal modules use common patterns that help define expected conventions. While Drupal has its own patterns, Drupal builds upon existing patterns from both PHP and Composer. All of these help ensure there is consistency, uniformity, and validated patterns for developers to follow when addressing the specific use cases of the application.

Module definitions

One of the most direct ways to understand these concepts is to see actual code. For example, the following fake `hotel_feed` module demonstrates various Drupal module capabilities based on a public, free API of hotel information (`https://rapidapi.com/apidojo/api/hotels4`).

Configuration

The following files demonstrate the standard configuration found in a Drupal module:

- `composer.json`: Maintains the module's composer definitions:

```
{
  "name": "drupal/hotel_feed",
  "description": "A sample module that processes and renders
hotel information from a feed.",
  "type": "drupal-module",
  "require": {
  }
}
```

- `hotel_feed.info.yml`: Maintains the module's high-level metadata:

```
name: Hotel Feed
type: module
```

```
description: A sample module that processes and renders hotel
information from a feed.
core: 10.x
package: Custom
```

- `hotel_feed.services.yml`: Defines the Symfony services that exist in the module:

```
services:
  hotel_feed.information_service:
    class: Drupal\hotel_feed\Service\InformationService
```

- `hotel_feed.routing.yml`: Provides the routes defined by the module:

```
hotel_feed.search:
  path: '/find-hotels/{location}'
  defaults:
    _controller: '\Drupal\hotel_feed\Controller\
SearchHotelController:find'
    _title: 'Search hotels'
  requirements:
    _permission: 'search hotels'
```

- `hotel_feed.permissions.yml`: Defines the permissions provided by the module:

```
search hotels:
  title: 'Search hotels'
  description: 'Be able to search hotels by location.'
```

PHP code

Drupal modules contain PHP files tied to the expected patterns, some of which are demonstrated here:

- `hotel_feed.module`: The standard file in which hooks are invoked and procedural code can be found:

```php
<?php

/**
 * Implements hook_theme().
 */
function hotel_feed_theme($existing, $type, $theme, $path) {
  return [
    'hotel_feed.search' => [
      'render element' => 'children',
      'variables' => [
        'location' => 'New York, New York',
        'results' => [],
```

```
        ],
      ],
    ];
}
```

- `src/Controller/SearchHotelController.php`: An example controller file:

```php
<?php

namespace Drupal\hotel_feed\Controller;

use Drupal\Core\Controller\ControllerBase;

/**
 * A controller to search hotels.
 */
class SearchHotelController extends ControllerBase {

  /**
   * Returns a render array for a search page.
   */
  public function find($location) {
    $results = \Drupal::service('hotel_feed.search')
      ->find($location);
    return [
      // Your theme hook name.
      '#theme' => 'hotel_find.show_hotels',
      '#results => $results,
      '#location => $location
    ];
  }

}
```

- `src/Service/InformationService.php`: A file exemplifying a service:

```php
<?php

namespace Drupal\hotel_feed;

use Drupal\Core\DependencyInjection\ContainerBuilder;
use Drupal\Core\DependencyInjection\ServiceProviderBase;
use Symfony\Component\DependencyInjection\Definition;
use Symfony\Component\Finder\Finder;
```

```
class InformationService extends ServiceProviderBase {
  public function find(string $location) {
    $response = \Drupal::httpClient()
     ->get('https://hotels4.p.rapidapi.com/locations/v3/search',
[
        'q' => $location,
      ]);
    $json_string = (string) $response->getBody();
    return json_decode($json_string);
  }
}
```

Templates

Templates provide the markup that bridges theming and rendering in a specific Twig format (https://twig.symfony.com/):

templates/hotel_feed.show_hotels.html.twig: Shows the markup of the listing mapped to the data in the service:

```
<p>You searched for this text: <b>{{ location }}</b></p>
<ul>
  {% for item in results %}
    <li>
       {{ item }}
    </li>
  {% endfor %}
</ul>
```

The example module showed a simple use case tied to a hotel web service feed that demonstrated PHP code, Twig templates, and the common configuration files found in a module. While the demonstration files are not comprehensive, they are intended to show some of the patterns and provide a starting example to build from.

Summary

Developing modules in Drupal is an important way to solve the 80/20 rule and to contribute back to the community. Drupal has a robust framework that allows for modules to extend out of the box Drupal and observe standard conventions that all modules follow. Modules often make use of patterns in both Symfony and Drupal. Modules have defined best practices across configuration, PHP code, and more through constructs such as the composer.json file, automated tests, and more.

The next chapter explores theme development in Drupal, important for the visual styling of a Drupal application.

19
Theme Development

In this chapter, you'll learn about theming Drupal. Drupal theming is different from many other content management systems (including WordPress) because the functionality (which is typically handled at the module layer) is separated from the theme layer. Nevertheless, Drupal gives the developer nearly full control over the markup, styles, and **JavaScript** (**JS**) interactions of the frontend, which enables the developer to display data however they wish.

In this chapter, we're going to cover the following main topics:

- Set up
- Working with Libraries (JS and CSS)
- Working with Templates
- Preprocessing data and PHP
- Working with CSS
- Working with JavaScript
- Single directory components
- Drupal Accessibility tips
- Contributed modules that help with theming

Technical requirements

Given this is an advanced chapter, some specific technical knowledge is assumed. Themes in Drupal leverage CSS, JavaScript, and HTML. This book does not cover these topics in depth given they are not specific to Drupal.

As stated earlier, functionality built in Drupal is typically put together using entities, views, display modes etc. All of these exist outside of the theme layer. The theme layer exists to change markup around existing functionality, and add the ability to style and add interactivity to it.

As of the time of this writing, Drupal's paid theme ecosystem is very small (compared to other CMSs such as WordPress) because of several reasons:

It's hard to style functionality that the theme author doesn't know will exist

Most Drupal sites tend to be on the larger side, and require custom bespoke designs

Setting up for theme development

Drupal gives you several tools to help you develop your theme, but you'll need to enable them. Theme development capabilities should only be enabled on development systems, not production.

Disabling CSS and JS aggregation

Drupal will bundle CSS and JS files together. While this is great for performance, it makes development difficult. To disable this, navigate to **Admin | Configuration | Development | Performance**. You'll end up at `admin/config/development/performance`. The following figure shows the options for **Aggregate CSS files** and **Aggregate JavaScript files**:

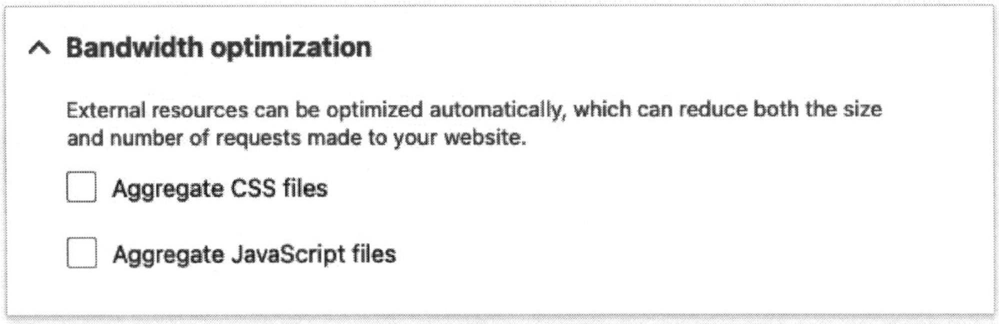

Figure 19.1 – Aggregation settings

Note you can also disable these via code, by adding the following to your `sites/default/settings.php` file:

```
$config['system.performance']['css']['preprocess'] = FALSE;
$config['system.performance']['js']['preprocess'] = FALSE;
```

That ensures that aggregation is turned off for development.

Setting up theme debugging and disabling caches

Theme debugging enables Drupal to output the current Twig template within comments, within the HTML markup that Drupal creates. The following figure shows the debugging output inline with the HTML source:

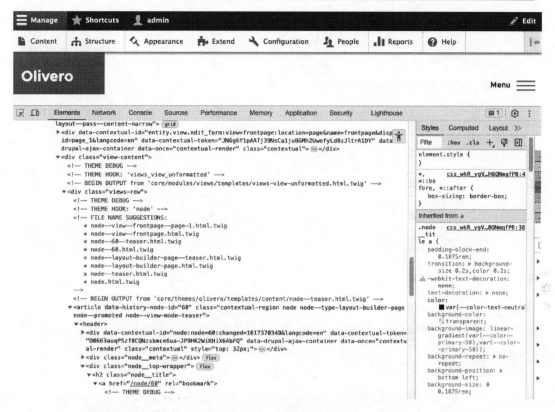

Figure 19.2 – The browser view source with the debugging comments enabled

In addition, theme debugging also enables you to use the dump() function within your Twig templates to output a list of variables.

If you're running Drupal 10.1.0 or later, navigate to **Admin | Configuration | Development | Development settings**. You'll arrive at /admin/config/development/settings.

Here, you'll find a form where you can enable Twig development mode. You'll want to check both boxes (note the first box will expose multiple options, which you'll want to keep checked). The following figure shows these settings:

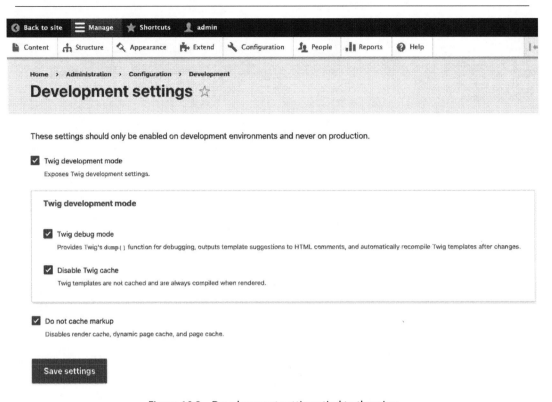

Figure 19.3 – Development settings tied to theming

Note that if you're on a version of Drupal before 10.1, you have to edit two files to accomplish the same.

Edit `sites/development.services.yml` to get the following:

```
parameters:
  http.response.debug_cacheability_headers: true
  twig.config:
    debug: true
    auto_reload: true
    cache: false
services:
  cache.backend.null:
    class: Drupal\Core\Cache\NullBackendFactory
```

Then, add the following to the bottom of your `sites/default/settings.php` file.

```
$settings['container_yamls'][] = $app_root . '/sites/development.
services.yml';
$settings['cache']['bins']['render'] = 'cache.backend.null';
$settings['cache']['bins']['page'] = 'cache.backend.null';
$settings['cache']['bins']['dynamic_page_cache'] = 'cache.backend.
null';
```

After making that change, you'll need to clear Drupal's cache at `admin/config/development/performance`.

Turning on verbose error messages

When you're doing Drupal development (including frontend development), you'll want to make sure that Drupal outputs the full errors to the screen. To do this, navigate to **Admin | Configuration | Development | Logging and errors**. You'll end up at `admin/config/development/logging`.

Select the option to display **All messages, with backtrace information**. Note that it's also recommended to add the following to your development environment's `settings.php` to do the same:

```
$config['system.logging']['error_level'] = 'verbose';
```

Verbose error messages will ensure that when (not if) you make a mistake in Twig or PHP, the proper error shows on the screen.

Creating a new theme using the theme generator tool

The official method to create a new theme is to use Drupal core's included theme generator tool. At the time of writing, the only theme that can be cloned is core's included Starterkit theme, although work is currently being done to make the Olivero theme cloneable.

Note, that this tool is intended to be run from the command line, and it requires a local version of PHP to be installed on the development computer:

```
php core/scripts/drupal generate-theme mytheme
```

This will generate a new theme, called `mytheme`, which is a clone of the Starterkit theme. The theme is extremely barebones and has only minimal styling.

Creating a new theme from scratch

Even if you don't create your theme from scratch, it's important to know how everything works in conjunction.

When you create a new theme, you'll want to start by creating a new directory within the /themes directory, with the name of your theme. For our example, we'll call our theme dexter (named after the author's dog).

> **Note**
>
> You'll need to clear the cache to see changes after modifying any of Drupal's YAML files.

Creating your dexter.info.yml

The definition of the theme is held in the theme's info.yml file. This contains the primary definitions of the themes, including which libraries (CSS and JS) are loaded by default, regions (where you place your blocks), library overrides (where you override the modules' CSS and JS), dependencies, and so on:

```
name: Dexter
type: theme
description: 'A theme named after a lovable but dumb dog.'
core_version_requirement: '>=10.1'
libraries:
  - dexter/global-styling
regions:
  header: 'Header'
  content: 'Content'
  content_below: 'Sidebar first'
  footer: 'Footer'
```

Regions

Regions are areas where you can drag and place Drupal blocks within the block layout page. You can either rely on Drupal's default regions (check Drupal's page.html.twig for a list) or you can define them yourself, using the preceding pattern.

Libraries

Libraries are defined in your dexter.libraries.yml file, and point to the CSS and JS that you want to load when that library is loaded. Within your dexter.info.yml file, you can do several things with libraries.

- You can define your global libraries (which will always be loaded) with the libraries key.

- You can override a module or theme's library with the libraries-overrides keys. This is useful to swap out CSS or JS files. You can also disable libraries completely by setting the library key's value to false. You can also granularly override or disable specific CSS or JS files.

- You can extend a library using the `libraries-extend` key. This lets you load your additional libraries when another library is loaded.

Creating your dexter.libraries.yml file

Your theme's `libraries.yml` file contains definitions for all of your theme libraries (which hold the definitions and paths to all of your CSS, and the JS that you want to load). Working with libraries is covered in a section later in this chapter.

Creating your CSS directory and files

You can put your CSS files pretty much anywhere, but it's common to place them in the a `/css` directory within the theme. Frequently, they're organized within a directory tree. The organization of this is the developer's choice, but my personal preference is the following:

```
dexter/
  css/
    base/
      - contains base styles, CSS variable definitions, resets, etc
    components/
      - contains a CSS file per component
    layout/
      -  contains layout styes, grid systems, etc
```

Note that Drupal 10.1.0 and later comes with Single Directory Components. These allow you to group templates, definitions, CSS, and JS for a component in its directory, under a `/components` directory. This means that CSS components can exist here. We'll cover Single Directory Components later in this chapter.

Creating your templates directory

Drupal uses the Twig templating language, and your theme's Twig files will live within the `/templates` directory within your theme. You can define an arbitrary directory structure within this if needed.

Typically, you'll want to copy over the Twig templates from Drupal core to populate the directory. One of the main benefits of Drupal's `theme generator` command is that it automatically populates this directory for you.

Creating your JS directory

JS can be placed in any directory within a theme, but it's standard practice to create a `/js` directory within the root of your theme, placing the respective file types into their directories.

Creating a new theme from a base theme (subtheming)

Drupal supports a concept of *subtheming*, where you can declare your theme a *subtheme*, and it will inherit everything from the parent theme. This is useful when you want to implement a framework such as Bootstrap or **U.S. Web Design System (USWDS)**.

Popular base themes

The community offers several base themes that can be found on `Drupal.org`:

- Bootstrap barrio (`https://www.drupal.org/project/bootstrap_barrio`)
- Radix (`https://www.drupal.org/project/radix`)
- USWDS base (`https://www.drupal.org/project/uswds`)

Working with Libraries API (and where to put CSS/JS)

The method by which themes and modules attach CSS and JS to a page is through Libraries API. This is extendable, very flexible, and easy to use.

To create a library, first create a `themename.libraries.yml` file in the root of your theme. Within this file, you can create a library using YML syntax:

```
card:
  css:
    component:
      css/components/card.css: {}
  js:
    js/card.js: {}
```

This library can then be loaded through one of many following methods.

Loading the library globally through your theme's *.info.yml file

You can tell your theme to always load the library by specifying it in the theme's `*.info.yml` file:

```
libraries:
  - mytheme/card
```

Attaching the library through a Twig template

This will ensure the library is loaded once whenever the Twig template is in use:

```
{{ attach_library('mytheme/card') }}
```

Loading the library programmatically through preprocess

If you have complex logic that determines when and where to load your library, you can do so via PHP within `preprocess` (there'll be more on preprocess later):

```
$variables['#attached']['library'][] = mytheme/card;
```

Overriding another module's or theme's libraries

You can override or disable other module's libraries within your theme's `*.info.yml`'s libraries-override section:

To override a library, use this:

```
libraries-override:
  some_module/card: mytheme/card
```

To disable a library, use this:

```
libraries-override:
  some_module/card: false
```

To override a specific asset within an external library, use this:

```
libraries-override:
  some_module/card:
    css:
      component:
        old/path/to/css/card.css: new/path/to/css/card.css
```

To disable a specific asset within an external library, use this:

```
libraries-override:
  some_module/card:
    js:
      old/path/to/js/card.js: false
```

Managing dependencies

In practice, many libraries depend on other libraries. To ensure that a library is loaded, use the `dependencies` key within your library.

```
dependencies:
    - core/jquery
    - core/drupal
```

Notes on CSS grouping

When adding CSS to your library, you need to organize it under one of several categories. These categories will enable Drupal to load the CSS in order.

- **Base**: CSS `reset`/`normalize` plus HTML element styling
- **Layout**: Macro arrangement of a web page, including any grid systems
- **Component**: Discrete, reusable UI elements
- **State**: Styles that deal with client-side changes to components
- **Theme**: Purely visual styling ("look-and-feel") for a component

In practice, the vast majority of CSS will be within the component grouping.

Setting weights and other options

You can set loading weights of CSS and JS by specifying the weight value within the object for the asset:

```
card:
  js:
    js/card.js: { weight: -18 }
```

If an asset is already minified, you can tell this to Drupal:

```
card:
  js:
    js/card.js: { minified: true }
```

You can specify additional attributes:

```
card:
  js:
    js/card.js: { attributes: { defer: true, type: module } }
```

Working with templates

Templates help provide variables inside of HTML markup to define the rendering of content in Drupal. The following sections outline how to work with templates.

How to find and create templates

One of the first things you'll need to do is figure out what template to use and create. You can find current templates that enable Twig Debug (which we talked about earlier) at `/admin/config/development/settings`.

Doing so will tell Drupal to output HTML comments in the markup that indicate what templates are in use, and what templates are available. Note that your theme's templates (except Single Directory Components) will reside in the theme's /templates directory.

```
<!-- THEME DEBUG -->
<!-- THEME HOOK: 'node' -->
<!-- FILE NAME SUGGESTIONS:
   * node--60--full.html.twig
   * node--60.html.twig
   * node--layout-builder-page--full.html.twig
   * node--layout-builder-page.html.twig
   * node--full.html.twig
   x node.html.twig
-->
<!-- BEGIN OUTPUT from 'core/themes/olivero/templates/content/node.html.twig' -->
<article data-history-node-id="60" class="contextual-region node node--type-layout-builder-page
l"> </article>
<!-- END OUTPUT from 'core/themes/olivero/templates/content/node.html.twig' -->
</div>
</div>
<!-- END OUTPUT from 'core/themes/olivero/templates/block/block.html.twig' -->
```

Figure 19.4 – Template suggestions in rendered HTML comments

In the preceding example, you can see under FILE NAME SUGGESTIONS: that six items are listed, with X next to the last (node.html.twig). This means that node.html.twig is in use, and if the others are created, they will take precedence.

If I want to create a new template for this specific template, copy and paste the currently used template (in this case, the node.html.twig in the theme's /templates directory), and then rename it as one of the names in the list (e.g., node--60--full.html.twig).

Twig basics

Drupal uses the open-source Twig templating language to create markup interspersed with data. This section of this chapter doesn't have time to conclusively cover Twig, but we will cover the basics and Drupal-specific implementations. Fortunately, Twig has excellent documentation (https://twig.symfony.com).

Outputting a variable in Twig

Within the Twig templating language, you'll want to intersperse the desired markup with variables that represent the live data from the site. To output a variable, simply wrap it in double curly braces – {{ my_variable }}.

Working with conditionals in Twig

Very frequently, you'll need to use `if/else` statements. To do so, you'll want to wrap it with a single curly brace and a percent sign `{% if my_var %}`.

You can also use the same syntax to set variables:

```
{% set my_var = true %}
```

The Drupal node system will give you a large content array that contains Drupal's content. To output a single field and associated markup, you can group all of these:

```
{% if content.field_my_field.0 %}
  <div class="my-field">
    {{ content.my_field }}
  </div>
{% endif %}
```

Note the `.0` within the `if` statement. Sometimes, Drupal will have an array defined even if the field has no value. Adding `.0` at the end of the conditional tells Twig to only output if data exists.

Twig ternary operators

Twig gives you options for ternary operators, which is a shorthand for if/else statements:

```
{{ variable ? 'value1' : 'value2' }}
```

This is a shortcut for the following:

```
{% if variable %}
  value1
{% else %}
  value2
{% endif %}
```

You can also use shortcuts such as the following:

```
{{ variable ? 'value1' }}
```

This is a shortcut for the following:

```
{% if variable %}
  value1
{% endif %}
```

Twig include, embed, and extends

Twig includes various functions and tags that allow a template to utilize other templates.

Include function

The `include` function allows you to include another template from where you're calling it:

```
{{ include('@olivero/_header.twig', { my_var: true, color: 'pink' },
with_context = false) }}
```

In the preceding `include` function, we call the `_header.twig` file from the Olivero theme. This function will tell Drupal to look for the file in the `/templates` directory of the Olivero theme. Note that the underscore in the filename isn't significant, other than to indicate to other developers that this file is to be included by other files. We pass in two variables. The first, `my_var`, is a Boolean set to `true`, and the second color variable is a string set to `pink`. We also pass in `with_context = false`, which tells Twig to only pass in the variables that are explicitly declared. Otherwise, `include` would have access to all the variables that the original template has access to.

The extends tag

The `extends` tag is very similar to the `include` function, but it does not pass through variables, instead passing data in `block` which are arbitrary groupings of markup and variables:

```
{% extends '@olivero/_meta.twig' %}
{% block meta %}
  <div class="meta">
    {{ content.field_meta }}
  </div>
{% endblock %}
```

In the template that this file extends, you will have corresponding `{% block meta %}` and `{% endblock %}` tags.

The embed tag

The `embed` tag combines the best of both the `include` function and the `extends` tag. In the following case, we prevent additional data from being passed to the embedded template by using the `only` keyword:

```
{% embed '@olivero/_meta.twig' with { my_var: true, color: 'pink' }
only %}
  {% block meta %}
    <div class="meta">
      {{ content.field_meta }}
```

```
    </div>
  {% endblock %}
{% endembed %}
```

Twig filters

Twig has several built-in *filters* that transform the data of the variable that they're applied to.

These are applied using a | symbol, followed by the filter's name, and then any parameters. Note that Twig filters can be chained.

Some useful Twig filters include the following:

- `capitalize`: Capitalizes the string
- `date`: Formats the data according to the passed-in parameters
- `length`: Returns the number of items in an array or sequence
- `striptags`: Strips HTML tags from a string

Drupal implements several of its filters:

- `t`: Invoke Drupal's translation for the provided input
- `clean_class`: Formats a string to be in the format of aN HTML class name
- `clean_id`: Formats a string to be in the format of aN HTML ID
- `format_date`: Formats a timestamp
- `raw`: Skips twig auto-escaping – use with care!
- `render`: Converts a render array to HTML
- `safe_join`: Joins together strings with a passed-in separator
- `without`: Creates a copy of a render array and removes keys that are passed in
- `add_suggestion`: Adds a theme suggestion to the render array
- `clean_unique_id`: Ensures a string is unique (to be used with an HTML ID)

Twig functions

Twig has several built-in functions available, including the following:

- `include`: Returns the rendered content of another template
- `random`: Returns a random number (or letter from a string)
- `date`: Converts an argument to a date to allow comparison

Similar to filters, Drupal also includes several custom filters:

- `attach_library`: Attaches the specified library to the page where the template is rendered

- `active_theme_path`: Returns the relative path of the active theme

- `create_attribute`: Creates an `attributes` object

- `dump`: Outputs a list of variables available to the template

- `file_url`: Returns a relative URL to a file

- `link`: Creates a hyperlink

- `path`: Returns a reactive path from a route name

- `URL`: Returns an absolute path from a route name

Finding what variables are available

Twig is relatively easy, but finding out what variables are available can be a bit tricky. Luckily, Drupal has your back with the `dump()` function. Note that for this to work, you have to enable Twig development mode and disable caching at `/admin/config/development/settings`.

```
array:27 [▼
  "elements" => array:20 [▶]
  "theme_hook_original" => "node"
  "attributes" => Drupal\...\Attribute {#1794 ▶}
  "title_attributes" => Drupal\...\Attribute {#1851 ▶}
  "content_attributes" => Drupal\...\Attribute {#1847 ▶}
  "title_prefix" => []
  "title_suffix" => array:1 [▼
    "contextual_links" => array:2 [▶]
  ]
  "db_is_active" => true
  "is_admin" => true
  "logged_in" => true
  "user" => Drupal\...\AccountProxy {#1396 ▶}
  "directory" => "core/themes/olivero"
  "view_mode" => "full"
  "teaser" => false
  "node" => Drupal\...\Node {#1034 ▶}
  "date" => "9 October, 2023"
  "author_name" => Drupal\...\Markup {#1529 ▶}
  "label" => array:23 [▶]
  "url" => "/node/1"
  "page" => true
  "content" => array:5 [▶]
  "author_attributes" => Drupal\...\Attribute {#1829 ▶}
  "display_submitted" => true
  "#cache" => array:1 [▶]
  "layout" => "layout--content-narrow"
  "theme_hook_suggestions" => array:5 [▶]
  "classes" => array:7 [▶]
]
```

Figure 19.5 – The rendered output of a variable dump

To use the dump() function, simply add {{ dump() }} to your template. You can also dump specific variables such as {{ dump(content) }}. You can then expand/collapse arrays and objects to see what variables are available.

You can also use a code debugger, such as Xdebug (https://xdebug.org/), to get variables in your code editor if configured. While more difficult to configure, it often provides for a better developer experience.

Working with the attributes object

Many, but not all, templates have an object variable called attributes available. This is used to set HTML attributes on the tag on which it is applied:

```
<article{{ attributes.addClass('my-class') }}>
```

Allowing Drupal to set HTML attributes without modifying templates allows contrib modules to set these as needed for their functionality.

If an attributes object is not available, you can create one with the create_attribute() function within the template.

There are several methods available for this, including the following:

- addClass: Add a CSS class to the HTML attributes
- removeClass: Removes a CSS class
- setAttribute: Sets an attribute
- removeAttribute: Removes an attribute

Preprocessing data and PHP

Frequently, you want to modify or create variables before they reach the template. You can do this within the theme's themename.theme file. This is a pure PHP file in which you can use hooks to do so.

To find the hook that you're looking for, enable theme debugging at /admin/config/development/settings. When you inspect the markup for the template, you'll see THEME HOOK.

```
<!-- THEME DEBUG -->
<!-- THEME HOOK: 'node' -->
<!-- FILE NAME SUGGESTIONS:
   * node--view--frontpage--page-1.html.twig
   * node--view--frontpage.html.twig
   * node--60--teaser.html.twig
   * node--60.html.twig
   * node--layout-builder-page--teaser.html.twig
   * node--layout-builder-page.html.twig
   x node--teaser.html.twig
   * node.html.twig
-->
<!-- BEGIN OUTPUT from 'core/themes/olivero/templates/content/node--teaser.html.twig' -->
<article data-history-node-id="60" class="contextual-region node node--type-layout-builder-page node--promoted node--view-mode-teaser">...</article>
<!-- END OUTPUT from 'core/themes/olivero/templates/content/node--teaser.html.twig' -->
```

Figure 19.6 – An example of a theme hook in the rendered markup

In the preceding screenshot, the hook is `node`.

To make use of this, you can create a function called `themename_preprocess_node` within your theme's `themename.theme` file. It takes an array as a parameter, `$variables`. This array contains all the variables that are available in the template:

```
/**
 * Implements hook_preprocess_HOOK() for node.html.twig.
 */
function themename_preprocess_node(&$variables) {
  // Create an additional variable for use in the template
  if ($variables['view_mode'] === 'full') {
    $variables['my_variable'] = true;
  }
}
```

The preceding function will add a `my_variable` variable and set it to `true` if view mode is full.

Working with CSS

Drupal expects specific conventions when it comes to implementing CSS. Typically, CSS files go into a `themename/css` directory, but that's not necessary. Drupal themes are free to use Sass, PostCSS, or other build processes as they see fit.

For the theme to load a CSS file, the file must be referenced from a library. Then, the library must be called from either the `themename.info.yml` file, attached in preprocess, attached within the template through the `attach_library` function, or loaded by a module.

Drupal core has a set of CSS standards that requires the use of **block element modifier** (**BEM**) architecture. Generally, this is best practice within all themes, but it isn't required. In addition, many popular utility-based CSS frameworks such as Tailwind or Bootstrap negate the need for BEM.

The basics of BEM is that you give your component (aka a "block") a name. In this case, the name will be a `card`. Then, any elements inside of that will have a class with an "element" appended to it, after double underscores. So, a child `div` can have the class of `card__media`. Any modifiers will have a "modifier" name appended to the class, after double hyphens. So, a landscape version of the card component might have a `card--landscape` CSS class on the same element as the card CSS class. For more information, see `https://getbem.com`

Drupal core has a couple of built-in CSS custom properties (aka CSS variables). They are used within the responsive grid view plugin, as well as the `Drupal.displace` JS library. The latter uses the variables to inform the theme on how tall or wide fixed Drupal administration elements are, so the theme can position against that. In the case of Drupal Displace, the custom properties are attached to the `<html>` element through JS.

Working with JS

Much like CSS, for JS to be loaded, the script needs to be referenced by a library, and then the library needs to be loaded by the theme. The JS can be placed in any directory but is typically placed in the `themename/js` directory.

Drupal behaviors

Drupal behaviors is the term for the JavaScript API that allows JS to process elements that are injected via AJAX.

It usually runs multiple times when a page is loaded. It'll run first and pass in the *document* as context. The subsequent times it loads it will then pass in the AJAX element as context:

```
((Drupal) => {
  Drupal.behaviors.myBehavior = {
    attach(context) {
      context.querySelector('.my-element')?.addClass('is-processed');
    },
  };
})(Drupal);
```

In the preceding example, we create a behavior called `myBehavior`. We add this to the `Drupal.behaviors` array that Drupal runs whenever it injects content. Within that, we pass in context to the `attach` function. On page load (or when data gets AJAX'd in), Drupal loops through all the behaviors in `Drupal.behaviors`. It then runs the `attach` function on each and passes in either the document or the AJAX element as context.

Note that to ensure that Drupal behaviors are available to your JS, create a dependency for `core/drupal` within the library that's referencing your script.

To ensure that behaviors do not process elements multiple times, you can use the Drupal `once()` JS utility.

```
((Drupal, once) => {
  Drupal.behaviors.myBehavior = {
    attach(context) {
        once('my-feature', '.my-element', context).forEach(el =>
el.addClass('is-processed'))
    },
  };
})(Drupal, once);
```

To load the `once` library, be sure to create a dependency for `core/once` within the library that's referencing your script.

Passing data from PHP into JS

You can pass data from PHP into JS using the `drupalSettings` object. This can be done from Drupal modules or your theme's `themename.theme` file:

```
$variables['#attached']['drupalSettings']['my_setting'] = 'my-data';
```

Once added, this gets added to inline JS within the HTML, and it is available through the global `drupalSettings` JS object.

Single Directory Components

Single Directory Components (**SDC**) were added to Drupal 10.1 as an experimental module, and they are expected to be stable in Drupal core around 10.3.0. They are Drupal's implementation of component-based architecture.

While experimental, the SDC module needs to be explicitly enabled. After SDC stabilizes, it will just be part of the theme system, with no separate module.

To use SDC, you'll need to create a `themename/components` directory, with a minimum of `componentName.component.yml` and `componentName.twig` files. You can add `componentName.css` and `componentName.js` as well, and they'll be included when the component is loaded. Once the component is created, it can be included in another template using Twig's built-in `include()` function or `embed` tag.

The benefit of using SDC is that relevant code is grouped, and libraries are automatically generated. In addition, it enables quick reusable components that can be moved from project to project.

For more information on SDC, see Drupal's documentation at `https://www.drupal.org/docs/develop/theming-drupal/using-single-directory-components/`.

Drupal accessibility tips

While Drupal core's accessibility is top-notch, custom themes rely on a frontend developer to ensure proper web accessibility. While most accessibility techniques are out of scope for this book, Drupal does contain several techniques to help save you time.

The visually hidden CSS class

The *visually-hidden* CSS class will hide an element visually, but it will still be apparent to the accessibility tree so that screen readers and other assistive technologies can access it.

Drupal announce JS API

The `Drupal.announce()` JS function is a way to easily add text to an `ARIA` live region so that screen reader users will be aware of the text that is passed in:

```
Drupal.announce('The application has been updated.');
```

Using buttons as menu items

While more content than theming, be aware that menu items can take `<button>`, which will generate a `<button>` HTML element. This is useful to show/toggle child menu items. Note that you still have to write the JS/CSS to show/hide the submenus.

Contributed modules that help with theming

Many people have created contributed modules to help theme Drupal. Some of the most popular ones are as follows:

- **Twig Tweak** (`https://www.drupal.org/project/twig_tweak`): This creates several Twig filters, functions, and so on that allow you to do things, such as placing blocks/views/entities in templates.
- **Twig Field Value** (`https://www.drupal.org/project/twig_field_value`): This creates a couple of Twig filters that allow you to generate the value of a field in a template and bypass the field template.
- **Components** (`https://www.drupal.org/project/components`): This allows you to create custom Twig namespaces, so you can reference templates more easily.

There are many more modules than these. If you run into issues, search and you'll likely find what you're looking for.

Summary

Drupal provides theming as a means of controlling the visual display of a Drupal application. Themes exist for both frontend and administrative visuals and adding them is a non-trivial development task. This chapter covered the major aspects of a theme in CSS, JS, Twig templates, and the expected Drupal directories and configuration. Best practices were covered for development, debugging, and so on. Emerging concepts such as single-file directories and community-related contributions also can help address specific use cases.

The next chapter covers Drupal's features tied to web service APIs that enable decoupled and headless application use cases.

20

Delivering Drupal Content through APIs

Drupal's structured content capabilities can be used beyond just rendering content in Drupal. Modern JavaScript frameworks, such as ReactJS and Vue.js, and more, often rely on third-party web services. Drupal is a natural fit for this use case and has features out of the box. This chapter extends what was already covered for structured content by configuring web service APIs through Drupal's JSON:API and REST capabilities. This helps configure web service endpoints that follow standard conventions and manage access to those endpoints. The chapter finishes by using and testing web services that can be called from any third-party system.

In this chapter, we're going to cover the following main topics:

- Web services primer
- Web service APIs in Drupal
- Using web services

Web services primer

Web services is a general concept that is used to promote systems interoperability. Companies often adopt or purchase products. Some of those products may be the source of truth for certain data or perform specific business functions. However, the technical implementation of these products and systems is often very different. Some of the implementation details, such as those found in SaaS products, are even abstracted from those who procured the service. But products often do not run in isolation and the need for interoperability has become a critical requirement for many businesses.

Let's take the simple example of a website. Many websites, such as those in Drupal, have means of engagement. This engagement may come through a web form on a website to inquire about services or products for that business. But businesses often have different departments. The marketing or sales departments may be the recipients of the engagement. While Drupal could easily send an email notification, there are many popular sales and CRM products that a business may have already adopted. In favor of using an email notification, it would be ideal to integrate a web form with a third-party product. Web services aim to solve this problem.

Web services define and promote common standards so that systems have common definitions when performing interoperability. Some standards include REST or JSON:API for the format of requests and responses. Other standards apply to the format of the data, such as JSON and XML. Web services are implemented as APIs commonly with support for specifically adopted standards. APIs are offered as specific endpoints that perform one specific action.

Interoperability follows similar patterns to CRUD concepts discussed in earlier chapters. Some endpoints may be used only to retrieve specific data. Others may be used transactionally to create, update, or delete a record in another system or, more generally, perform an action.

The standards help abstract the underlying technical details. The system that is hosting the APIs may be a Java application, while a system calling the endpoints may be in PHP, JavaScript, or practically anything else. While businesses also may seek to standardize their technical tools and stacks, web services allow businesses to procure best-of-breed solutions that are interoperable and can work with other technologies they have adopted.

Web service APIs in Drupal

Drupal, which commonly maintains structured content and has features other systems may need, can play an important role in both calling and providing web services.

Drupal commonly refers to its backend and frontend. Out of the box, it offers both. But Drupal's frontend can be replaced, often through the use of Drupal's backend APIs. This approach is known as decoupled or headless Drupal. The frontend is not assumed. It could be an app on a mobile phone, an Internet of Things device, or even another web application.

A lot of recent focus has has harnessed web service features in Drupal to pull content for modern JavaScript frontend applications. Frameworks such as ReactJS and Vue.js can interface with any third-party web service and create performant, innovative web frontends. Drupal's technology stack, given that it spans systems, backend, and frontend, often drives specific types of experts, such as a backend or frontend engineer. But Drupal's web service APIs allow Drupal to be used by others already trained outside of Drupal. Developers familiar with ReactJS or Vue.js can make web service requests to Drupal's backend without necessarily having to be an expert in all of Drupal. And it solves problems in making use of the underlying structured content, which does not necessarily presume how that content will be rendered.

Concepts

Drupal leverages common API concepts to promote the most interoperability with other tools and systems.

Drupal's web service APIs manage the serialization of its data structures and conversion to standard response formats. Out of the box, web services can be configured to serve **JavaScript object notation (JSON)** and **Extensible Markup Language (XML)**. These formats are widely adopted by frameworks that often have parsers for these data formats. Consistency in data formats helps developers to focus on their applications by reusing tools that can both serialize and parse the data.

Drupal also harnesses common standards in REST API and JSON:API, both of which have specific conventions that promote consistency and interoperability. **REST**, which also goes by RESTful APIs, stands for **representational state transfer**. REST APIs were created to manage and return information about resources at the time the request was made (its current state). JSON:API also focuses on resources but is a convention of the format of a JSON request and response. This convention is adopted by Drupal and is especially beneficial for JavaScript-based applications.

All APIs are built around the concept of endpoints. An endpoint is an interface that processes a request, interprets the request, and returns a response. In its simplest form, an endpoint is a URL to the Drupal application with its own expected parameters.

Given that both REST and JSON:API emphasize resources, an endpoint often represents Drupal entities. It is common to have CRUD through endpoints based on request methods (GET, POST, PATCH, and DELETE). Each request type has a semantic meaning. GET retrieves resources, POST creates, PATCH updates, and DELETE removes. APIs can extend these conventions with specific actions. For instance, users can log in to create a session within the Drupal application.

> **Important note**
>
> API requests still observe Drupal's built-in permissions. Drupal's configurable permission system also applies to APIs. Anonymous requests without authorization credentials would largely be blocked from performing administrative actions (unless explicitly authorized to do so). Actions that are performed through APIs, such as POST requests that create an entity, will be subjected to the corresponding permissions for that entity. It is important to understand that Drupal does not simply open up an API without the proper checks in place that requests are valid.

Requests to web service APIs make use of several HTTP conventions. Aside from the URL, the header and request body are critical for web service APIs given the conventions for both JSON:API and REST. The header is common to provide authorization, specify the type of request, and specify the desired data format. The request body also must provide the correct format and data. For instance, a POST request to create a user must have a request body with all of the relevant structured content for the user and provide all of the necessary credentials in the header.

Modules and configuration

Drupal core offers two common modules that provide web services. Both are tied to their specific web standards and can be configured to provide different functionality.

JSON:API

JSON:API works more seamlessly with Drupal entities. It can automatically create API endpoints for Drupal entities tied to standard request types, formats, and more.

Once enabled, the module configuration is quite simple, as seen in the following figure from **Home | Administration | Configuration | Web services | JSON:API**:

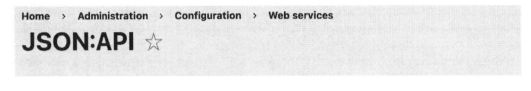

Allowed operations

⦿ Accept only JSON:API read operations.

◯ Accept all JSON:API create, read, update, and delete operations.

Warning: Only enable all operations if the site requires it. Learn more about securing your site with JSON:API.

Save configuration

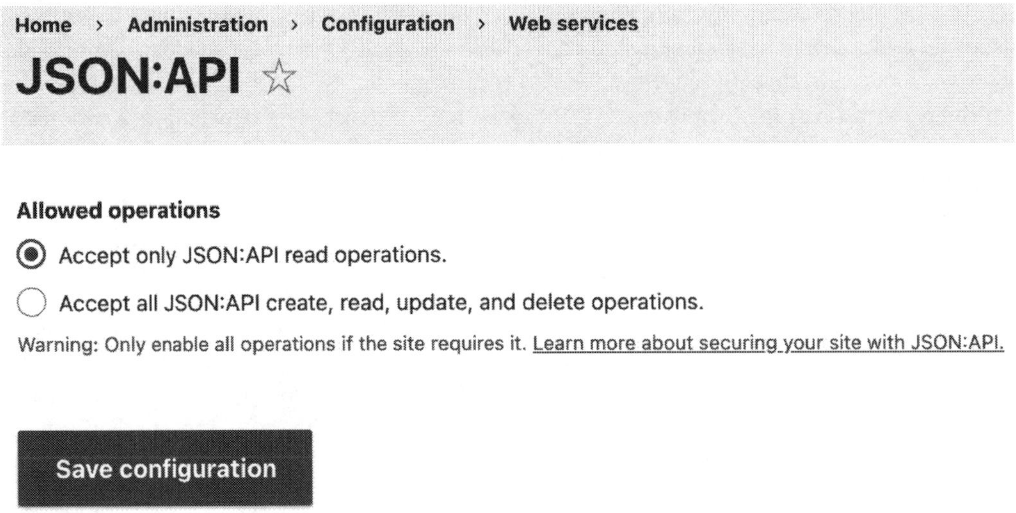

Figure 20.1 - Configuration page for the JSON:API module

As shown in *Figure 20.1*, the module differentiates between read operations and other transactions that can modify data in the Drupal application. The module handles the rest. All entities are then exposed as resources with their specific operations.

Sometimes, more granular configuration is welcomed, such as being able to enable or disable what resources are exposed. The contributed **JSON:API Extras** module provides this. The following figure shows additional configuration added by the module, found at **Home/Administration/Configuration/Web services/JSON:API/Extras**:

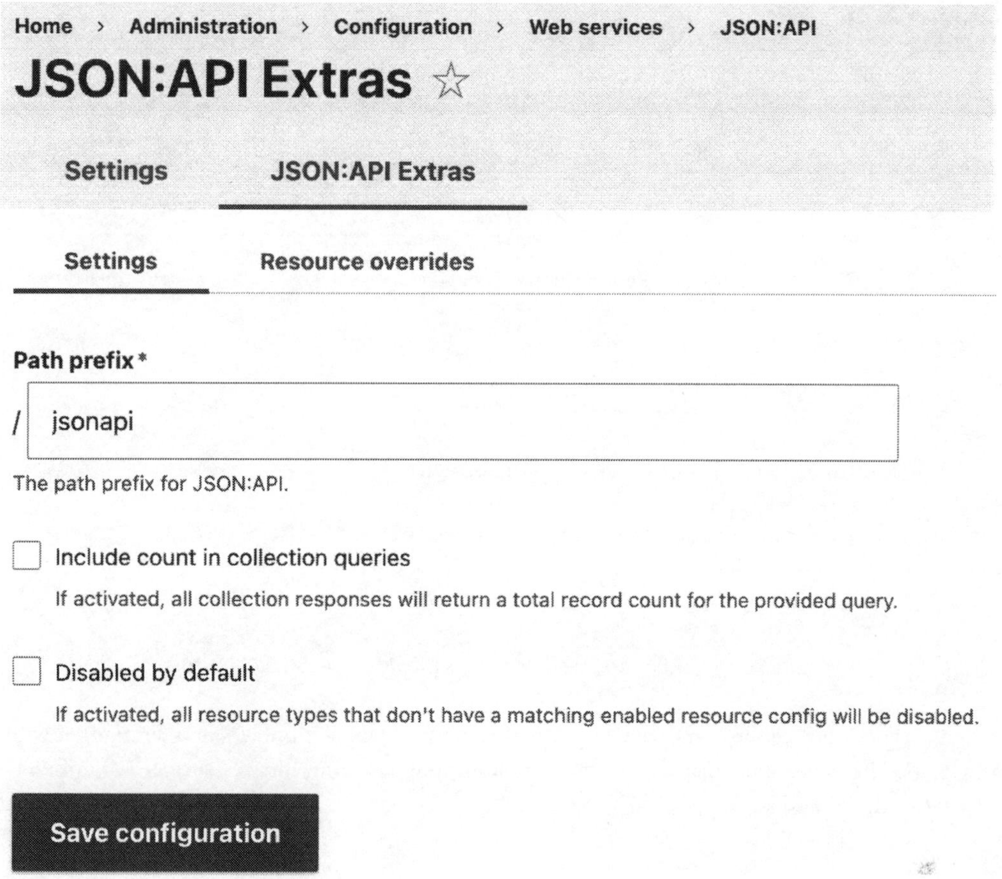

Home > Administration > Configuration > Web services > JSON:API

JSON:API Extras ☆

Settings   **JSON:API Extras**

Settings   **Resource overrides**

Path prefix *

/   jsonapi

The path prefix for JSON:API.

☐ Include count in collection queries

If activated, all collection responses will return a total record count for the provided query.

☐ Disabled by default

If activated, all resource types that don't have a matching enabled resource config will be disabled.

Save configuration

Figure 20.2 - Additional configuration provided by JSON:API Extras

The path prefix allows a site builder to override the out-of-the-box location for the JSON:API endpoints. Also, the option for disabled by default changes JSON:API's automatic behavior of enabling everything. The **Resource overrides** tab, found at `Home/Administration/Configuration/Web services/JSON:API/Extras/ resource_types`, provides the ability for fine-grained modification of which resources are enabled or disabled. This is shown in the following figure:

^ **Enabled Resources**

Name	Path	State	Operations
block--block	/jsonapi/block/block	Default	Overwrite
block_content--basic	/jsonapi/block_content/basic	Default	Overwrite
block_content_type-- block_content_type	/jsonapi/block_content_type/block_content_type	Default	Overwrite
comment--comment	/jsonapi/comment/comment	Default	Overwrite
comment_type-- comment_type	/jsonapi/comment_type/comment_type	Default	Overwrite
contact_form--contact_form	/jsonapi/contact_form/contact_form	Default	Overwrite
contact_message--feedback	/jsonapi/contact_message/feedback	Default	Overwrite
contact_message--personal	/jsonapi/contact_message/personal	Default	Overwrite

Figure 20.3 - Configuring resource types provided by JSON:API Extras

Resource types, such as those shown in *Figure 20.3*, can be enabled, disabled, and configured within JSON:API. This is the logic for configuring specific endpoints within the web service API, often tied to specific entities and bundles.

REST

Drupal's RESTful Web Services module provides a general framework for web service APIs. It offers common data formats (JSON, XML, and more) and allows for custom REST resource definition. This framework is extensible programmatically. Out of the box, the module does not have an administrative UI as it primarily relies on modules and the application's configuration. Once enabled, all node-related REST web services are enabled.

Drupal core also has a module for HTTP Basic Authentication. This complements the REST API, as a username and password can be passed through the request header. Once enabled, this provides a mechanism for API requests to pass Drupal credentials through a request. Doing so provides the authorization with Drupal's permission system.

The contributed module REST UI (https://www.drupal.org/project/restui) offers a UI to view and configure REST web services. This helps offer more conventional configuration methods and helps administrators see what is configured. The following figure is what is available from this UI:

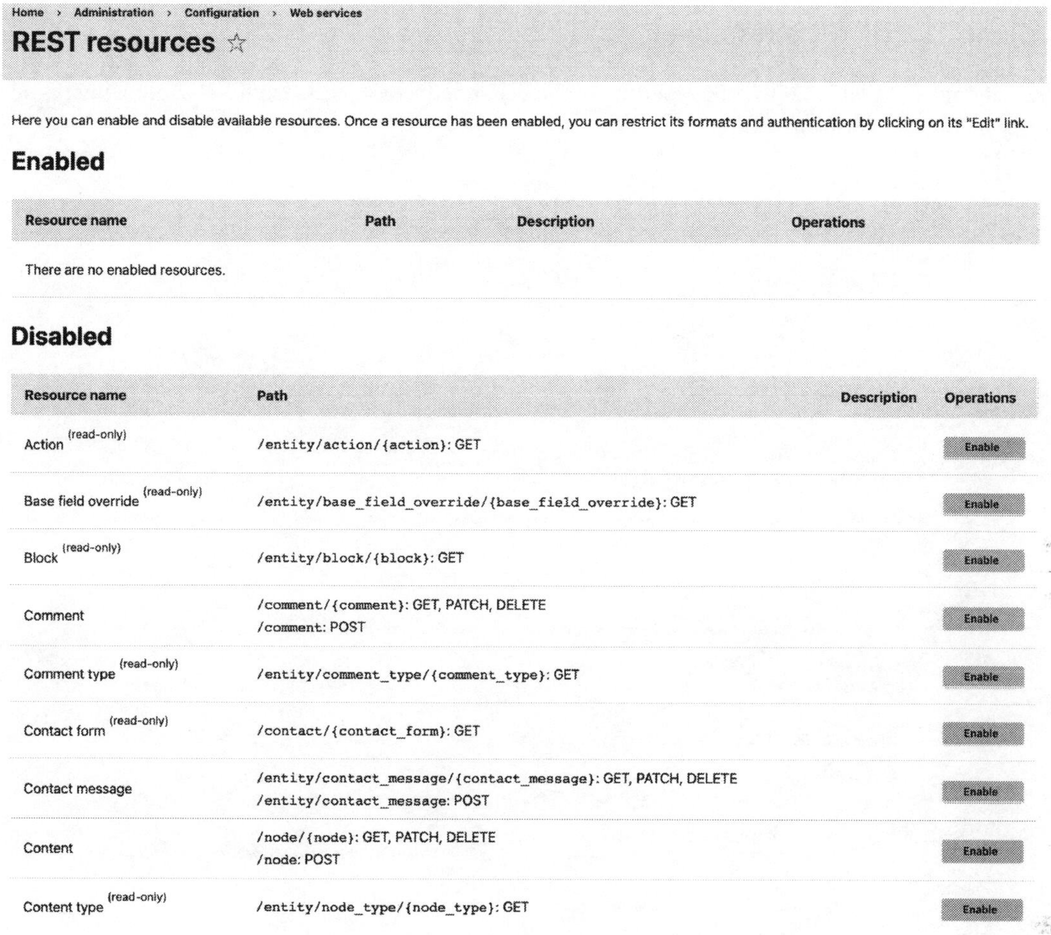

Figure 20.4 - Endpoint management by REST UI

REST UI shows which modules, such as the node module, provide REST resources and allow for these resources to be enabled or disabled individually. The figure also shows the available request types tied to the resources.

After configuring endpoints in Drupal, API endpoints can then be invoked through tools that use web services for interoperability.

Using web services

Any system that is capable of making an HTTP request can use web services. Covering those topics would be outside of the scope of this book given many different languages, platforms, tools, and capabilities have some support for web services. This section outlines how to invoke endpoints in Drupal using the aforementioned features.

Basic JSON:API examples

A catalog of available JSON:API requests can be generated from /jsonapi. The following figure shows part of a sample response:

```json
{
  "jsonapi": {
    "version": "1.0",
    "meta": {
      "links": {
        "self": {
          "href": "http://jsonapi.org/format/1.0/"
        }
      }
    }
  },
  "data": [],
  "meta": {
    "links": {
      "me": {
        "meta": {
          "id": "bb1ed17f-1c56-411b-ac42-eef44a0afdbc"
        },
        "href": "https://master-kglzbh5lomngac76tms8gf9hqv8irafd.tugboatqa.com/jsonapi/user/user/bb1ed17f-1c56-411b-ac42-eef44a0afdbc"
      }
    }
  },
  "links": {
    "action--action": {
      "href": "https://master-kglzbh5lomngac76tms8gf9hqv8irafd.tugboatqa.com/jsonapi/action/action"
    },
    "base_field_override--base_field_override": {
      "href": "https://master-kglzbh5lomngac76tms8gf9hqv8irafd.tugboatqa.com/jsonapi/base_field_override/base_field_override"
    },
    "block--block": {
      "href": "https://master-kglzbh5lomngac76tms8gf9hqv8irafd.tugboatqa.com/jsonapi/block/block"
    },
    "block_content--basic": {
      "href": "https://master-kglzbh5lomngac76tms8gf9hqv8irafd.tugboatqa.com/jsonapi/block_content/basic"
    },
    "block_content_type--block_content_type": {
      "href": "https://master-kglzbh5lomngac76tms8gf9hqv8irafd.tugboatqa.com/jsonapi/block_content_type/block_content_type"
    },
    "comment--comment": {
      "href": "https://master-kglzbh5lomngac76tms8gf9hqv8irafd.tugboatqa.com/jsonapi/comment/comment"
    },
    "comment_type--comment_type": {
      "href": "https://master-kglzbh5lomngac76tms8gf9hqv8irafd.tugboatqa.com/jsonapi/comment_type/comment_type"
    },
    "contact_form--contact_form": {
      "href": "https://master-kglzbh5lomngac76tms8gf9hqv8irafd.tugboatqa.com/jsonapi/contact_form/contact_form"
    },
    "contact_message--feedback": {
      "href": "https://master-kglzbh5lomngac76tms8gf9hqv8irafd.tugboatqa.com/jsonapi/contact_message/feedback"
    },
```

Figure 20.5 - JSON:API catalog response

This response provides a machine-readable response with a series of links to get to the configured resources. Each of the links provides more detail based on the resource. For instance, clicking on the link for block--block provides a catalog of blocks (metadata and block placement), as shown in the following figure:

```json
            }
        },
    {
        "type": "block--block",
        "id": "be73a0c2-9ab8-4e41-9ab2-c094c8791b78",
        "links": {
            "self": {
                "href": "https://master-
                kglzbh5lomngac76tms8gf9hqv8irafd.tugboatqa.com/jsonapi/block/block/be73a0c2-9ab8-4e41-9ab2-
                c094c8791b78"
            }
        },
        "attributes": {
            "langcode": "en",
            "status": true,
            "dependencies": {
                "theme": [
                    "claro"
                ]
            },
            "drupal_internal__id": "claro_primary_local_tasks",
            "theme": "claro",
            "region": "header",
            "weight": 0,
            "provider": null,
            "plugin": "local_tasks_block",
            "settings": {
                "id": "local_tasks_block",
                "label": "Primary tabs",
                "label_display": "0",
                "provider": "core",
                "primary": true,
                "secondary": false
            },
            "visibility": []
        }
    },
    {
        "type": "block--block",
        "id": "a4249f6b-e324-4854-88e3-73884e41fd72",
        "links": {
            "self": {
                "href": "https://master-
                kglzbh5lomngac76tms8gf9hqv8irafd.tugboatqa.com/jsonapi/block/block/a4249f6b-e324-4854-88e3-
                73884e41fd72"
            }
        },
```

Figure 20.6 - JSON:API block catalog response

Getting to the structured data for each block is available through the link from the block catalog. This type of functionality can be expected for each entity and entity type given they are exposed as resources.

Basic REST API examples

The REST UI module provides an administrative interface to manage REST API endpoints outside of configuration. To enable node content to be served via REST API, the `node/{node}` endpoint must be enabled with the `GET`. A `_format` parameter and a data format value must be passed to access a node. The following figure shows an example of a node with an ID of 1 generated from `node/1?_format=json`:

```
← → C    🔒 master-kglzbh5lomngac76tms8gf9hqv8irafd.tugboatqa.com/node/1?_format=json
```

```json
▼ {
  ▼ "nid": [
    ▼ {
        "value": 1
      }
    ],
  ▼ "uuid": [
    ▼ {
        "value": "90ee4135-a73f-41f3-9d9f-03c17a8fa82a"
      }
    ],
  ▼ "vid": [
    ▼ {
        "value": 1
      }
    ],
  ▼ "langcode": [
    ▼ {
        "value": "en"
      }
    ],
  ▼ "type": [
    ▼ {
        "target_id": "article",
        "target_type": "node_type",
        "target_uuid": "2ef589a8-3963-4c81-b99b-33409698a441"
      }
    ],
  ▼ "revision_timestamp": [
    ▼ {
        "value": "2023-09-24T18:36:06+00:00",
        "format": "Y-m-d\\TH:i:sP"
      }
    ],
  ▼ "revision_uid": [
    ▼ {
        "target_id": 1,
```

Figure 20.7 - Example REST API response for a test node

The response returns JSON structured data for all of the entity's fields and metadata. Please note that there is not a base API endpoint like there is with the JSON:API module. Simply going to `node/1` without a `_format` parameter would attempt to render node 1 as HTML through Drupal's standard rendering.

REST clients

Several REST API clients are available to help with debugging. Tools such as Postman or various REST-related browser extensions can be very helpful in debugging requests, modifying headers, passing various parameters, performing basic authorization, and more. This can help work locally as well.

Summary

Drupal offers native web service API features that are complementary to its structured content. APIs leveraging Drupal's RESTful Web Services or JSON:API modules can be used for decoupled or headless applications that build custom frontends outside of Drupal or connect with the Internet of Things, mobile apps, and more. Drupal helps provide serialization, authorization tied to its permission system, and common data formats (JSON and XML). Various contributed modules help manage these APIs and provide fine-grained controls.

The next chapter covers the basics of Drupal's migration system, which is the primary tool used to migrate content into a Drupal application.

21
Migrating Content into Drupal

Drupal offers a migration system named Migrate that allows for one-time or continuous content migration into Drupal. Migrate is built on a set of standard concepts and tooling that help offer a standard to perform content-related migrations. This includes common **extract, transform, load (ETL)** practices such as source-to-destination mapping and data transformation. Migrate also offers a framework that can be used for more customized needs. It enables various use cases, such as moving content from Drupal 7 to Drupal 10, moving from WordPress, and performing ongoing feed-based content updates.

In this chapter, we're going to cover the following main topics:

- Migration concepts
- The Migrate system
- Use cases

Migration concepts

Enterprises often have their existing websites and systems, but they may wish to move onto Drupal. To accommodate this, Drupal has a core Migrate system to perform migration. Migration is then made easier through a common set of tools, practices, systems, and frameworks that offer repeatability, predictability, and consistency.

Migrate itself is built from a conventional ETL convention. This is a common design pattern in software engineering and not specific to Drupal. Drupal applies this concept through sources and destinations. Content is extracted from a source. Migrate's tooling, including features within Drupal, processes that content into a raw data format. Finally, the raw data is loaded into the destination through serialization. This process maintains the foundational, underlying design of the Migrate system.

Migration brings a lot of complexity to both the sources and destinations involved in migrating content. Sources can be any content source, and that content, in a general sense, can be both structured and unstructured. As a destination, Drupal itself allows for open-ended configurability in its underlying content structures. This mandates a lot of application and use case-specific complexity to be introduced to every migration. While a site builder should have as much automation as possible to perform migrations, it is not practical to expect every configuration and every contributed and custom module to have a smooth path. As such, migrations can be a lot of work and require significant effort in both code and configuration to get them perfect.

Migrations are a way to promote data integrity. A migration is transactional. It presents an opportunity to transform data from one source to a destination. It is not assumed the data in the source promotes data integrity. It's common to find edge cases where content authors did not follow conventions. Maybe an author did not use a conventional date format, misspelled words, or even placed content in the wrong place. Migrations present opportunities to clean up mistakes to promote data integrity, and the Migrate system offers the capabilities to do so.

The Migrate system

Foundationally, the Migrate system is a backend API framework built around ETL concepts. Given the need to support diverse source and destination requirements, it must be highly configurable to work properly. This framework has been used to allow developers to address all of the migration-specific needs with defined plugins, configurations, and so on.

Beyond the API, the Migrate system includes the state of the migrations specific to the Drupal application in which migrations are run. This state maintains useful information, such as which migrations are registered on the application, what content has been successfully or unsuccessfully migrated per migration, what content has not yet been migrated per migration, and execution logs of every migration execution. Given the Migrate system is specific to a Drupal application, developers are empowered to run migrations on their local systems or non-production environments before running a migration on production.

Three Migrate modules come with Drupal core. The first is the `migrate` module that provides the underlying framework. The `migrate drupal` module is a utility built on top of the framework that tries to provide an automated migration utility from Drupal 6 or 7. That module also has an optional UI module named `Migrate Drupal UI`.

A significant portion of migration definitions are declarative YAML files. Modules can define their migrations by placing a YAML file within a `migrations` directory of a module. The convention follows a `[migration-id].yml` file with the configuration of the migration. The following shows an `example_migration.yml` file, which was exemplified on `drupal.org` (`https://www.drupal.org/docs/drupal-apis/migrate-api/migrate-api-overview#s-glossary`):

```
id: example_migration
label: 'Example migration'
source:
  constants:
    title_suffix: ' (example)'
```

```
      text_format: plain_text
  plugin: embedded_data
  data_rows:
    - unique_id: 1
      src_title: 'DRUPAL MIGRATIONS'
      src_content: 'Example content'
    - unique_id: 2
      src_title: 'DRUPAL UPGRADES'
      src_content: 'Example content'
  ids:
    unique_id:
      type: integer
              process:
  pseudo_title:
    - plugin: callback
      source: src_title
      callable: mb_strtolower
    - plugin: callback
      callable: ucwords
  title:
    plugin: concat
    source:
      - '@pseudo_title'
      - constants/title_suffix
  body/value: src_content
  body/format: constants/text_format
destination:
  plugin: 'entity:node'
  default_bundle: page
```

The migration YAML file shows how a migration definition invokes plugins. Three primary types of plugins map to the ETL process. All plugin types are provided by code in a module:

- **Source plugins**: A source plugin allows for data extraction

- **Destination plugins**: A process plugin is responsible for the transformation

- **Processor plugins**: A destination plugin manages where the data is loaded in the Drupal application

This example demonstrates the ETL primitives in the following ways.

Extract

Under source, the migration definition leverages the *embedded_data* plugin and provides the plugin-specific parameters necessary to process the migration. This helps identify unique identifiers, titles, and various processing logic.

Transform

The process block provides the mapping and the transformations. Every child element listed under process is a field that is either generated or directly pulled from the source. The example demonstrates transformations through rudimentary PHP functions, such as ucwords and mb_strtolower, to perform transformations of specific field values.

Load

The destination block provides the specific mapping into Drupal. In this example, content is imported into a node entity with a page bundle. The default_bundle attribute is a specific parameter of the specified plugin. Note that the example YAML file provides the entire definition for the ETL.

Before developing a new plugin, check out the out-of-the-box plugins available in core, which are defined here: https://api.drupal.org/api/drupal/namespace/Drupal!migrate!Plugin!migrate!source.

Custom events

One other aspect of the framework is events. Events provide another means for modules to customize at specific points in a migration. Events can be implemented by harnessing the EventSubscriber capabilities when developing Drupal modules. For instance, events exist for pre- and post-import that can alter a Drupal application before and after a migration occurs. A pre-migration event is common to disable **CRON (a Linux-based job scheduler)**, turn off any email notifications triggered by new nodes, or disable specific modules that may interfere with migration. A post-migration event can then restore the overrides after the migration finishes. The migration system has several other events that can perform actions where relevant. A full list of events can be found on drupal.org (https://www.drupal.org/docs/drupal-apis/migrate-api/migrate-api-overview#s-events-and-hooks).

Operating migrations

The Migrate system does not formally have an administrative UI, although one is contributed on drupal.org. Drush commands are the best means of getting the status of migrations and performing migration-related actions. The following examples highlight how to use Drush to perform some common commands. Note that each of these commands has various options that can readily extend the basic commands captured here:

```
$ drush migrate:status
```

This reports the status of all migrations found in the Drupal application; more details can be found on drush.org (https://www.drush.org/12.x/commands/migrate_status/):

```
$ drush migrate:import [migration-id]
```

This performs the migration for the specified migration; more details can be found on drush.org (`https://www.drush.org/12.x/commands/migrate_import/`):

```
$ drush migrate:rollback [migration-id]
```

This rolls back a specific migration within a Drupal application; more details can be found on drush.org (`https://www.drush.org/12.x/commands/migrate_rollback/`):

```
$ drush migrate:message [migration-id] -verbose
```

This shows all relevant messages captured during the execution of a migration with various levels of verbosity; more details can be found on drush.org (`https://www.drush.org/12.x/commands/migrate_rollback/`).

Contributed modules

Several contributed modules extend the out-of-the-box Migrate system found in core. While these are optional, the use cases are common and the modules are often used.

The first is the Migrate Plus contributed module. Most notably, it provides a robust set of extended ETL plugins that extend support for file-based streams, JSON, XML, various processors, and so on. Migrate Plus allows for migrations to be managed within the site config. It also provides a useful migration grouping that can help organize various migrations.

Migrations do not need to only run on demand. Migrations can be scheduled or triggered through CRON. There are contributed modules for both `migrate scheduler` and `migrate cron`. This use case is covered in more detail in the following section.

The Migrate system provides all of the tooling, systems, and processes to customize, run, manage, and roll back migrations within a Drupal application. A comprehensive overview of the Migrate system can be found in drupal.org's online documentation (`https://www.drupal.org/docs/drupal-apis/migrate-api/migrate-api-overview`).

Use cases

There are several use cases in which the Migrate system can be used.

Migrations often are designed as one-time or ongoing (continuous migrations). One-time migrations pull from sources only once. It is common to move from one **content management system (CMS)** to another, where Drupal is the new destination and the old system gets shut down. The migration moves the data only once into the new system. Ongoing migrations are often used when data is pulled from a third-party destination that changes with time and is leveraged by the Drupal application. Ongoing migrations can be executed periodically via drush calls with CRON directly on the server, or through the use of the migrate scheduler or migrate Cron contributed modules.

An example of this could be a daily migration that pulls from public JSON web service feeds into Drupal. The following YAML file, which leverages the Migrate Plus and Migrate Tools modules, defines a migration definition that pulls articles from the *New York Times* RSS feed and stores it into a hypothetical nyt_articles content type:

```yaml
id: nyt_migration
label: 'New York Times RSS feed'
status: true

source:
  plugin: url
  data_fetcher_plugin: http
  urls: 'https://rss.nytimes.com/services/xml/rss/nyt/HomePage.xml'
  data_parser_plugin: simple_xml

  item_selector: /rss/channel/item
  fields:
    -
      name: guid
      label: GUID
      selector: guid
    -
      name: title
      label: Title
      selector: title
    -
      name: pub_date
      label: 'Publication date'
      selector: pubDate
    -
      name: link
      label: 'Origin link'
      selector: link
    -
      name: summary
      label: Summary
      selector: 'description'

  ids:
    guid:
      type: string

destination:
  plugin: 'entity:node'
```

```
process:
  title: title
  field_remote_url: link
  body: summary
  created:
    plugin: format_date
    from_format: 'D, d M Y H:i:s O'
    to_format: 'U'
    source: pub_date
  status:
    plugin: default_value
    default_value: 1
  type:
    plugin: default_value
    default_value: nyt_articles
```

After defining the migration, the Migrate Scheduler module can be configured to invoke the migration daily. The following code can be added in `settings.php`:

```
$config['migrate_scheduler']['migrations'] = [
  'nyt_migration' => [
    'time' => 86400,
  ],
];
```

The code added to `settings.php` will then trigger the `nyt_migration` migration each day (84,600 seconds).

Other use cases are also relevant. When moving from an existing CMS, Drupal has capabilities for common use cases. A contributed module exists to migrate from WordPress. As mentioned, Core has a module to migrate from Drupal 6 or 7. Several source plugins already exist for various web service feeds, which are offered by a broad set of CMS systems. This aids in creating migrations based on XML, JSON, and so on.

The contributed module Migrate Tools also has useful features. Its main use case is providing a migration UI. Before Drush 11, it was also used to offer all of the Drush commands related to the Migrate system. Those were subsequently moved into Drush itself.

Debugging migrations can also be tricky. Migrate Devel extends the popular Devel module, which is a common tool for developers to create modules. The module offers more fine-grained reporting of rows and statuses as a migration is run. This helps expose what happens during migrations.

Summary

Drupal's Migrate system provides a standard ETL-based framework used for one-time and ongoing migrations. The ETL is implemented through YAML file definitions, `source/processing/ destination plugins`, and common tools to run, roll back, and view the status of migrations. Modules can be developed to extend the out-of-the-box plugins and harness Migrate's event system for custom processing. The Migrate system helps address use cases where an existing CMS needs to be moved to a Drupal application, or periodic processing of web service feeds.

The next chapter covers multisite management in Drupal, which can be helpful to run multiple sites from the same code base.

22
Multisite Management

Drupal allows you to manage many sites with the same code through its multisite feature. This can be useful in many settings where it's desirable to have parity across a large number of Drupal applications. Leveraging one codebase allows for a level of scale where you can manage a lot of sites uniformly way. However, this comes with some benefits and drawbacks that adopters should be mindful of before they implement.

In this chapter we're going to cover the following main topics:

- The multisite feature
- Benefits
- Drawbacks
- Automating deployments across many sites

The multisite feature

Every Drupal codebase has a site's directory. Single site instances leverage a `sites/default` directory to store the Drupal application settings, which includes its corresponding database. Another standard convention is to place custom and contributed modules within the `sites/all` directory. The intention for this convention is to potentially share code. The "default" site still has access to the code found in `sites/all`.

`Default` does not have to be the only site if used at all. Suppose a university wants to offer each department its website but wants to maintain all websites through centralized IT. One Drupal codebase could be leveraged that has a specific site directory for every department in the university. The same modules and features can then be installed on each site given they're all running the same code.

Each Drupal application has a `sites.php` file that helps map a domain to its corresponding site directory. This is not fully required. Site directories can also be a full domain name, but this is less ideal when working with environments. An example of a `sites.php` file is shown here:

```
$sites['compsci.university.com'] = 'compsci';
$sites['physics.university.com'] = 'physics';
$sites['literature.university.com'] = 'literature';
```

The example helps Drupal process requests from specific domains to the corresponding compsci, physics, and literature site directories.

Also, note that leveraging multisite requires work on servers. If you're leveraging Apache, each domain would need to be its virtual host that points to the same Drupal docroot where the code is installed. The code does not need to be copied for each docroot since the Drupal application can derive the correct size from the `sites.php` file.

Multisite is a feature that helps the same Drupal codebase run multiple websites. This can easily be configured and often requires additional databases and filesystems per site.

Benefits

Drupal developers get major benefits and significant drawbacks with the multisite feature.

The main benefit is consistent governance to help manage sites at scale. Imagine having to manage hundreds or even thousands of similar Drupal applications. Performing code updates site by site would be extremely laborious.

Another benefit is growth. New sites can be added at any point and they can build off of the existing systems and code implemented. Practices established for leveraging multisite can readily be extended to more sites.

Drawbacks

The main drawback is failure at scale. Code updates can be problematic, especially given Drupal's value proposition is its extensibility. Updates that introduce regressions are not caught on just one or two sites, they're deployed to all of them. And, once the code is updated, the Drupal application needs to be updated. This must happen immediately. It is impossible to manage failures in just one site; each site needs to be remediated. And, it's common that a code-level failure applies to one if not all, sites.

To do any level of testing before deploying to a large number of sites, it is important to use environments and perform rigorous testing against multiple sites. Check logs for anomalies and run automated tests. All of these steps should be done before a production deployment to mitigate risk.

A similar approach is leveraging a shared codebase with orchestration but without multisite. Developers often use Git repositories to manage Drupal codebases. The same Git repositories can be cloned for any number of sites, even a large number. Some orchestration can exist to perform updates, but developers have the discretion to create orchestration capable of updating sites in batches through progressive updates.

Automating deployments across many sites

When leveraging multisite, it is important to consider automation. Updating every site in a large-scale Drupal multisite implementation would be difficult, especially given the frequency with which updates happen.

Drush provides helpful commands to manage this.

```
$ drush site:alias > list-of-sites.txt
```

The preceding command prints a list of site aliases for a Drupal application (https://www.drush. org/12.x/commands/site_alias/).

```
$ while read s; do \
drush sql-dump > backup-$s.sql \
drush "@$s" deploy \
done <list-of-sites.txt
```

This small script takes the results of each alias from the previous command and performs a deployment. While it is a simple example, a script could then invoke rollback logic upon error.

```
$ if grep -Fxq "error" list-of-sites.txt \
then \
while read s; do \
drush "@$s" sql-import -y < backup-$s.sql \
done <list-of-sites.txt \
fi
```

It is highly recommended that you stage down multisites into non-production environments to test a production deployment.

Summary

Drupal multisite can be an option if you wish to run a large number of similar sites with the same codebase. The benefits of consistency and centralized management of multisite can be appealing over maintaining a large number of single Drupal applications. However, code deployments and testing can become complicated, especially if regressions are introduced.

That concludes this book. Drupal is a powerful tool that covers different personas, such as a site builder, developer, site administrator, and even user. It has many features that can be enabled and configured based on the needs of an application. It also has an underlying framework that can be used to extend for custom modules and themes. While the book would not effectively be able to cover every topic and every technology in depth, hopefully, the book offered a broad overview that proved useful.

We express our sincere gratitude for accompanying us to the end of this book. Again, thank you and wishing you success!

Appendix A - Drupal Terminology

Drupal has a lot of "Drupal-isms" that define key concepts or features. This terminology is fairly niche. Understanding this terminology is critical for ongoing success building Drupal applications. It can be as simple as being able to understand documentation to being able to effectively file issues in project issue queues. Terminology is commonly used on project pages and builders can rapidly evaluate what a module does simply by reading the description and understanding the problems solved.

Drupal leverages common words or phrases that have specific meaning in the community. Understanding this terminology is a significant enabler for those wanting to learn Drupal. Site builders who know the terminology can more rapidly evaluate community projects. Developers who read documentation can more effectively create custom modules. And, any community member up to speed on "Drupal-isms" will be far more prepared to collaborate and get help from community members. While this chapter may not cover everything, it should provide a foundation for your journey in Drupal.

This chapter can serve as a quick reference to help review terminology, as needed.

Terminology

- **Drupal**: An open source digital experience application and framework.
- **Core**: The basic features and framework required for any Drupal application.
- **Project**: A feature or capability that builds upon Drupal's framework
- **Module**: A project that changes or enhances Drupal's backend behavior or functionality
- **Theme**: A project that changes the look and feel of Drupal's rendering or administrative area
- **Site Building**: An activity that installs and configures projects within a Drupal application without hands-on coding
- **Theming**: An activity that creates Drupal themes that includes CSS, JavaScript, templates, and metadata
- **Templates**: Markup and variables represented as Twig that get converted to rendered content during the render pipeline
- **Issue**: A specific bug, feature request, or help request filed into a project's issue queue by a community member with a status, comments, relevant project version, and other metadata.

- **Issue Queue**: A record of all issues for a specific project.

- **Entity types**: A data structure that consists of fields and properties.

- **Entity**: An instance of an entity type

- **Bundle**: An extension of an entity type for categorization and/or additional fields or properties.

- **Property**: Static metadata of an entity

- **Field**: A specific, atomic attribute of an entity used to organize content with a defined field type

- **Field Type**: A specific definition and validation of field values for data integrity

- **Fieldable**: A behavior of an entity type that allows for fields to be added to entity types.

- **Node**: An entity of a content type that renders content

- **Content Type**: A bundle for nodes

- **Taxonomy**: A type of entity for hierarchical categorization

- **Term**: An entity within a specific taxonomy

- **Blocks**: A fieldable type of entity used for structuring reusable content segments that are shared across pages

- **Block Type**: A bundle for blocks

- **Block**: An entity of a block type

- **Paragraphs**: A popular contributed module that provides structured, fieldable content components, similar to blocks, that has a vibrant ecosystem of sub and contributed modules

- **Paragraph Type**: Different paragraph content structures

- **Menu**: A hierarchical entity type used for handling navigation links as menu items

- **Path**: The URI used for Drupal's routing to map a browser request to Drupal's rendering system

- **Revision**: A log of changes to an entity that allow for reversion and tracking of changes

- **Watchdog**: Drupal's logging system that covers system logs, Drupal application logs, and more

- **Migrate**: A subsystem in Drupal used to manage and execute ETL (extract, transform, and load) commonly used to load content into a Drupal application

- **Migration**: Logic and directives executed to migrate specific content, typically creating Drupal entities

- **Configuration**: A Drupal subsystem used to manage Drupal core and project settings that modify Drupal behaviors; loaded by the database but managed and synchronized through the filesystem

- **Contrib**: A synonym for Drupal's open source contributed community projects, often differentiated from core

- **Custom**: Drupal projects that are created only for specific application requirements and not contributed to the open source community

- **Drush**: Drupal's contributed command line interface with commands that execute on a Drupal application

- **Files**: A subsystem used to manage file content for file fields or files uploaded through the WYSIWYG

- **Media**: A subsystem that manages uploaded and external digital assets within a Drupal application; has a large number of submodules and contributed community projects capable of commonly supporting advanced features and external platforms

- **Image Styles**: Configuration that transforms uploaded image files to various sizes and formats

- **Views**: A feature of Drupal that queries entities, offers display settings, and manages different dynamic outputs like pages, blocks, or various data formats

- **User**: A subsystem used for allowing people to authenticate into Drupal to perform content management, site building, operations, or manage configuration

- **Permission**: A capability granted to a Drupal user to perform a specific action.

- **Static**: Aspects of a Drupal application that are fixed and cannot readily be updated through the content management features or through configuration

- **Dynamic**: Aspects of a Drupal application that are not fixed and can readily be updated through the content management features or through configuration

- **Composer**: Drupal's selected code dependency management tool widely adopted by the PHP ecosystem

- **Render**: The logic used by Drupal's application to leverage the context of a specific request, perform processing, and return dynamic output that represents the provided context

- **Platform**: Often refers to the environments, tools, and servers that are used to run and manage a Drupal application

- **Framework**: A collection of APIs and conventions provided by Drupal core and installed projects that allow for developers to create custom projects that extend Drupal's application

- **API**: A defined, standardized interface used to allow developers to create software that integrates with a specific Drupal subsystem

- **JSON API**: Drupal core's adopted web service standard often used to deliver Drupal content in a conventional data format to external clients

- **WYSIWYG**: A type of field in Drupal that allows for less structured content by giving content authors more autonomy to style and organize content within one field

- **CKEditor**: An external open source project adopted by Drupal core for a WYSIWYG feature

Index

A

administrative backend 5, 6
administrator 100
admin theme 14
advanced search 144
anonymous role 100
Antibot module 13
application architecture 19, 20
  code 19
  database 19
  files 19
ArgoCD 200
assets 123
  use cases 124, 138, 139
attributes object
  working with 234
automated testing
  reference link 214
automatic updates 44

B

backend architecture 21, 22
backend development 59
base entities 82

base themes 226
  Bootstrap barrio 226
  Radix 226
  theme, creating from 226
  USWDS base 226
basic configuration 60
  configuration changes 61, 62
  post-installation configuration 61
basic JSON:API examples 248, 249
basic REST API examples 250, 251
block element modifier (BEM)
    architecture 235
blocks 175
  managing 175-177
Bootstrap 226
Bootstrap barrio
  URL 226
Breakpoints 130
Drupal 10 44
  automatic updates 44
  decoupled menus 45
  project browser 45
  recipes 44, 45
bundles 82

C

caches
  disabling 220-223
case studies 8
CKEditor 5 41
Claro 14, 23, 42, 43
codebase 50
code maintenance process 69
  typical code maintenance process 70-72
code management and deployment concept
  reviewing 69, 70
code-related maintenance 68
common patterns 211
  Drupal patterns 213, 214
  PHP patterns 211, 212
  Symfony capabilities 212
community
  resources and tools 37, 38
community modules 13
  Antibot 13
  Google Analytics 13
  Metatag 14
  Pathauto 13
  Redirect 13
  Sitewide Alerts 14
  Taxonomy Menu 13
  Webform 13
Components 238
  URL 238
Composer 50
  basics 204
  commands 52-54
  common commands 205
  projects 51, 52
  reference link, for documentation 204
  setup 204
composer.json file 21, 50, 204

composer.lock file 50, 204
concepts 209, 210
  early Drupal concepts 210
  modern Drupal concepts 210
configuration entities 83
configuration schemas 83
contact forms 97, 151
  advanced forms 156
  basic information 151
  configuring 154
  Contact Block project 156
  extending 155
  management 152, 153
  robust email notifications 156
  spam prevention 156
  submissions 154
  submissions, viewing and managing 155
  user profile configuration 155
Contact module 151
  personal forms 152
  site-wide forms 152
container 213
content authoring 161, 162
  menus 170, 171
  nodes 162-170
  taxonomies 171
Content Construction Kit (CCK) module 13
content delivery network (CDN) 75
content editor 100
content entity 82
content management 102
content management system
    (CMS) 3, 4, 10, 79, 106, 257
Content Moderation module
  reference link 193
content translation module 92, 93
content-type listing 84
content types 83

Continuous Integration (CI) systems 72

continuous integration/continuous delivery (CI/CD) 25

contributed projects 183
  Gutenberg 184-187
  Paragraphs 184

contribution impact 37

contributions 14

Controllers 210, 212

core API 84

core themes 14
  Claro 14
  Olivero 14

create, read, update, and delete (CRUD) operations 129, 151

CSS
  working with 235

CSS and JS aggregation
  disabling 219, 220

CSS directory and files
  creating 225

custom block types 177, 178

D

data
  passing, from PHP into JS 237
  preprocessing 234, 235

database management system (DBMS) 106

database normalization 80

dblog module 27

decoupled menus 45

default layout
  configuring 179, 181

default roles
  administrator 100
  anonymous 100

  authenticated 100
  content editor 100

dependency injection 213

deployment 25

DevOps
  practices 205-208

dexter.info.yml
  creating 224
  libraries 224, 225

dexter.libraries.yml file
  creating 225

digital asset manager (DAM) 124

digital assets
  authoring 172-174

display modes
  defining 109
  overview 109
  RSS feed display, creating 120
  teaser display mode, creating
    for blogs 111, 112
  use cases 110

distributions 44

Drupal 3
  hosting 17
  installation 54
  installation, performing with Drush 58
  installation preparation 54
  post-installation 58
  UI-based installation 54-58

Drupal 10 39
  built 44
  new features 40-43
  platform requirements 40
  upgrade considerations 40

Drupal 11 39

Drupal accessibility tips 238
buttons, using as menu items 238
Drupal announce JS API 238
visually hidden CSS class 238
Drupal application
maintenance 24, 25
operations 25-27
Drupal architecture 18
application architecture 19-21
backend architecture 21, 22
frontend architecture 22, 23
infrastructure technical stack 19
Drupal Association 37
Drupal behaviors 236, 237
Drupal Commerce 37
DrupalCon 37
Drupal core 9, 10
contribution 32
development 12
features 10, 11
project page 31, 32
systems 11
Drupal modules 13
Drupal.org
basics 29-31
projects 32-36
Drupal patterns 213, 214
Drupal projects 12
Drupal themes 14
Drush 53
basics 202
common commands 203, 204
reference link, for documentation 202
setup 202

E

early Drupal concepts 210
endpoint 243
entities 81, 90
environments 25
EventDispatcher 212
events 212
EventSubscriber 210, 212
example models 83
extensibility 4, 5
Extensible Markup Language (XML) 243
extract, transform, load (ETL) 253

F

facets 149
fieldable 81
field formatters 82
fields 81
field storage 82
field types 82
field validators 82
field widgets 82
files 124
modules and configuration 125-128
subsystem 125
first normal form (1NF) 80
frameworks 4, 5
frontend architecture 22, 23
front-end development 59
frontend presentation layer 7, 8

G

GD2 129
Git
basics 200
common commands 201, 202
reference link, for documentation 200
setup 200
GitHub 200
GitLab 200
GitOps 200
Google Analytics module 13
graphical user interface (GUI) 200
Gutenberg 184-187
URL 184

H

help 62
hook system 210

I

images 129
modules and configuration 129-133
infrastructure platform maintenance 69
infrastructure technical stack 19

J

JavaScript
working with 236
JavaScript object notation (JSON) 243
JS directory
creating 225
JSON:API 244-246

L

**LAMP (Linux, Apache, MySQL,
and PHP) stack** 17
language module 91, 92
Layout Builder 175, 178, 179
setting up 183
Libraries API
CSS grouping 228
dependencies, managing 227
library, attaching through Twig template 226
library, loading globally through
theme's :.info.yml file 226
library, loading programmatically
through preprocess 227
module's or theme's libraries, overriding 227
weights, setting 228
working with 226
locale module 93, 94
logging and reporting 63-65

M

Macromedia Dreamweaver 3
maintenance
code-related maintenance 68
infrastructure platform maintenance 69
types 67
maintenance, best practices
backups 73
edge systems 75, 76
environment differences 73
managed platforms 74
product life cycles 75
SaaS services 74
system monitoring and tools 75
update frequency 75

major releases 40

Media 133

  modules and configuration 133-136

menus 170, 171

Metatag module 14

Migrate system 254, 255

  contributed modules 257

  custom events 256

  Extract 255

  Load 256

  operating migrations 256

  Transform 256

  use cases 257-259

migration

  concepts 253, 254

modern Drupal concepts 210

module definitions 214

  configuration 214, 215

  PHP code 215, 216

  templates 217

modules 13, 91, 103, 209

  content translation module 92, 93

  language module 91, 92

  locale module 93, 94

multilingual features 91

multisite feature 261, 262

  benefits 262

  deployments, automating

    across many sites 263

  drawbacks 262, 263

N

new features, Drupal 10

  CKEditor 5 41

  Claro 42, 43

  Olivero 41, 42

starter kit themes 43

Symfony 6.2 40

node-based default displays 110

nodes 82, 162

node-specific layouts 182, 183

npm 27

O

object-oriented (OO) 12

Olivero 14, 23, 41, 42

open-source community 29

operating system (OS) 24

out-of-the-box contributed modules,

    for paragraph types

  references 184

P

Paragraphs 184

  URL 184

patching

  reference link 60

Pathauto module 13

permissions 101

  access control 102

  content management 102

  definition 103, 104

  managing 102, 193

  types 102

personal forms 152

PHP

  preprocessing 234, 235

PHP patterns 211, 212

platform requirements

  hosting 18

Plugin API

reference link 213

procedural 210

project browser 45

projects 31, 209

on Drupal.org 32-36

R

Radix

URL 226

recipes 21, 44, 45

Redirect module 13

regions 224

relational database

best practices 80

release methodology 39

repository 200

**representational state transfer
(REST) 243-247**

requirements gathering 59

responsive image 131

REST clients 251

REST UI 247

URL 246

role entity 100

roles 100

configuring 101

default roles 100

routes 212

reference link 212

RSS feed display

creating 120

S

Scheduler module

reference link 193

Search API Autocomplete project 149

search configuration 145-147

search engine optimization (SEO) 14

search feature 141

backend 144

frontend 142-144

use cases 150

search function

implementing 141

search pages 147, 148

second normal form (2NF) 80

Services 210, 213

Single Directory Components (SDC) 237

reference link 237

site building 59, 60, 84-90

Sitewide Alerts module 14

site-wide forms 152

source of truth (SOT) 80

Stage File Proxy 71

Stark 23

Starter Kit themes 23, 43

states 190

managing 189

string-based translation 93

structured content 79-81

subscribe to and dispatch events

reference link 212

subtheming 226

Symfony 6.2 40

Symfony capabilities 212

container 213

controllers 212

dependency injection 213

events 212

routes 212

services 213

T

taxonomies 170, 171

Taxonomy Menu module 13

teaser display mode 110

   creating, for blogs 111, 112

templates

   creating 228, 229

   finding 228, 229

   working with 228

templates directory

   creating 225

theme debugging

   setting up 220-223

theme development

   setting up for 219

themes 14, 23

   creating, from base theme 226

   creating, from scratch 223

   creating, from theme generator tool 223

third normal form (3NF) 80

third-party indexes 149

transitions 191

   managing 190

Twig

   basics 229

   conditionals 230

   embed tag 231

   extends tag 231

   filters 232

   functions 232, 233

   include function 231

reference link, for documentation 229

ternary operators 230

variable, outputting in 229

Twig Field Value 238

   URL 238

Twig Tweak 238

   URL 238

typical code maintenance process 70-72

U

use case 83

user entity 95

users 90, 95

   features 96, 97

   management 97-100

USWDS base

   URL 226

V

verbose error messages

   turning on 223

Views 90

   creating, for blog listing with fields 115-118

   creating, for blog listing with teaser display mode 113, 114

   customizing 108

   defining 105

   editing interface 118, 119

   features 106-108

   overview 106

   using 110

Views Bulk Operations (VBO) 108

Violinist

   URL 74

visual content management 175

W

watchdog 65

web application firewall (WAF) 75

Webform module 13
  URL 156

Webform REST
  URL 156

Webform Validation
  URL 156

Webform Views
  URL 156

web service APIs 242
  concepts 242, 243

web services 241, 242
  using 247

workflows
  configuring 189
  managing 190-192
  use case 195
  using 193-195

WYSIWYG 125

www.packtpub.com

Subscribe to our online digital library for full access to over 7,000 books and videos, as well as industry leading tools to help you plan your personal development and advance your career. For more information, please visit our website.

Why subscribe?

- Spend less time learning and more time coding with practical eBooks and Videos from over 4,000 industry professionals

- Improve your learning with Skill Plans built especially for you

- Get a free eBook or video every month

- Fully searchable for easy access to vital information

- Copy and paste, print, and bookmark content

Did you know that Packt offers eBook versions of every book published, with PDF and ePub files available? You can upgrade to the eBook version at packtpub.com and as a print book customer, you are entitled to a discount on the eBook copy. Get in touch with us at customercare@packtpub.com for more details.

At www.packtpub.com, you can also read a collection of free technical articles, sign up for a range of free newsletters, and receive exclusive discounts and offers on Packt books and eBooks.

Other Books You May Enjoy

If you enjoyed this book, you may be interested in these other books by Packt:

Drupal 10 Module Development - Fourth Edition

Daniel Sipos

ISBN: 978-1-83763-180-3

- Gain insight into the Drupal 10 architecture for developing advanced modules
- Master different Drupal 10 subsystems and APIs
- Optimize data management by modeling, storing, manipulating, and processing data efficiently
- Present data and content cleanly and securely using the theme system
- Understand helpful functions while dealing with managed and unmanaged files
- Ensure your Drupal app has business logic integrity with automated testing
- Implement secure coding in Drupal

Modernizing Drupal 10 Theme Development

Luca Lusso

ISBN: 978-1-80323-809-8

- Map design systems made by Storybook components to Drupal structures
- Understand and use render arrays and Twig templates
- Get familiarized with the new Single Directory Component feature introduced in Drupal 10.1
- Define, import, and use CSS and JavaScript libraries
- Discover how to style content created with fields and paragraphs
- Define, place, customize, and style blocks
- Explore advanced topics like extending Twig, making a theme configurable, and boosting performance and accessibility
- Find out how to build a decoupled website using json:api and Next.js

Drupal 10 Development Cookbook - Third Edition

Matt Glaman, Kevin Quillen

ISBN: 978-1-80323-496-0

- Create and manage a Drupal site's codebase
- Design tailored content creator experiences
- Leverage Drupal by creating customized pages and plugins
- Turn Drupal into an API platform for exposing content to consumers
- Import data into Drupal using the data migration APIs
- Advance your Drupal site with modern frontend tools using Laravel Mix

Packt is searching for authors like you

If you're interested in becoming an author for Packt, please visit `authors.packtpub.com` and apply today. We have worked with thousands of developers and tech professionals, just like you, to help them share their insight with the global tech community. You can make a general application, apply for a specific hot topic that we are recruiting an author for, or submit your own idea.

Share your thoughts

Now you've finished *Drupal 10 Masterclass*, we'd love to hear your thoughts! Scan the QR code below to go straight to the Amazon review page for this book and share your feedback or leave a review on the site that you purchased it from.

`https://packt.link/r/1-837-63310-X`

Your review is important to us and the tech community and will help us make sure we're delivering excellent quality content.

Download a free PDF copy of this book

Thanks for purchasing this book!

Do you like to read on the go but are unable to carry your print books everywhere?

Is your eBook purchase not compatible with the device of your choice?

Don't worry, now with every Packt book you get a DRM-free PDF version of that book at no cost.

Read anywhere, any place, on any device. Search, copy, and paste code from your favorite technical books directly into your application.

The perks don't stop there, you can get exclusive access to discounts, newsletters, and great free content in your inbox daily

Follow these simple steps to get the benefits:

1. Scan the QR code or visit the link below

https://packt.link/free-ebook/9781837633104

2. Submit your proof of purchase
3. That's it! We'll send your free PDF and other benefits to your email directly

Made in the USA
Monee, IL
20 August 2024

64186713R00171